Aesthetic Animism

Aesthetic Animism

Digital Poetry's Ontological Implications

David Jhave Johnston

The MIT Press
Cambridge, Massachusetts
London, England

This book was set in Stone Serif Std by Toppan Best-set Premedia Limited. Printed and bound in the United States of America.

Library of Congress Cataloging-in-Publication Data

Names: Johnston, David Jhave, author.
Title: Aesthetic animism : digital poetry's ontological implications / David Jhave Johnston.
Description: Cambridge, MA : The MIT Press, 2016. | Based on the author's dissertation (doctoral)—Concordia University, 2011. | Includes bibliographical references and index.
Identifiers: LCCN 2015039944 | ISBN 9780262034517 (hardcover : alk. paper)
Subjects: LCSH: Computer poetry—History and criticism. | Computer Poetry—Technique. | Literature and technology.
Classification: LCC PN1059.C6 J86 2016 | DDC 809.1/911—dc23 LC record available at http://lccn.loc.gov/2015039944

10 9 8 7 6 5 4 3 2 1

Contents

Acknowledgments

This book grew from doctoral work. My PhD dissertation advisers provided crucial counsel: Ollivier Dyens, Chris Salter, Sha Xin Wei, and Jason Lewis. Excerpts have appeared in EBR (*Electronic Book Review*), LARB (*Los Angeles Review of Books*), and *POEMM*: The Album (a book of essays released by Obx Labs in 2015).

Stephanie Strickland read through and commented on early drafts with meticulous intensity. School of Creative Media (City University of Hong Kong) colleagues and friends Daniel Howe, Roberto Simanowski, Ingrid Hoelzl, Jane Prophet, Bobo Lee, and many others tolerated my anxieties. Poets and critics whose conversation contributed to my thought: Loss Pequeño Glazier, Chris Funkhouser, Amaranth Borsuk, Nick Montfort, and John Cayley.

Short lists exclude the many helpful, gracious, and thoughtful individuals whose insights nourish. I thank you all. I am grateful also to the editors and competent staff at MIT Press.

There are innumerable dedicated authors/artists/critics whose creative works are not covered at all or sufficiently as befits their merit in this volume. These include Kathi Inman Berens, Alan Bigelow, Abigail Child, Roderick Coover, M. D. Coverley, Maria Damon, Jeremy Douglass, Natalia Fedorova, Taras Mashtalir, Ottar Ormstad, Marjorie Luesebrink, Will Luers, Hazel Smith, Mark Marino, Kate Pullinger, Scott Rettberg, Maria Mencia, Patricia Tomaszek, Mark Sample, Special America, Rainer Strasser, Illya Szilak, Steve Tomasula, Rob Wittig, Judy Malloy, Peter Ciccariello, Chris Funkhouser, and many others. Apologies; go read them.

Finally, thanks to Mom for years of solid, intelligent conversation, and my family for their effervescence. And to my dear friends Sophie, Janusz, Serge, Thanh, Ouadane, Anke, Pascaline, Jericho, and Susan: thank you.

How-to (Read This Book)

In this era of compressed attention, the following information might prove useful.

Chapter 1: Contexts

Read this if you are arriving from the humanities or literature. It *introduces* and *outlines* the general argument, and provides an overview of the subject of digital poetry and the approach. It also *defines terms*, including TAVs (textual audiovisuals) and TAVITs (textual audiovisual interactives).

Chapter 2: Critiques

For literary theorists, critics, students, and philosophically inclined readers: this chapter provides an overview of theories about language that leads toward a notion of *spoems* (poetic objects), outlines a brief *history of image-texts*, attempts a *symbiotic merger* between two historically distinct ways (materiality and ontologies) of considering poetry, and contains *central arguments about aesthetic animism*. These concern the plausibility of living language as an outcome of the convergence of literature and computation, the volumetric possibility that archetypal letterforms relate to internal physiognomy, and discourse on how these archetypal forms might be attained in ways that are both synesthetic and synergetic.

Chapter 3: Practices

Digital poetry case-studies. The chapter begins with precedents, typographic explorers, and parallel practitioners. The bulk of the chapter offers numerous *case-studies* of contemporary digital poetry (and/or language-art in mediated contexts) grouped by thematics.

Chapter 4: Softwares

Software defines what digital poetry is. This chapter explores the temporal implications of animation time lines on the literary imagination. Read it if you are concerned with *software studies* and/or *creative media*.

Chapter 5: Futures

The final chapter proposes a few seemingly ludicrous, perhaps-prescient *prophecies*. Auto-writing bots, emotive reverse-engineering, and an inexhaustible muse. I'm an artist taking refuge in academia. I make "big" claims. In this era of advanced entropy, it seems appropriate to suggest the edges, to surrender into a contingent infinite.

Appendices

Tangents for elliptical thinkers: Ekphrasis in the digital meadow, neuroscience of semantics, Simondon and the Singularity, poetry as cryptography.

1 Contexts

I think electronic expression has come not to destroy the Western arts and letters, but to fulfill them.

—Richard Lanham, 1995

Consider this book a semipopulist decoder for some of the new forms of poetry emerging. It is not simple nor does it move in a straight line, but it does strive to describe a poetics appropriate to the digital era and establish digital poetry's connection to traditional poetry's concerns with being.

Aesthetic Animism is a compendium of critical approaches to literary practices, with a concentration on poems, utilizing digital technology in the period 1994–2014. Pure literati scholars may be challenged by the fact that many of the "poems" cited are not "poems" and are not written by "poets"; some are ads, conceptual art, interactive displays, performative projects, games, and apps. As fields open, boundaries dissipate, and often, exterior catalysts contribute to core transformations. Digital poetry is not simply a descendant of the book.

As Patricia Crain notes in *Reading Childishly: A Codicology of the Modern Self*, "The book form is often represented as a container for aspects of the self that can only be acquired there" (quoted in Hayles and Pressman 2013). The aspects of self found in digital poems are difficult to decipher and frequently more easily diffused acquisitions. The horizons of our attention contract in inversely proportional ways to the opportunities of the network. The copies we own of digital works are ephemeral, nontactile installations on machines that will be obsolete within years; digital poems do not sit in the hand or on the shelf but rather on a hard drive and servers; old computers and dysfunctional software are rarely considered as heritable traditions. Digital work does not confirm selfhood as poetic literacy did; instead it distends selves toward collectivities that remind it of oblivion, redundancy, arbitrary obliteration, obsolescence, and overlap. The speed of replacement often precludes the forms of emotive attachments once developed over books as a tradition: aspects of identity, ways of knowing. Yet this book operates on the premise that *the digital form operates as a container for aspects of a networked self that can only be acquired there.*

So even though reading may feel like being lost among a wasteland of upgrades (Harpold 2009)—the debris of publishing methodologies with life spans less than decades and modes of writing that change seasonally— there is an emergent self arising. This emergent self displays signs of being lithe, immediate, opportunistic, and distributed; it still cares for the word but sees the containers as disposable. In the perforated space of handheld or wearable augmentation, lines between inanimate and animate language blur. It is within the richness of these temporary contradictions orbiting soft/hardware release dates that digital poets play, and that this book both finds and reveals its paths.

Poetics before Computation Era (BCE)

Before the computer (let us assume), poetics was the study of poetry. It studied words structured into poems; words as media for consciousness; words as markers of events, memories, homages, and psychological rivers. Poets configured words into formal units: verses contained lines; phrases contained morphemes, beats, strophes, and so on. Poetry was supposed to capture, commemorate, or convert events into literary process. The technology of poetry was voice (rhythm, stress, meter, and prosody); its diffusion media: oration, pen, pamphlets, printing press, and books; its concerns primarily oriented around consciousness (love, death, and war). After the birth of modern linguistics, poetic concerns expanded to include conceptual considerations (materiality, appropriation, and language as self-referential contextual archive), and literary critics absorbed terminology and analytic methods from conceptual art.

Poetics among Digital Entropy (ADE)

After the digital, poetics becomes the study of mediated processes involving language: video, sound, animation, interactivity, and code. Poetic tools expand to include algorithms, browsers, social networks, Markov chains, sensors, and data. Poetics absorbs concerns and terminology from media studies, cybernetics, network theory, phenomenology, and cognitive science. And as the Internet blooms into ubiquity, blogs and then social networks become publication platforms; collective creations mutate into poems; and poets appropriate info surfing, hack search engines, or release bot poets to diligently produce verse with the meticulous regularity of metronomes.

Along the way, digital poetry reengages themes active at the origin of poetry: animism, agency, and consciousness. Improvements in the power of speech/text generation transform oral poetry into computationally tractable, publishable material. Animated, dynamic content modulates responsiveness to use. Writing becomes an augmented act, spontaneous and lucid. Language is grown using code; poems are manipulated and printed in 3-D, on Web sites, in CAVEs (Cave Automatic Virtual Environment), and as apps, installations, and augmented reality. The page becomes vestigial; the screen dominates for a while; and now we are entering an era of mediated things, poetic objects, and poetic organisms.

Questions Expand Maps

As poetry increasingly merges with digital media, there's a significant need in traditional literary communities for maps to digital poetry and the implications (philosophical, critical, and technological) generated by this new terrain. At issue is a redefinition of what constitutes poetry, language arts, and literary criticism. *Aesthetic Animism* examines many of the strange technological vectors converging on language. It does this by tracing spaces where computation and literature merge. It belongs to an interdisciplinary and emergent species of speculative literary criticism concerned with the philosophical implications of digital media.

This book is not so much interested in the establishment of a canon or a theory that dominates as it is in the general implications of questions with large ramifications—questions that are at once nonspecific (ontological and societal) and personal (emotional). This paradoxical (both large and small) scope of scrutiny emerges from an acceptance of the personal as political, intimacy as insurrection. It induces a discourse style that is rigorous yet also informal.

How can literary criticism deal with animated, volumetric letterforms, code, and the incorporation of interactive audiovisual media? Philosophically, does coded language entail an ontological shift from representation to being/enactment? What technology optimally empowers the poetic? Do software interfaces constrain and empower imaginative processes? Does intuition need to modulate in order to engage with the rational aspects of digital media? What is the future of poetry?

Most psychology or cognitive science experiments try to control for as many variables as possible. They strip away the superfluous and heighten specificity. In doing so, they constrain their conclusions to specialized niches. By contrast, when approaching questions holistically (as a generalist) and originating inquiry in artistic "research creation" (where practice and theory intimately interweave), a methodology emerges that allows intuition a prominent role and permits variables to proliferate.

Predictions and Definitions

I define *digital poetry* idiosyncratically: as a memory resource unit (inducing long-term potentiation from the cruft and spam of experience), GPU-accelerated lyricism (multimedia lamentations and celebrations), compression utility (compressing narratives into epiphanies), and translation algorithm (converting the cultural heritage of bards into interactive and generative formats). Beyond this, on the singularity horizon, I predict digital poems will blossom as proto-organisms, endowed with quasi-mitochondrial code, drifting across an ontological divide between abstraction and embodiment. In a hypothetical future, digital poets program, sculpt, and nourish immense immersive interfaces of semiautonomous word ecosystems

Structural Spasms

Because we live in an information-saturated era, this book is written in bite-size modules that link to form aggregates. It can be read in spasms, nonlinearly.

Each section of the book focuses on a different methodology or way of examining the material: contexts (foundation), critiques (history, analysis, theories, and approaches), practices (creative examples), softwares (implications of writing tools), and futures (promises, warnings and synthesis).

There is no glossary; by the time this book is published, I suspect the search for word definitions to be ubiquitous.

Terminology: TAVIT

Inquiry expands through embracing new terminology. The word *text* (derived from the fourteenth-century root *weave*) is not inclusive enough to incorporate dynamic, animated type. Multimedia digital poetry renders the term insufficient. Future theorists will require terminology specific to the domain. I suggest the adoption of acronyms: TAV (textual audiovisual) and TAVIT (textual audiovisual interactive).

Why Digital Poetry?

What does digital media offer to poetry? Speculatively, a chance again for words to live as if born from the breath of "gods," but this time on the waves of networks, in the minds of algorithms, from the heat at the core of an intense, complicated, modularized, international formal system of language interchange.

What does poetry offer to digital media? A profound awareness of the potency of precise language erupting in packets (meter and foot tracing breath), an irreverence amalgamated with compassion, and a dense serenity that encompasses systems transcending time and space.

Poetics and Technology

For Aristotle, poetics was an inquiry into the structure and principles of poetry. For most contemporary literary theorists, poetics is to some degree a conceptual investigation of language structure and literary forms, emphasizing the social construction of meaning and material contexts of language. For me, however, poetics arises when language explores unstable technological edges—edges being spaces where potential resides.

Aristotle's analysis implied a stable, eternal continuum. Twentieth-century conceptual inquiry foregrounded a fluctuating, subjective, postmodern contextual process. In this book, poetics is mutated by proximity to ongoing technological change: it is time mediated and embodied. Letters burrow into flesh (inserted into databases or networks, or conceived as DNA), and poems writhe into new information-inflected embodiments.

Interdisciplinary State Change

In our era, in the networks that we use, in the ads that we watch, in the generative text that fills in-boxes, language is undergoing an ontological state change from inert to active, from isolated to interconnected, from tool to quasi-proto-organism. Wherever digital tools influence the creation and diffusion of language, the symptoms of this phase transition appear: in motion graphics, generative typography, *language arts* that use computation, e-lit, networked narratives, dancing logos, and digital poetry. What these works often share is a defiance of easy answers or categorization as poetry; they are flagrantly interdisciplinary. Within this immense interdisciplinary pressure, poetics becomes an open-state excursion that incorporates insights from science, advertising, media design, and so on.

A Continuum

One of the most ancient conceptions of the author is of a conduit, the empty reed, the vessel through which the wind speaks. The oracular vessel is analogous to the perforated fiber-optic networks, the server nodes, or the platform codebase deep-learning bundles that analyze, recognize, and generate speech. The architectural parallel between ancient reeds and contemporary technology connects digital poetics to ancient animist roots, shamans and soothsayers, readers of subtle riddles, and reawakeners of the muse. In contemporary networks, language generated by code becomes autonomous of authorial intent. Autonomy of language (coded and embodied) resonates with the deepest roots of writing.

A List

Consider the following topology of events in language arts history: in 1913, Guillaume Apollinaire's static *Calligrames* outlined an eye-drop heart; ... in 1996, John Cayley developed navigable poems using HyperCard; in 1997, Matthew Kirschenbaum began investigating the textual possibilities of VRML (Virtual Reality Modeling Language) as inscription surface; in 1998, Eduardo Kac created Genesis, a language arts BioArt installation that transcoded a Bible excerpt into bacterial DNA, a living text that could be edited (mutated) by Internet viewers with ultraviolet light; in 1999, Camille Utterback and Romy Achituv's Text Rain creates poems that follow the contours of flesh; in 2000, Ben Fry harvested websites and converted their text into a writhing tumescent animation called *Tendril*; in 2005, Andreas Müller created *For All Seasons*, an interactive text-poem in 3-D space; in 2008, Karsten Schmidt grew a font using algorithms, extruded it, and then 3-D printed it; in 2010, Craig Venter announced the creation of Synthia, a synthetic life-form, its DNA etched with a line from James Joyce ("To live, to err, to fall, to triumph, to recreate life out of life"); in 2011, Christian Bök announced the creation of a poem written into the DNA of a radiodurans (an extremophile bacteria) that would write another poem in proteins (his announcement was later rescinded but the research continues).[1]

These are new forms of writing in which myths mingle with code. They provoke relations between literature, genomics, and computation. Texts sense stimuli from networks of data and react. Letterforms swell off the flat page (in HyperCard, interactive, or bacterial form). Three-dimensional printed letterforms, grown from living processes; tubular networks of language scraped from the Internet and animated; letterforms adhering and responding to environments and bodies: each engages notions of sensorial awareness and distributed intelligence. In the first fever of youth, awkward, illicit, and occasionally tactile, quasi-intelligent, reactive, augmented, embodied letterforms demand to be received as structures that are far from abstract; they demand to be known as selves.

Where Are We Now?

In spite or perhaps because of all the tech hype, the e-poetry examples that we have now (in the second decade of the twenty-first century), while frequently astonishing, are often rudimentary, troglodytes, or cave dwellers compared to the parametric, deep neural net, autogenerative, viewer-responsive, variation-exploring poet modes that are imminent. We live in an era where it is possible to perceive the obsolescence in the new, ancestors in the youths. Contemporary digital poems are technically no more than a sketch of a shadow of potential: latent process evolving toward a state where the activated granules of many tender oscillations merge into a reactive experience, where rapid machines read us and produce the literature that corresponds to our desires and deliriums.

Proposal (the Heart of It)

Emerging predominantly from intellectual institutions where the brain is superior, in literary criticism the heart sometimes gets left behind. In an eagerness to investigate the superlative digital devices that proliferate around us, the actuality of lived embodied experience, aesthetics, nuance, and story gets abandoned. The result is art that is invigoratingly investigative yet meaningless to the masses. Elitist culture and populist marketplace bifurcate. If meaning is (as Alfred North Whitehead suggests) primarily emotional and instinctual before it rises up through abstract cognition into subjective passion, then love is meaningful.[2] I propose we remarry elite and folk, fuse heart and head, bind the digital into poetry, leaving behind neither body nor analysis.

2 Critiques

A man of my occupation seldom claims a systematic mode of thinking; at worst, he claims to have a system—but even that, in his case, is borrowing from a milieu, from a social order, or from the pursuit of philosophy at a tender age. Nothing convinces an artist more of the arbitrariness of the means to which he resorts to attain a goal—however permanent it may be—than the creative process itself, the process of composition.

—Joseph Brodsky, Nobel lecture, 1987

Critical approaches offer not dogma but rather potential modes of reasoning to open and gain insight into cultural work. Yet it is common for disciplines to seek closure, define themselves as exclusive practices or apply singular methods, to preach modes of approach. Practitioners and critics rely on labeling to demarcate space and define territory. In digital poetry, however, disciplines fuse, methods confuse, and lines blur. The following section outlines several analytic frames or critical lens.

Digital poetry implies composites, so it is not accidental that the following sections examine amalgamations of philosophical/critical threads. Language conflates with code. Text combines with image. Media-specific analysis (materiality) mixes with a close reading (ontological approaches). Beauty (aesthetics) mingles with an apprehension of life (animism). In each case, symbiotic relations between digital affordances and poetry necessitate these structural, critical composites.

Language and Code

Richard Rorty (1979) identified philosophy as a series of turns. Like the head of a small bird, the orientation of philosophy pivots to find new concerns each generation. In the early twentieth century, Ludwig Wittgenstein's linguistic turn precipitated a concentration on language. In 1994, the pictorial turn (Mitchell 1994) described a visual focus, ocular-centric and inundated in photons. The pictorial turn is living in parallel competition (and partial completion) with many other concurrent turns: the media turn, hybrid turn, nonlinear turn, interactive-tangible turn, agency turn, augmented turn, and network turn.

The primary turns of the twentieth century (language, pictorial, and media) orbit the concept of life (which invokes unresolved questions of agency, determinism, and ethics). An unprecedented capacity for 3-D rendering (representations of life) parallels biomedical manipulation and the development of genetic organisms (molecular biology). In 3-D and genetics, code (computational and biological) is at the core.

Poetry, at its roots, involves a radical openness to the possibility that there is life operating within language and things. Poets have experience reading matter (muttering the moods of things, writing the thoughts of systems), and that makes them credible candidates to explore moments where dry silicon competes with moist mentation. Poet skills at decoding events, eliding life in objects, and converting premonitions into language can be considered as antecedents to the contemporary fields of genomics and computer code.

Code, like ancient poetry, is a structured, constrained subset of language; in both new media, 3-D representations and biologically constructed organisms, life arises from manipulations of structured language. The current confluence of life and language appears poised to precipitate a transition in collective beliefs about what is alive; this change might occur slowly, insidiously, over generations. As proteomics decode the codes that code us, microbiomes enter into normal speech, and computational language gains quasi-metabolisms (words spewed across networks within knots of data; autogenerated sentences fluctuating inside animated skins), collective attitudes might swivel to consider abstract language and letterforms as alive.

Language: What Is It?

What is this thing we use all the time, that you are reading now, that Ferdinand de Saussure calls a "concrete natural object in the brain" (de Saussure, 1916 in Pulvermüller, 2002, 270)? Is it William Burroughs's infamous virus? Possibly. But that's a way of seeing it that requires a little psychotic torque.

Or is language (take a deep breath here) an inanimate, functional, formal system of amodal symbols generated by recursive grammatical transformation rules occurring within a human cognitive architecture? Perhaps. But even though there's clear explanatory power in linguistic or logical descriptions, structural definitions rarely touch or attempt to explain ambiguous intimate meanings—language's emotional/expressive capacity. Language evades easy reification; all definitions are contingent, no size fits all.

In linguistics, language is an abstract system, neither object nor thing nor animal; within computation, however, language metamorphosizes into objects (given form, on/in images, within 3-D worlds). Code also visually endows language with apparent volition like an animal. And now, data science may give computers the capacity to speak, spew out massive tides of language, emulate and explore the fringe careening unobvious collisions where surrealists and Dadaists bred. This change in the ontological status of language from abstraction to entity to ecological force is one of the contemporary emergent results of computation, and it is here that poetry dwells where it has often dwelled: in the living word.

Recursion: Language, Computation, and Creativity

If language is understood linguistically as hierarchical, recursive relations of bounded sets (of symbols that form unbounded sets of words, phrases, and meanings, etc.), then a conceptual parallel with mediated data structures is clear. Recursive hierarchies are inherent to the structure of both language and digital media; digital media wraps, duplicates, and enhances the structure of language itself. Recursive, symbiotic symmetry between language, poetry, and digital media results.

Herbert Simon, one of the founders of systems theory and artificial intelligence (AI), identified hierarchical recursion as a fundamental feature of computational systems. In a seminal 1962 paper, "The Architecture of Complexity," Herbert Simon claims that "it may not be entirely vain, however, to search for common properties among diverse kinds of complex systems" (Simon 1962, 467). This search for common properties (patterns, harmony, rhythms, and more) in complex systems (emotions, death, time, and more) is fundamental to poetic inquiry. Simon's broad sense of hierarchy, which refers "to all complex systems analyzable into successive sets of subsystems" (ibid.), has ramifications for many systems (from mathematics to physiology to ecosystems). Recursion (L-systems, fractals, and more) in living structures, linguistics, and digital systems points to a deep continuity between life, language, and computation.

Reading poetry is innately recursive (as is program execution in a computer). The eye enters the poem, follows a line of meaning, feeds what is found back into what is seen (what has been known, felt, touched, or heard), and this loop occurs again and again, in an iterative, cyclic process. Semantic epiphanies are proximal to chaotic blossoms in the brain. Code and poetry, poets and programmers, share a common concern with efficient, taut, resilient language (Jhave 2001).[1]

Metadata Memory and Heritage

When words, phrases, sentences, paragraphs, and books are transmitted in digital networks, they become data structures; data structures collect metadata. As texts/words/letters accumulate complex nets of contextual metadata, texts (like bodies) fill with memories (structured traces that represent past events). Locative data, about where text packets have been, function as spatiotemporal memory, incipient narrative. Packets communicate, connect into chains, navigate, and burrow into the psyche like bugs.

If metadata memories (organized hierarchically and recursively attached at the level of glyph, word, phrase, paragraph, article, corpus, or discipline) plug into a distributed intelligence (network-monitoring software, packet sniffers, Internet servers, P2P mesh networks, open data repositories, or the quantified self), then simple phrases will be able to tell us who said them (and where and when), who first wrote them, who modified them, and who read them. What eye lingered on this word?

As big data techniques discover how to classify texts into families, replicate variations of writing in styles that never occurred, language itself disattaches from the author. Future experimental authors will watch the machines write, exploring variational state spaces where words comb potential for the unsaid. This form of passive interaction deepens and enriches literary intertextuality, expanding the conversations between tomes that constitute heritage.

From Spimes to Spoems

Language originates inside bodies, and its curved, sinuous, wet origins suggest that a lineated format on a paper page is not the optimal, final, or only mode that poetic expression can take. Poetry will transform more as computation extends further into devices, homes, and minds: autonomous sensors embedded into daily objects, interfaces contacting neurons, screens diving through optic nerves.

Bruce Sterling (2005) calls evolving mediated networks-of-things that intercommunicate *spimes*. Spimes are emerging rapidly as ubiquitous computation incorporates itself into many objects around us. Language is not exempt. As Kevin Kelly (2005) has presciently noted, with every keystroke the web grows, nourished by collective contributions, evolving into a creature.

Poems may merge with *spimes* to become *spoems*.

Spoems (like poems) will be languaged spaces where poets establish networks of resonance between things and experiences, memories and intuitions. One example: Allison Parrish's (2009) *Autonomous Parapoetic Device (APxD mkII)* is a tiny box that displays tiny poems; it is designed to be carried around, as a companion volume.[2] Spoems may also be poems that read the network and even read the reader (Who is this reader? What are their skills? Interests? Eye focus?), modulating and adapting themselves to fit/evoke/transgress the reader with variable effects, surfaces, depths, vocabularies, speeds, and other parameters. Jichen Zhu, who researches AI-generated narrative, speculates that it may be "possible to generate an experience that is only possible with AI" (quoted in Jhave 2012b).

Bursty, crowdsourced language play (that might be harvested by spoems) abounds in text messaging, social networks, and anarchic net-spaces like 4chan or Reddit; these have spawned second-order meme hunters whose single-line, aphoristic, image-text micropoems now operate as viral diagnostics to global collectives. Ancient poet orators used the footstep to measure meter and space as a repository for memory (Yates 1992). Future poets may use network traffic to set meter/pace, and network space as the repository and orchard for generating spoems: reservoirs of networked spimes contributing to a recursive spoem. The unowned (crowdsourced), innate (fluctuating), animate epic poet of the next era may be a bot.

Animism Becomes Animation

From a philosophical perspective, thinkers as diverse as Thales of Miletus (often referred to as the father of philosophy and science), Arthur Schopenhauer, and Alfred North Whitehead have adopted animism (or variants sympathetic to it). In contemporary discourse, the terms used to tacitly refer to animism include *object-oriented ontologies, panpsychism,* and *hylozoism.* I prefer the term *aesthetic animism*: an estuary where reception of beauty invokes an apperception of aliveness.

Animism is often conflated with a naive idolatry of everything natural, as if Henry David Thoreau and Lucretius were idiots. Yet an alternative interpretation exists: animism evidences an increased sensibility to the speech of things, phrases in wind, the force of phenomena coalescing into a singular evocative system that communicates. It also reflects, at another level, thought congruous with scientific insights that reveal material flux permeated by life-forms (from the gut to the stars).

Not Object-Oriented Ontology, Not Panpsychism, Not Hylozoism
Animism has a compelling history; a contemporary compendium, *Panpsychism in the West* (Skrbina 2005), chronicles the complexity and controversies of hundreds of reputable (and disreputable) philosophers sympathetic to animist notions across millennia. This sympathy is unceasing even when it seems distant. Craig Venter, the scientist responsible for sequencing the human genome and creating Synthia, the first synthetic life-form, contends that life will be emailed, broadcast, and printed. Information is the contemporary crucible, a pattern that "now moves at the speed of light" (Venter 2013, 187).

Digital poetic aesthetic animism does not belong completely to any of the preceding spectrums: not object-oriented ontology, not panpsychism or hylozoism or purebred animism, not shamanism, not prophesy, not alien phenomenology, and certainly not genetics research.

Aesthetic animism proposes an interdisciplinary poetics that engages with these strands as a composite. Combining these threads in practice converts abstract categories into entities. Language itself flips over, seemingly eager for embodiment; the flip reveals a covert continuity, an aspect of language that always existed. Aesthetic animism is a birth term emerging out of the latent context of language as the binding bridge behind animate matter—a discourse tool that bridges the past and braids the preceding references into a palpable, palpitating form.

Endowing with Life
The link between poetry and animism is ancient: oral and epic poetry arose from the mouths of oracles who read messages in matter,

naturalists-farmers-hunters-warriors-midwives who chose to evoke the vividness of fields-forests-mountains-deserts-villages-jungles-oceans, love-struck suitors and political poets appealing with incantations to wrathful deities for helpful intervention. In antiquity, there is a sense of an animate world thick with animating forces; to be *animated* is to be alive. Etymologi-cally, animation is either endowing with movement or life. According to Alan Cholodenko (1993), in the twentieth-century animation was referred to as the "illusion of life" by the Lumière brothers, Walt Disney, and Orson Welles. Soon after the birth of motion graphics, advertising adopted life-like mobile text specifically for its dynamic affect and capacity to capture attention. Among the first poets to link digitally animated text to notions of aliveness were Jason Lewis and Alex Weyers in their 1999 ActiveText pro-totype application called *It's Alive!* "Its functionality is best summarized as the mutant offspring of a text editor and Adobe AfterEffects" (Lewis 1999).

Neurology, Empathy, and Entities

It may be that as digitized letters swirl (chaotically, interactively, or with Brownian motion), they evoke neurological reflexes similar to those evoked when witnessing a flock of insects or birds. Researchers into *neurological aes-thetics* have shown that when viewing paintings, "our brains can reconstruct actions by merely observing the static graphic outcome of an agent's past action" (Freedberg and Gallese 2007, 202). And experiments on witnessing handwriting have shown that "actions are simulated while being observed" (Knoblich et al. 2002, 1097). Extending those insights into animated text, it is plausible to expect that as a textured and volumetric letterform moves through a 3-D scene (casting shadows and respecting collisions), the human mind may apprehend it as an objective (perhaps even autonomous) thing. Volitional being will be projected onto letterform things that exhibit coherent programmatic behaviors. When injected with code, animated let-terforms (in addition to being abstract, symbolic pointers) might become subconsciously perceived as embodied entities. This possible shift in per-ception suggests that mediated language exists in ways that are ontologi-cally unprecedented. It also indicates that poetics needs to evolve ways of describing and understanding such apparitions so as to chart the nebulous resonances of new modes of reading proximal to seeing (being).

Digital Oracles and the Virtual Muse

There's a website that claims to allow the user to ask a question and have it answered by the Delphic oracle. Pythia of the mystical pronouncements, inexorably connected to the Internet underworld (reputedly sitting over a hallucinogenic chasm of intuitive servers), yet intimate with the "gods" (virginal, a sacrifice, in beta), her poetry reflecting language that is metatemporal, beyond time, guided by a muse (algorithm) that originates in the cloud (network). The website unfortunately, when you enter the page that is the temple, reports: "Unable to connect to MySQL."

Poets and their forebears, shamans and mystics, throughout history have faced similar connection problems: the divine database is elusive, and inspiration often fossilizes. Yet across cultures, a preoccupation with visionary states results in words given elevated status, words claimed to come from the mouth of god-creator-void, from or via a "Muse." Talan Memmott's (2006) *The Hugo Ball* jests with this impulse to attribute prophetic grace to computer speech; in this online work, when the cursor touches a magic ball face, it releases streams of Dada drivel.[3]

The Bible, the Koran, and the *Tao Te Ching*, Ovid, Sappho, and Walt Whitman, each claim that their words originate from a consciousness beyond normal—these words are, to the devout, vivid, awakened rivers of light, capable of quickening the mind. These words, and the chanting of them, implement an ontologically divine and alive app.

To the contemporary secular mind, prophecy is rabid, contingent, and delusional ranting; devotional incantations are mute; all ontological claims are canceled. The living words of gods, or Allen Ginsberg's or William Blake's encounters with flaming eyes/mouths/vulvas, erupt from a deranged, atavistic, evolutionary subconscious that cannot tolerate the vast unknown weight of mortality and human ignorance. In response, much of contemporary poetry has quietly retreated from the exorbitant passion of Pythia hallucinating at Delphi; shamans are exiled, and instead poets quietly delineate a litany of days. Poems often now either concentrate on the quotidian world (meek, normal moments) or conceptually engage with the texture of language (pulling apart the devious apparition that provokes their tongue).

At the same time, semi-ironic contemporary theorists like Ian Bogost flirt with notions of *alien phenomenology*, "the parallel universes of private objects cradled silently in their cocoons." (Bogost 2012, 79)

Programmer-philosopher Brian Cantwell-Smith claims that "we are not getting to the heart of computation ... until the ontological wall is scaled." (Cantwell-Smith, 1996, 17)

Image and Text

We are coming to recognize visual literature as a distinct genre whose measure is simply the visual enhancement of language. Once the concept of a distinct genre is in mind, we can acknowledge that visual literature can appear in many media, only one of which is books.

—Richard Kostelanetz, 1992

A Synergy of Eyes, Ears, Muscle, and Brain

Visual language, in its broadest form as *language on a page that is read*, is a relatively recent phenomenon. Walter J. Ong maintains that of the "3000 languages spoken that exist today only some 78 have a literature"; for Ong, the "basic orality of language [is] permanent" (Ong 1982, 7). Ong also notes that literature literally means letters. Etymology, however, is not always trustworthy as a categorical tool. From an alternate perspective, literature (the dreaming of a story) may have begun long before letterforms. Seeds began to sprout in the mouths of ancient primates muttering stories by fires, and literature arose with glyphs and cave paintings (narratives of hunted creatures smeared onto rock), with grunts, growls, and gestures. It started with eyes, ears, and muscles. From unknown roots, poetry mutated into cuneiform, papyrus, epic, folio, volume, book, print, poster, mail art, cassette, personal computer, BitTorrent, PDF, video, hologram, immersive cinema, augmented reality, website, app, and (eventually) implant. Over several thousand years, in the salient title of Christian Vandendorpe's (1999) history of writing, literature transitioned "from papyrus to hypertext."

In many branches of literary evolution, sight and hearing operate together. André Leroi-Gourhan (1993) suggests also that gesture (muscle path memory) informs language. Bernard Stiegler refers to written language as *grammatization*, a form of "intellectual technology" (Stiegler 2014, 57) that colonizes cognition. The roots of symbolic language representation permeate us as creatures; the implication is that language is a creeping, rooted weed that constitutes cognition.

In most literate individuals, reading-listening-thinking fuse; eyes, ears, and brain act in tandem; audiovisual hybrids (television, YouTube, ads, and film credits) invoke such synchronization. Spoken (oral), read (written), and viewed (mergers of textual audiovisuals, or TAVs) are simply modes of language flow. This reflects a long history of cross-modal representations of language. Multimedia poetry amplifies that continuity; it intensifies the blurring between domains.

Image-Texts

Convergence ... results in conditions proportionally able to undermine the expressive distinctness that separates art and literature.

—Francisco Ricardo, 2009

No process is immediate; few assimilations are total, and some are reciprocal. In digital environments, images are in the process of assimilating text, and texts are in the process of assimilating images.[4] W.J.T. Mitchell (1994) refers to these composites as *image-texts*. When audio is added, these become TAVs. In image-texts or TAVs, there is a reciprocal convergence on synthesis (of perceptual modes).[5] The synthesis is complicated by code and interactivity. Each additional vector entails a redefinition of reading: Where does it occur? At the juncture between modes of perception, or in the crevice where meaning ignites? Is seeing reading? Is being reading? Computers operate through read/write operations. Will machines *read* (in the sense of absorb and relate words to life)?

Poetry is a fertile space for such questions. Some poets would suggest that literature is the externalization of an embodied ontological process of being. Mark Amerika (a hybrid VJ, postmodern-novelist, and poet-polemicist) describes "nomadic Net Artists, who are wholly immersed in the digital flux of a drifting Life Style Practice[,] ... really have no choice but to activate themselves" (Amerika 2007a, 12) Other writers might point out that literature transcends instantiations as words or sights or sounds; it operates beyond sensory modalities, as in Caitlin Fisher's augmented-reality pop-up books that utilize the physical form of a book to deliver multimedia hybrids of children's and feminist literature.[6] Still others view poetry as experimenting with the granular logic of computer programming. Ian Hatcher's (2007) dynamic browser-based poems and performances operate at this level: they perform a coded and sonic archaeology on language debris discovered within networks; in Hatcher's work the image is nonexistent, and instead words operate as image, ephemeral knots of sound woven into tides, iterations of code aligned with obsessional yearning.

Sometimes, as in young TAVs, text imagines itself as image; at other times, text inhabits image, and the idea of image-as-habitat emerges. In that habitat, text may sit on top of image, still occluding it perhaps, but it has left behind womb-page. During preliminary contact between text/image, each remains distinct, in proximal intimacy but not contacting.

Evolutionary time lapse: a photo with a logo superimposed, a caption, a box/brand label, animated text swimming in a field, 3-D extruded text melting into backgrounds, or augmented text on every surface of a city.

Coexistence   Poetic history already contains a lot of TAVs, yet in spite of the extensive history of cross-modal image-text combos, a bias implicitly suggests words are mind (objective logic, serious science, etc.) and images are sensual (foolish desire, distraction, etc.). Pop cartoons ("lowbrow" entertainment) struggle to be considered philosophical ("high-brow," education); text-based motion graphics and film credits are rarely venerated as serious cultural artifacts; language arts installations are rarely the subject of "close readings."[7] The traditional view is that words and images are distinct, and should remain that way. In the November 18, 2010, *London Review of Books*, Peter Campbell writes, "Images tend to drown out words. Why not let them? Well, words and images need different kinds of attention. Words tend to reduce pictures to illustrations, pictures to reduce texts to captions." In Campbell's view, conjunction leads to reductions, disruptions, and ruptures in concentrative force; since image-texts "drown" and "reduce" each other, sensory apartheid is optimal.

Nevertheless, historically, text assimilated into imagery, reading fusing with viewing, oral poems performed with gestures, are quite common. As is the experience of synergy: word-images that evoke more than they are individually, with typography and layout imbuing words with character and texture. Interpreting design parallels literacy. For some critics, TAVs can (if utilized judiciously) be more potent than text or image alone.[8] Lev Manovich states that the ensuing result of convergence or assimilation (or whatever terminology is used) will be "more species rather than less" (Manovich 2013, 319) The paradox of convergence is its radiant divergence.

4K Aural Poetics (Jim Andrews)

The primal or the harmonic/dissonant reveries of pure sound or the meaningful repetition, variance, trance, and pattern of the drum.

—Jim Andrews, 2001

Consider the oral epic poem as the prehistoric analog of a 4K action film, an ancient poetic gold standard.[9] At one level, printing rendered the old oral-poem standard obsolete. Yet the integral structures of chant and rhythm remain preeminent in multiple modalities (rap, lyric, gospel, etc.—forms where authentic voice and bodies sing). And the values of oral language reincarnate even in digital works, most notably Andrews's *Nio*.

In *Nio*, the drum circle consists of interactive audio clips of spoken word, and letterform glyphs dance like flames. *Nio* burns code: programmed audiovisuals for the ear and the eye, an interactive ritual. Digital capacities augment oral concerns. The circle returns in numerous ways: the flames are animated vectors, and the poems gather around that fire as polyphonic voices triggered by the touch of the viewer's mouse (mouth).

Cartoons versus Cognition (Jason Nelson)

When oscillatory attention arises due to a TAVIT (textual audiovisual inter-activity is inherently oscillatory: Where should we look? What should we hear? Is reading primary?; multimedia is like a multimodal party), there are also risks of binocular rivalries between eye-ear-mind, between cartoons and cognition. Hybrid literacy may require knowledge of film, television, animation, cartoon, websites, 4chan, Reddit, memes, and moving, time-based media. It does not ask to see your library card; it rewires you and asks the viewer to regurgitate a surfing history. Compounding the challenge of allocating time to simultaneous sensory modalities is the extra cognitive effort to disentangle thickets of cultural references, to engage in cyclic read-ings across networks of pop culture, branding, philosophy, and so on.

Games may be poetic, and poems may appear to be satiric, absurd games, as on Nelson's (2009) online portal.

Nelson's sophisticated subversions borrow aesthetics of art brut doodles, gutter trash graphics, plonk audio, and frustrating glitch interactivity: to read, the reader needs to play; to play involves figuring it out; and read-ing becomes infected with navigating absurdity. Yet disguised behind the sardonic shifting textures and acerbic, brash, frustrating interactivity, a sizable, serious poetic oeuvre exists. Kitsch visual remix meets poetic instincts: Nelson is Jonathan Swift's, Laurence Sterne's, and Tristan Tzara's progeny. He directs a derelict mayhem arcade where animation and glitch gaming blends with a lo-fi, Super Mario circus of poetry. In Nelson's work, parallel modalities (microlyrics, postmodern idioms, junk food, and eight-bit arcade games) propagate TAVITs until the antagonistic competitiveness of image-text and high-low culture annihilate.

In these and numerous other TAVITs, hybrid media and network froth increase semantic throughput. And these TAVITs, instead of being at the periphery of culture, populate the center, propagate a multimedia literature—in ads, art installations, film credits, music videos, experimental videos, and other pop culture. Motion graphics in advertising operate as visual conversations, citing and remixing tropes and styles just as poets mixed (mashed and rehashed each other's riffs) for centuries. In motion graphics, images inhabit semantic spaces previously reserved for words. Low and high, ad and poem, trash and transcendence, audio and visual merge into an estuary where new species of encounters with the literary emerge.

Assimilation of Text by Image: Overlay and Word-Art

Assimilation suggests loss of identity; yet assimilations also create splicings, cross-fertilizations, and tenable mutations. There are several ways image-texts occur on the path toward the assimilation of text by image and image by text. The first and simplest is a label or caption. On the cave wall, there is a scratched glyph near a smeared figure. Both picture and text inhabit distinct worlds. There is no visual overlap. Reading and viewing are activated separately. But already there is a shared space. As reading and viewing oscillates, a meaning emerges that is the product of the two activities: viewing and symbolic analysis.

The corollary of the caption is text overlay. In overlay, text juts out a pier of translucent or opaque color; it appears above the ground of the page, paving over image. The text's world (the printed page) protrudes unapologetically into the world of the image. An oscillation between reading and viewing occurs; the text makes no concessions to imagistic style; each remains separate even though superimposed. In fact, the text's background ignores and occludes the image. Text in this scenario is antagonist to viewing the image as a whole. It breaks the frame and obscures a segment. The overlay-with-background is implicitly hierarchical, privileging the language act. Explicative process trumps integrative absorption. At a rough level of granularity, this layout reflects the widely held bias of logic over sensuality. As the text works to make the image comprehensible, it becomes the context.

The next step in the evolution of text-image toward symbiotic fusion was popularly referred to as "word-art" when Microsoft Word integrated a meager subset of static functions (skew, shadow, curve, bevel, etc.) into its software (circa 1990s).[10] When text as image discards the image entirely by becoming it, representative or mimetic functions are subsumed by the placement of words. Guillaume Apollinaire is the obvious progenitor of this branch. His *Calligrammes* precipitated concrete poetry and led to language sculpture. Steve McCaffery exemplifies and extends this graphic-language tradition; in *Carnival*, McCaffery utilizes the typewriter and masks in direct reaction to the claustrophobia of the page. Idiosyncratic commercial-art practitioner Robert Bowen's *Textscapes* uses a similar approach when he wraps landscapes in text; iconically, *Alice in Wonderland* wrapped over a wormhole. Camille Utterback and Romy Achinov's iconic *Text Rain* is another example of what Ricardo refers to as "that tradition where the text is the image and vice versa, so that neither is fully itself autonomously, separately, individually" (Ricardo 2009, 76).

Illuminated Manuscripts

Illuminated manuscripts form the first occidental example of a highly sophisticated integration of graphic *into* letterform; this is different from a graphic that is a letterform (as in hieroglyphs) or an ideogram (as in Chinese). Instead, both semantic and sculptural-visual meanings operate in the same figure, on the same level. It is the origin of image-text integration, the ongoing assimilation of text by image.

Illuminated letters can be read as both sculpture and texts. When presence imposes itself on the eye, eye becomes visceral and absorptive. Interwoven recursive forms evoke ancient actualities: fire smoke and cloud paths, intestinal entrails and molten lava. In illuminated manuscript, the letter is *world* made flesh; it becomes more than its semantic meaning, a composite hybrid perched between reading and witnessing. For this reason, illuminated manuscripts are the ancestors of 3-D modeled typography, networked attention (mobile roaming fractured into packets and spasms), motion graphics (After Effect ribbons unfurling), and visual language in poetry.

It might seem heretical to put illuminated manuscripts into the same typographic box as glass sign painting in pubs and psychedelic record covers, but the aesthetic lineage is the same in each: both reflect the urge to recursively decorate letterforms until they appear as entities or vitalist forces within foliage. The curlicue swirls that adorn these letterforms are the typographic equivalent of the death flourishes of Sarah Bernhardt or guitar licks of Jerry Garcia: torsional excess, magnetic vortices seeking to entice, archetypes of thirst, path labyrinth, forest, breast.

What is expressed in folding, flowing, illuminated scripts? I would guess that it is a complex knot of luxury (honey or melted gold), heraldry (status or shields), labyrinth (reading over and over until a message at the center like a lure is taken or takes), and solidity (a sense of the letter as a thing that has weight, and by association its message is heavy and profound). What these features share is that they are all primarily attributes of matter. They reference the world directly in ways that do not require literacy; they are read by experienced, embodied subjectivity. As humans, we have tasted honey, known or heard of gold, walked a labyrinth (or studied a curl of smoke), and held things in our hands. So the typography is speaking to the body at a lived level. It is engaging with the energy of our hands, muscles, and tongue.

The Soft Pressure of a Stick
The vast history of known glyphs from prehistory contains few 3-D letterforms as monumental as the contemporary CGI-carved Twentieth Century Fox's logo or Robert Indiana's aluminum sculpture *LOVE*. Instead, prehistory contains a plenitude of fragments and tiny monuments: handheld vases and tablets engraved, etched inward, and carved; symbols pressed into moist, wet clay, sketched on pottery, and carved into bone. Malleability and gesture conjoin at the source of semantics. Clay and mud were among the first substrates for typography: erasable, tactile, and supple glyphs. Prehistoric fragments of language etched into clay are at the origins of a lineage of the tablet personal computer or handheld PDA; both have a size and weight appropriate to the hand. Digital etymologically originates with the digit: a finger.

It is plausible to suggest that the soft pressure of a stick or finger probably lies at the origin of language. And at the origin, several disciplines are fused: the impulse to make marks and leave trace is an aspect of sculpture (scratching the surface), painting (marking the wall), and writing (which might have developed as an outgrowth of counting and transactional memory). It is only as systematized symbols torque indecipherability toward shared sentience that written arts separate from the abstract or representational disciplines of sculpture and painting.

Literature then evolved independently of touch for millennia until the printing press made the masses "literate."[11] Now digital media is once again making typography malleable and tactile. Writing has come full circle to its roots in mud. Fingertips that touch the screen are touching ancestral processes.

Kabbalists and Alchemists (Florian Cramer)

In *Words Made Flesh*, Cramer documents how ancient Kabbalists used generative systems of symbols to construct taxonomies of divine language. These systems often took the form of wheels of categories. While Cramer is concerned with the programmatic, permutational implications of these constructions (and how process permutation informs computational poetry), I am fascinated by the visual implications of these typographic wheels for digital poetry.

Imagine ancient spinning mandalas used for oracular divination. As the wheel spun, eager alchemist mystics might have leaned over blurred letters, anticipating the next revelatory package of divine data. Speculatively, renegade mystics resembled Internet users awaiting emails (bent over the spinning hard disk, reading results that surface through layers of abstraction), eyes groping for an aesthetic impact that emerges when mobile text finally stops.[12]

Anemic Cinema (Marcel Duchamp)

The spinning wheel is a fundamental trope of an early example of animated text: Duchamp's 1926 film *Anemic Cinema*.[13] In *Anemic Cinema*, phrases painted in spirals onto a flat disk are rotated at constant speed and filmed. The result is a film that expects the reader to read inward from the edge to the phrase's end near the spinning center. *Anemic Cinema* seems to reference the algorithmic alchemists with their circular charts and spiraling meanings as it simultaneously anticipates the mobility and motility of digitally animated text pulled along curved paths. In Duchamp's film, spirals of text painted onto wheels are spun in ways that only permit a reading if the eye slips in or out along a serpentine labyrinth. Vinyl LP grooves in gramophone recordings may have been the inspiration. Certainly the vortices of Brion Gysin's *Dream Machine* are descendants.

Anemic Cinema derives its visual energy from mechanical rotation. This evokes the origin of malleable language: the clay potter's wheel spinning so that fingers dragged from the center to the edge form nebulae. In *Anemic Cinema*, spirals punctuate the text. The text segments revel in puns, spoonerisms, and aphorisms; they semantically spin spirals of potential meaning. The geometric interludes form a visual counterpoint or rest to allow the text's spiraling meanings to be digested. Several of the geometric segments succeed in conveying a 3-D quality that anticipates the slab extrusions of CGI cylinders.

The overexposure strobes of the early film stock date it to contemporary eyes as an antiquarian project; yet this is a project that for its era, must have required the use of technically advanced equipment combined with idiosyncratic vision. In this sense, it is close in practice to digital poets who extend software and work with new media: it leverages the edge of tech. *Anemic Cinema* places Duchamp at the origin of animated text and visual poetry in high art, and forms a useful link between ancient clay glyphs, potter's wheels, and petroglyphs, and current motion graphics and spinning digital media: disk drive, laser disk, CD-ROM, and DVD.

The Concrete Intervase (The Rise of Opaque Typography)

In an age of theme parks and progressing semi-analphabets, in an age of boundless media spectacles should one not, in such a world, stand up against the sell-out of meaning and fight for artifacts, which still demand to invest and practice hermeneutic energy?

—Roberto Simanowski, 2004

Concrete poetry is the obvious twentieth-century precursor of visual digital poetry. Concrete poetry situated itself as "a revolt against [the] transparency of the word" (Perloff 1991); as such, it is the hermeneutic antithesis of fluff; opacity demands attentive reading. Just as in concrete poetry, digital poetry often revolts against the transparency of both machine and typography. Opaque typography induces a semantic oscillation between the pictorial and the literal. Opaque machines/interfaces provoke oscillations between awe and frustration. This oscillation challenges the foundation of typography and interface design's transparency dogma, and complicates stable interpretations. It invites/expects as entrance fee, in the words of Simanowski, *hermeneutic energy*. In the following segment, I examine one key concrete poet—Mary Ellen Solt—as part of an argument for an expansion of visual poetry beyond the boundaries that concrete poetry initially conceived for itself. I advocate a hermeneutics of ease, for the transparency of the opaque.

Concrete is a technological substance: a synthetic hard surface, impermeable, roadworthy. The intention of concrete poetry's founders (Eugen Gomringer in Switzerland and simultaneously the Noigandres group in Brazil) was to differentiate and distance *concrete* from the soft, emotional, labial ambiguity of traditional poetry; an inadvertent side effect of the initial intention is that a residual machismo clings to concrete poetry's exposition.

But there is a difference between the original motivation (as semantically pure attention to language's visual element) and the works produced by concrete practitioners, which are frequently sensual, aesthetic, organic, lush, and personal visions.[14] Solt's critical writing (notably, *Concrete Poetry: A World View*) echoes the ideology of concrete's origins, "there is a fundamental requirement which the various kinds of concrete poetry meet: concentration upon the physical material from which the poem or text is made. Emotions and ideas are not the physical materials of poetry. ... [T]he material of the concrete poem is language. ... [The concrete poem] places a control upon the flow of emotions" (Solt 1969, 59). Yet Solt creates (what I will call) *sensual concrete*. Her opacity is transparent. While Solt's critical work (like many avant-garde critiques) insists on the controlled exclusion of emotion from content, her practice can be read as a contradiction of that stance. In my view, Solt is a latent animist.

The history of literary movements oscillating between Friedrich Wilhelm Nietzsche's poles of Apollo (reason) and Bacchus (passion) resolve their tensions by establishing positions: symbolists, surrealists, de Stijl, James Joyce, Samuel Beckett, the Beats, OULIPO, L=A=N=G=U=A=G=E poetry, Jodi, new baroque, and so on. The landscape of poetry fluctuates between diverse ideological camps. Instability is innate; narcissistic subjectivity precludes cultural stability.

In Solt's *Flowers in Concrete*, the expressive tendency of visual poetry erupts: delicate, sinuous, graceful branches of letterforms invite a free flow of aesthetic emotion. A figurative thread palpitates Apollinaire's stylistic ghost. Solt's static visual poems explicitly emulate nature. Metaphors display as visual analogies of themselves: Solt features arboreal trees and flowers; Apollinaire utilizes an upside-down heart-tear. These pioneers are both representational traditionalists—of the painting tradition. In contemporary practice, concrete poet Anatol Knotek (2014) codes gravity and reframes a "falling alphabet"; programmer-poet Jörg Piringer (2012) performs the rising and falling, high-frequency trading of stock markets as a typographic poem with real-time video treatments in "Broe Sael." The Anipoems of Ana Maria Uribe explore myth, cities, nature, and sensuality. Made in 1997–2000, these simple, silent, monochrome animations "are typography and motion, in that order. And once motion is added, rhythm becomes all important, since I work with repetition and short sequences of elements" (Uribe 2003).

The strength of these works, as in Solt's *Flowers in Concrete*, is how they bridge contradictions: motion and reading, flowers and concrete, ontology and materiality. Theme and treatment express an agile, sensual softness that invokes oscillations between pictorial and literal. Any still frame of these preceding works could easily be mistaken for a concrete poem.[15] These are not words that deny emotion; these are works that exemplify intuition without sacrificing intellect. Thus, sensual concrete acts as a precedent for aesthetic animism in digital poetry, anticipating tactile and volumetric type that activates a sense of entity. Animation is implied in the gravity of Knotek, the volatile transitions of Piringer, Uribe's knots, and the branches and curls of Solt's letterforms; the gaze follows and folds. In spite of an external critical stance, sensual concrete anticipates text as organism, laden with metadata memories, palpitating the off page.

Syncretic Peripheries: Concrete Exile

Syncretic is defined as a merging of disciplines or beliefs; it suggests unity or continuity. Maria Engberg (2010) utilizes the term *polyaesthetic* to refer to a similar confluence: "media environments that call on more dimensions of the human sensorium than earlier media."[16] In the 1960 to 1990s, several major practitioners worked at the intersection of language and painting. Among the contributors to that syncretic tendency were Pierre Garnier and Ilse Garnier (1962), who wrote a manifesto for *Spatialism* proposing a confluence of influences converging between human and machine in painting, sculpture, and musique concrete. Max Bense (1965), in one of his first polemics supporting concrete poetry (on a foundation of cybernetic semiotics), begins: "The world is only to be justified as an aesthetic phenomena." He advocates a poetry based on linguistics, models, and schemata. Bense (ibid.) also argues presciently for a poem that is a "verbal, vocal and visual ... three-dimensional language object."[17] Parallel, in 1987, Dick Higgins wrote *Pattern Poetry: Guide to an Unknown Literature*, a thorough compendium of hybrid visual poetics through history. Joseph Kosuth's primitive, handwritten scripts conjoined with conceptual bravura to develop a space for poetry as plastic art probing the assumptions of the art market as well as repetition.

Yet resistance existed to any definition of poetry that challenged the conventions of pure text on page. As Paul Dutton notes, Gary Geddes removed all reference to concrete poetry from the 1985 edition of *20th Century Poetics* because he considered it "interesting but of limited significance" (Dutton 1988, 84). And in spite of decades of strong advocates for hybrid poetics, a 2012 search of the Academy of American Poets website (www.poets.org) for the keyword "concrete" returned a single relevant reference: to Apollinaire's *Calligrammes*, published in 1918. In a drop-down menu "concrete poetry" is an option, but there are only two poets listed, ee cummings (1894–1962) and John Hollander (1929–2013). This deficit of real pictorial poetry in the official narrative suggests a policy of strict exclusion (or cultured indifference).[18]

In actuality, there is no shortage of image-text or even interactive concrete poetry works that could be incorporated into a syncretic history. Consider one mediated example: Allison Clifford's (2008) clever interactive updating of ee cummings's *Sweet Old Etc.* plants (literally) his poetry as seeds in an animated landscape: "Initially, the landscape is bare but through gradual interaction, poetry grows from the landscape's soil and individual letters become protagonists of each story/poem."[19] Her accompanying text highlights how ee cummings's fractured play anticipates *computerese*, and how since his roots were as a painter, his work exceeds the arbitrary labels/ limits imposed by the traditional poetry canon.[20]

Irony became traditional as the machinic gestalt arose in the age of appliances, and advertising (tainted sincerity) distributed itself throughout public space and diffused into private space on televisions. Gloss photos, ricochet montage, and succinct subliminal text supplanted and corrupted the poetic impulse, purposefully leveraging libidinal energies as commercial drives. In twentieth-century sculpture, the metals and machines of industry became the materials of language; Mathias Goeritz developed steelworks such as *The Echo of Gold* (Solt 1969). In experimental novels and art brut poetry, Kenneth Patchen's sustained polemics from the 1940s through the 1970s created a parallel space for visual experimentation: quasi-mystical anarchy ruled as sentences spanned multiple pages. In the avant-garde, bpNichol and Steve McCaffery claimed the typewriter as a tool for dirty concrete; mail art flourished. Kitasono Katue (1966), in "A Note on Plastic Poetry," was one of the first poets to recognize that representational technology offered an expanded toolkit for poets: "The camera is fit to be used expressively by poets." For Katue, poems were *devices*. Poetry and image merged. Basically, marginalized radicals subsisting in interstices outside definition, iconoclast sculptors and photographers, academic e-poets creating multimedia investigations within insular conference-fed communities, and pop culture, manipulator ad makers—each in their own way, paralleled or extended the intimate flesh of concrete poetry's formal foundations.

Ontologies and Materiality

The medium is the message.

—Marshall McLuhan, 1964

Art is I; Science is We.

—Claude Bernard, 1928

Many late twentieth-century and contemporary developments in digital humanities and critical theory borrow insights from cybernetics and the methodologies of science. Implicitly, they are associated with quantitative evidence and validity. The logic in these disciplines and their tools (software, hardware, and terminology) influence the emergence of conceptual

writing, materiality, and media-specific criticism—literary schools concerned with language as apparatus and an examination of the media used
in writing. This mode of creation and criticism privileges "materiality." This
"hard" focus in some cases led to a neglect of ontological concerns (how
alive words seem) and expression (what it feels like to be alive). By merging
materiality with ontology, this neglect can be healed.

A Symbiotic Merger

The theoretical framework ... was Ernst Mayr's *Systematics and the Origin of Species*,
where the concept of "allopatric speciation" (allopatry = a homeland elsewhere)
explained the genesis of new species by their movement into new space. I took
forms as the literary analogue of species.

—Francesco Moretti, 2013

Evolution is how time overlaps itself while exploring space. This process
also occurs in the realm of ideas: literary criticism and forms optimize for
their cultural ecosystems. Opposing theories often eventually overlap and
occasionally merge to create symbiotic structures. A symbiotic merger is
possible in poetics between (orthogonal or tangential) theoretical modes of
criticism: materiality, modernity, and ontology.

What follows are metaphoric compressions. *Materialistic poetics* (also
known as materiality or media-specific criticism) applies the methodical
insights of evolutionary biology to poetry: it endorses poem as mechanism and erases poem as organism.[21] *Ontological poetics* (an umbrella term
for ancient poetic practices such as mysticism) foregrounds intuition and
being: it invokes language as living entity and lets the *Muses* write. Perched
between these two extremes of logic and spirit is *modernity*: a solid dwelling
for daily perception, gently ironic, pragmatic, and patient. Reconciling the
polarities of these positions permits the complexity of contemporary computational poetry to persist. Using their apparently irreconcilable opposi-
tions, it is possible to generate a taut, proficient, creative/critical practice.

Metaphorically, materiality uses a microscope; modernity accepts the
world as it is; and ontology aspires to a cosmological, expanded perspective. The following section outlines a history of materiality's ascendancy
to become the dominant literary criticism methodology, and also proposes
a merger of hard materiality with soft ontologies, a healing of the poetic

divide between brain (conceptualism) and body (inspiration), and a path to nourish neglected instincts without abandoning awareness of the impact of media on creation-reception (writing-reading).

A Strategic Response

Underlying this proposed merger of materiality, ontology, and modernity are the following recognitions. *Materiality* is not just an abstruse game played by academic literary critics; it is a science-based mode of research. It arose as a strategic response to cybernetics, incorporates notions of embodiment (from phenomenology to neuroscience), and argues for a complex, nuanced view of human-language-machine hybrids. *Ontological approaches* (or any engaged expressive poetic exploration that tends to privilege intuition, epiphanies, ecstasy, or animism) are not raw delusion; they offer modes of being beyond the normative. And *modernism* (in the sense of modernist poetry, the root of "normal" paper poetry) contains capacities for transforming temporal, physical events into just-enough suchness— moments where the "is" shines in all its routine richness, and objective precision cultivates a presence that is independent of transcendence. The approach advocated here is that each of these approaches supports aspects of poetic practice integral to a comprehensive understanding, and each continues to be relevant irrespective of the mediated substrate.

A Few Technoetic Cyborg Bridges

Bridges already exist between these disparate (material, modern and ontological) approaches. Donna Haraway's (1991, 2003) *Cyborg Manifesto* blurs the organism/machine dichotomy, blends technophilology into engaged feminism, and even flirts with cybermysticism (the problematic transcendence of machines). In 1997, Roy Ascott coined a word for the exploration of consciousness with technology: *technoetic*. Ascott (2007) fuses art, media, and mysticism. This work was preceded by decades of cybernetic research (Norbert Weiner and Claude Shannon), centuries of hylozoic or panpsychic thought (from Gustav Fechner to William James), and a few technoscience philosophers (Leroi-Gourhan, Gilbert Simondon). In contemporary discourse, Stiegler notes how "lodged between mechanics and biology, a technical being came to be considered a complex of heterogeneous forces" (Stiegler 1998, 2). Jane Bennett extends this notion of a liminal object perched between machine and biology, traces a path through

Félix Guattari to Henri Bergson, and suggests a "vital materiality" (Bennett 2010, 34, 80, 113) that offers agency to nonhuman assemblages. Digital poets appear amid this complex debris and shattered state-space of ideas to play in a new sandbox, innocently quilting toys (sensors), tools (GPUs), and tornadoes (emotion and ideas) together.

Close Reading Literary Phenotypes

After centuries of experimentation, the surface of printed poems, their aesthetic or experiential qualities, reflect habituated poetic modes that are well populated, domesticated, and comfortingly familiar. Lineated verses on paper; rhythmic or free; rhyming or assonant; introducing a theme, revising its contours, or delivering authentic aesthetic resonance—poems are a predictable, reassuring artifact. The critical toolkit of literary theory refined and resilient is like an old, visiting doctor's bag: it opens to reveal close readings, technical autopsies, biographical biopsies, and the occasionally controversial associational dissection. Yet when applied to digital poems, these tools don't heal the split between reader and poem; they inflame it.

Mainframe computers and transistor-based digital media emerged in the late 1950s; DNA was discovered in 1953; and McLuhan's *Understanding Media* was first published in 1964. Is there a causal chain? Probably not; but there is a confluence that suggests cross-fertilization. Close reading is/was literary criticism's scientific method. Jessica Pressman (2014) narrates how McLuhan imported close reading techniques into media theory. He used conceptual tools developed for reading difficult texts (like Joyce or Gertrude Stein) to probe the core of the media *instead* of the message.[22] As is widely accepted, according to biological theory, genetic mechanisms (DNA) encode proteins that form and regulate the bodies of individual organisms. Analogously, according to materiality critics (who descend from McLuhan), media DNA (frequently conceived as code) controls surface content. Prior to digital media, literary analysis most often viewed surface content (plot, characters, meter, etc.) as primary, and media (paper, papyrus, etc.) as secondary; materiality (modeled on the paradigm of genomics) inverts that paradigm; it perceives content as surface (phenotype) regulated or expressed by an underlying media (code context).

Occasionally, the terminology of genomics has been explicitly adopted by poet-programmer-practitioners, notably in the notion of *recombinant poetics* coined by Bill Seaman in 1995—"to articulate a set of generative virtual worlds"—which he continues to explore in contemporary work such as *Architecture of Association* (Seaman and Howe 2010). The *Architecture of Association* points toward an art ecosystem generated by code that combinatorially evolves using quasi-genetic algorithms to establish aesthetic fitness. This long-term goal explicitly influences many digital poets: automate writing so it creates a "genetically modified" creature capable of attracting readers; use "hard" materiality practiced toward an ontological goal.

Genetic-inspired methodologies implement/analyze the transcription/diffusion/reception of data/networks/abstractions that express bodies of digital literature; code operates as authorial intent; content operates as skin. Technically, this means that materiality theorists/practitioners (like geneticists) concentrate on operative processes/procedures/code/hardware beneath the surface or phenotype appearances of poetry; content is subsumed into context, and analysis transcends the individual entity (poem)—the meta-format of technology transcends culture.[23]

Materiality and Media Determinism as Central Dogma

Consider 2002, the year digital poetic materiality went mainstream. In 2002, in *Digital Poetics: The Making of E-Poetries*, Loss Pequeño Glazier stated, "By appreciating the material qualities of new computer media, we can begin to identify the new poetries of the twenty-first century" (Glazier 2002, 1). The same year, in *Writing Machines*, N. Katherine Hayles identified "media-specific analysis ... as a kind of criticism that pays attention to the material apparatus producing the literary work as a physical artifact" (Hayles 2002b, 29). Glazier traced materialistic criticism to Jerome McGann's 1991 notion of *textual condition*: "Poetical texts operate to display their own practices, to put them forward as the subject of attention" (McGann in Glazier 2002, 21). The roots of materiality also extend through Wittgenstein, the objectivist poets (Louis Zukofsky, George Oppen, and Lorine Niedecker), the Language poets (Lyn Hejinian, Leslie Scalapino, and Charles Bernstein), and permeates the new media theorists or theorist poets (Johanna Drucker, Hayles, Glazier, Stephanie Strickland, John Cayley, Talan Memmott, Adalaide Morris, and Manuel Portela).[24]

As Hayles has unequivocally noted, "Materiality of the artefact can no longer be positioned as a sub-specialty within the literary studies; it must be central, for without it, we have little hope of forging a robust and nuanced account of how literature is changing under the impact of information technologies" (Hayles 2002b, 19). Just as the central dogma in molecular biology eclipsed other formulations, media-specific materiality for a period of time formed its own dominant ideological system within the electronic literature community. And similar to how the *central dogma* of molecular biology explains how DNA sequences proteins, how environments regulate gene expression, and how phylogenetic variations relate to selective fitness, materiality theory (material apparatus poetics) explains how texts need to be read in media-specific contexts: media encodes meaning; poetry arises from within the constraints of technological production; and nature (the network) trumps nurture (intent/experience).

At a fundamental level, this stratagem constitutes the triumph of objective science over fallible subjective vision. From within this perspective, in order to be valid, digital poems *must* investigate media. Interpretations of poems that bypass questions of authorship consolidate media and systems theory at the core of credible literary criticism.

Historians of science critical of *biological determinism* emphasize how it operates as an ideological vector for assumptions and prejudices about social class and bloodlines. As Richard Lewontin observes, "Molecular biology is now a religion, and molecular biologists are its prophets" (Lewontin 2001, 137) and biological determinism is "the legitimating ideology of our society" (ibid, 19). Lewontin critiques how biology's central dogma reinforces privilege. An analogous critique of material analysis poetics might note how it privileges modes of academic discourse, highlights works that are amenable to critical modes of appreciation, amplifies a concentration on machinic elements, and discards pure aesthetic experimentation.[25]

Media Forensics: Unraveling Digital Threads

Yet in the same way that genomics research offers unprecedented explicative power, materiality offers unprecedented insights. Material forensics reads the digital "black box" in the same way that mid-twentieth-century structural hermeneutics unraveled literature using Sigmund Freud and Saussure. The insights are often revelatory, and occasionally oracular. The first sentence of Matthew Kirschenbaum *Mechanisms: New Media and the Forensic Imagination* is a proclamation: "Begin with a mechanism" (Kirschenbaum 2008, 1). Kirschenbaum then dives into an autopsy of hard drives and digital esoterica: hashing tables, data standards, and magnetic force microscopy. At its foundation, "*materiality*, will be the watchword of the book" (ibid., 9). And it is a materiality that Kirschenbaum explicitly connects to the nuanced work of Drucker, who sees materiality as "two major intertwined strands: that of a relational, insubstantial, and non-transcendent difference and that of a phenomenological, apprehendable, immanent substance[,] ... a process of interpretation rather than a positing of the characteristics of the object" (quoted in ibid., 9). Note Drucker's reference to "two major intertwined strands"—a DNA metaphor. In simple words, the intertwined strands are the practitioner's relation to media, and the media itself as physical structure.

Appropriation Constraint Networks

Metaphors do not just flow from biology and science into literature; osmosis also occurs between the arts. Jason Lewis (1997) refers to one of his early works, *WordNozzle* (which allowed the user to spray text on screen), as "an experiment in painting with text." It did this textual painting with a mouse using the metaphor of a hose. From a premodern ontological perspective, the hollow reed of the conduit-author waters an ecosystem of epiphanies; in modernity, the hose nourishes the lawn of the everyday; in materiality, viewers become writer-receivers controlling (or controlled by) network fiber filled with data.

If the network is a system of perforations, holes, and hoses that irrigate/contaminate minds with knowledge/debris, such systems also encourage leaks and deviations of fluids aka appropriations aka mutations. Paper-based appropriations as brilliant as the Brothers Grimm's *Fairy Tales* or Walter Benjamin's *Arcades* anticipate Flarf's search engine spew, Christian Bök's beatbox-merz, Kenneth Goldsmith's *Uncreative Writing*, the Twitter bot Metaphor-a-Minute, and Allison Parrish's @everyword.[26] In the past, paper and scissors, and/or pen collated texts; now, network spiders programmatically assemble immense criteria-driven poems from fragments of Internet data. A constraint-based-writing lineage also connects surrealist automatism, Dadaist ripped newspapers, Burroughs and Gysin's cut-ups, OULIPO's rule-based experiments, LAIRE's coded verse,[27] and contemporary, networked or big-data poetry generators-bots; in each technological incarnation, similar poetic constraints emulate the nonlinear flow of dream's disjunctions. A classic fusion of these techniques is *Apostrophe* by Darren Wershler-Henry and Bill Kennedy (2000). Originally a long conceptual poem (written by Kennedy), *Apostrophe* existed for a brief period as a website that used segments of Kennedy's seed poem to query search engines for other phrases to generate more of itself. This was a poem that foraged, digested, grew, and eventually died, leaving behind a fossilized, static form.[28]

Mental Flesh: Abstract and Figure

Digital poetry's development, as in painting and traditional page-based poetry, can be roughly demarcated into *figurative* works (emulating previous literary forms and exploring emotive meaning) and *abstract* works (exploring semiotic/linguistic/cultural structuralism). These creative dualities roughly parallel the difference between materiality and ontological approaches. The difference is palpably clear when reading. Emotive-aesthetic figurative works carry within them the intention to express experience with succinct linearity or metaphor; abstract-semiotic works more often defy linearity and banish experience in the hope that at the fracture of normative meaning, structural insights will leak out.

But even though the difference is frequently palpable, the distinction is not always stable; some abstract-conceptual works display significant aesthetic impulses, while to produce a convincing figurative replica of a previous literary form requires substantial comprehension of structural linguistics and prosodic rhythms (as seen in the case of Christopher Strachey; see Wardrip-Fruin 2005). So these categories are, as in most taxonomies, mildly arbitrary and prone to fall apart under the weight of significant anomalies. Yet this ambiguous abstract-figurative chasm is one way to perceive the origin of the contemporary theoretical concentration on materiality doctrines. At another level, perhaps the affect-analysis strands simply grew apart from each other. And it allows another (somewhat-predictable) generalization: entertainment (focused on affect and engagement) motivates *figurative* work while avant-garde art (focused on materiality and research) more commonly motivates *abstract-structuralist* poets.

Metaphorically, it is helpful to think of the divergent-reconvergent head-heart strands of poetic practice as emergent paths or living vines; from a conceptual perspective, it is plausible to consider them as symbiotic structures intertwined with communicative-technology ecosystems. That technology is currently digital. The apparent opposition conceals a coevolution. And that coevolution of emotion-cognition is paralleled in the cultural biosphere by the human–machine dichotomy.[29] This fundamental fulcrum of metal and flesh leads Charles Hartman to a question that transcends the dichotomy: "the question isn't exactly whether a poet or a computer writes the poem but what kinds of collaboration might be interesting" (Hartman 1996, 5).[30] Hartman's question about interest invokes meaning—meaning that occurs at the collaborative membrane between man–machine, entertainment–art, and materiality–aesthetics.

Merging Aesthetics and Formalism (Marc Adrian)

Marc Adrian's 1974 *Computer Poems* is a set of work that exemplifies the difficulties of demarcation (Reichardt and Institute of Contemporary Arts 1969). Adrian utilized thirty-five millimeter, black-and-white film as media for animation and was one of the artists featured in the Cybernetic Serendipity exhibit at Dover's Institute of Contemporary Arts in 1974; but Adrian had created films as early as 1963 using words generated by a computer. Often his films were based on procedural workings (what he called "methodic inventionism"). His "work is important for several reasons. The 'computer texts' are among the first examples of works presented with unconventional 'syntax,' permutation and aleatoric reordering of pieces of language" (Funkhouser 2007). Parallel to his conceptual focus, Adrian clearly concentrated on aesthetic-display issues. Yet he also can be considered one of the forerunners of kinetic poetry; a screenshot of Adrian's *Computer Poems* in the Cybernetic Serendipity catalog echoes the Flash-based work that proliferated in the first decade of the twenty-first century.

As mentioned earlier, a surplus of categories and nomenclatures exist for digital poetic techniques, but utilizing multimedia as a blanket term (for work concerned with the aesthetics of display), subsumes kinetic, animated, and video poems under a single umbrella. And following the analytic/affect, materiality/engagement, and abstract/figurative dualities established earlier, it is possible to add: *aesthetic* and *generative*. As usual with a dichotomy, it is nonexclusive: aesthetic concerns are often crucial to generative processes.[31]

Reductionism versus Layers

Accepting the premise that materiality borrows methodologically from science, the discourse of science might yield insights into how to create in literature a balanced, critical viewpoint encompassing both materiality and what might be termed *inspiration* (etymologically, inhalation of spirits: the emotional, irrational, and intuitive substrate of poetry's origins). In scientific discourse, pure reductionism posits that mechanisms of a prior layer of scale define the properties of a subsequent layer (i.e., the contentious claim that "DNA *creates* the body"). Yet at a practical level, pure reductionism rarely occurs. Existence is punctuated by duplex flows. DNA encodes proteins, but experience influences which proteins are made (regulation). Pure poetic materiality, the absolutely forensic foregrounding of the machine, delimits only a truncated domain. To ensure comprehensiveness, the body of poetry as an experience demands an approach inclusive of, yet operative at, scales encompassing human–machine environments.

As digital media dives toward a networked-perforated, handheld-augmented, implanted, and deep-neural-net singularity, the necessity increases for an inclusive, multiscale analysis of questions invoked by these processes. Author, programmer, viewer, and computational media—all operate as readers-writers. Within emergent, exponential technical growth, complexity may coalesce into a proxy-pseudo metabolism (a network where processes self-regulate and replicate). Will the breaching of this emergent threshold convey being and agency onto language and thereby poetry? In other words, can mechanism become metabolism? Does materiality (analysis of the machine) need to expand to include ontology? Can ontology accept its mechanistic, mediated foundation? Can poems be created that articulate and exemplify both a critical awareness of media and sensual intuition at both a personal and esoteric level?

Subjective, spiritual, and/or emotional digital poems (personalized and observation based) challenge the dogma of materiality by reintroducing the tropes of modernity and romanticism (the author, inspiration, and sensitivity) back into poetics. This reassertion corresponds to the rising legitimacy of epigenetics within biology: the heretical flow of experience writing itself back into the genome. Jean-Baptiste Lamarck may, after centuries of repudiation, be celebrated as an origin of evolutionary theory inclusive of writing that occurs downward into matter; so too may expressivity make a comeback among the avant-garde. Future poets may alter media, write into the hardware of the network, and etch experience into the evolution of future poems.

Materiality sees poetry like a river tracing contours of technological context; ontology considers how poetry erodes the surface of technology, changing its course. Comprehensive positions consider both.

Analog Materiality: Language Poetics

It's tempting to think that materiality had two phases: analog, and then digital. The actual chronology is more ambiguous: analog and digital interweave. Modes cross-pollinate, miscegenate, at boundaries between discourse networks. Yet two major strands to late twentieth-century material practice can be identified. Some analog poets (prone to what Marjorie Perloff identified as the "simple rejection" of digital methods) continued on (oblivious to Wittgenstein, Stein, and digital signs), seeking out lineated modes of making language expressive of experience; for these traditional poets, what mattered was a materiality of time, texture, and emotion. Other analog poets (intellectually restless and resistant to confession) joined forces to investigate language as a sociological material, a constructed structure, to (in the words of that master instigator Charles Bernstein) "do more than simply echo the past with memorable phrases ... [to] also invent the present in language never heard before" (Bernstein 2011, 105). As this invention occurred, it carved out a style that computationally enhanced and networked poetry would soon colonize.

The Language poets birthed forms of extreme, unintelligible virtuosity, rhapsodic, fetishistic smears of sociological slogan merged with engineered rhythm; they appropriated, collaging what they bartered or stole. They celebrated disjunction rather than harmony; they protested against the placid ingestion of language as apolitical. Technically these poets, in a quest for renewed relevance, scavenged outside the traditional realms of poetic vocabulary. The pastoral, sexual, and spiritual epiphanies of Romanticism receded behind a blur of propagandistic, genomic, and cosmetic ricochets. Bruce Andrews (1988) exemplifies a stylistic refutation of surreal transcendence, his voice descending into a basement of fragments and shards caught and woven: "I knew the signs by their tents, obligation for hire, lexicon seduces, personally notwithstanding, ad? Consummate alarm, ulterior, stain, fling incarceration by rumour, punctual beauty ... mechanics of sleaze ... aim of irony, prefix at discount ... a practice, doubt ... artisanal difference admission ... small whim capsized, subjugated toast, substance aghast."

Spambot before spambots were born. The Language legacy autogenerated code riffs using the analog stuff of newspapers, ads, and books. Stylistically, they were precursors and prophetic antecedents of generative methods before code-networked poetry matured into a discipline in the 1990s.

Aesthetics and Animism

I like thick socks and heavy shirts … but all my theories are threadbare. All I have ever asked a theory to do is to help me, like a bowline or a compass, get from one ledge or campsite to another.

—Robert Bringhurst, 2009

The literary theory advocated here borrows from animism (a desecrated strand of philosophy), a way of being in the world often associated with being primitive, and connects that soft, open, intuitive awareness to hard, logical, networked computation and science. By fusing formally incompatible contradictory principles, new synergetic modes and modalities emerge. What happens when an ancient, emotional, intuitive, cosmological attitude diffuses through a contemporary network of postmodern, deconstructed, conceptual kitsch? As William Poundstone (2001) notes in *New World Emblem*,

Before the dot.com bust, so much that was written about the web struck me as wrongheaded. People imputed what I can only call "magic" to web's feature set. Low-cost-per-million multimedia interactivity was going to change the world. I knew that people had said similar things about the emblem, and had offered, in outline, many of the same reasons for it. So the emblem, often literally magical, became a caricature of the web. (Poundstone 2001)

Poundstone's *New World Emblem* links the animist tendencies of antiquity (Bacchic festivals, talking masks, Kabbalists, etc.) to contemporary fetishes, renegade artists, and idea cults (Mark Rothko, Giuseppe Archimboldo, Henry Darger, OULIPO, etc.). He does so in the interests of skeptically querying the hype that surrounds each new invention—the hype that projects an anthropomorphic image onto the inanimate other. By bouncing from insane asylums to alchemists and medieval etchings, Poundstone (2001) highlights how "technology imposes on art a sense of morality that transcends the idea of art itself."

In contrast to Poundstone's quizzical satire, aesthetic animism adopts the psychological projection of life as leverage, and asks if in the engaged, immersed gaze there is a latent potential for ethical relation to others.

Definition

All bodies are causes. … [T]hese effects are not bodies, but, properly speaking, "incorporeal" entities. … We cannot say that they exist, but rather that they subsist or insist, having this minimum of being which is appropriate to that which is not a thing, but a non-existing entity.

— Jon Roffe, 2014

Aesthetic animism occurs when an animated emulation of life seems alive. In other words, it is a subjective attribution of life or livingness based on a perception of credible, autonomous motion or systemic beauty. This aesthetic-ontological act entails a cyclic reciprocity emergent between perceiver and perceived instead of a uniplex subject-object reception/projection. It does not necessitate worship, but it can invoke immersion and engagement with an implied immanence. It can be passive and implicit: often humans perceive the ecosystem (grass, flowers, and trees) almost without any thought, moving through fields immune to any contemplation of the field's livingness, because they know it is alive, and accept it as such.

Humans engage with living things emotively and complexly. Our knowledge of the world (our epistemology) arises from relational acts, experiences, physical systems, and the tactile presence of other organisms. Language is the abstract, systemic filter of these epistemic experiences; it is also the means by which experiences think within us. As life changes over time (through birth, growth, and death), understanding and the language used to express understanding changes.

Does not a fondness for a certain word or sound, the worship of a cadenced phrase, already constitute a form of relation with an entity? Does digital tech amplify that relation? Thinking through these questions involves accepting aesthetic animist language as credible. Poetry roots its visual origins in inscription and a quest for meaning. It has frequently been an ontological act that disrupts norms and asserts the incredible; the following arguments/*approaches* belong to that category of discourse.

Language's Latent Tongue

Up until now, occidental letterforms appear mostly arbitrary, bearing little resemblance to the structures of speech sounds (an observation attributed to de Saussure). Unlike ideograms, which often refer to real physical pictorial processes, occidental letters are arbitrarily conjoined to the sounds they elicit. Digital technology offers space to heal this gap between form and content. By modeling the geometric resonance of speech into visually expressive letterforms, digital media offers a means to construct letterforms that more closely approximate the actual structure of morphemes (the constituent sounds of language).[32]

The shape of these letterform objects might correspond to analogs of mathematical structures that arise from the acoustic resonance inside our bodies. It can be argued that much of proportional aesthetics (theories of golden mean and the like) arises from embodiment, evolutionary activity over millennia etching patterns in physiognomy.

What I am suggesting is that innate shapes already exist for letterforms. They implicitly underlie our oral audible language, they are subconscious sculptures intuited from the shape of diaphragm, larynx, mouth, lips, and tongue. They have been etched there by speaking. Some shapes are personal, some shapes are cross-cultural. Yet it is these shapes and vibrational presences that are being given birth and dimensional form within 3D animation, ads, and digital poetry.

Bouba/Kiki : Shape-Sound Synaesthesia

There is evidence that shape-sound-letter associations occur innately. These associations suggest that interpreting the emotive intent of volumetric typography (TAV and TAVIT) may emerge instinctively. In 1929, a gestalt anthropologist named Wolfgang Köhler reported evidence of correspondences between shape and sounds in letterforms. Round sounds like bouba were associated with round shapes; sharp sounds like kiki were associated with spiky shapes. The audio waveform, shape of our mouth, the physiological form of the musculature of the cheeks, the tension or looseness of breath all seem to merge together to create an associational nexus. This effect is sometimes called the Bouba/Kiki effect or sound symbolism. And it has seeded investigations by the neurologists Ramachandran and Hubbard into synesthesia that trace grapheme-color synesthesia to the angular gyrus: "a seat of polymodal convergence of sensory information." Interestingly, lesions to the angular gyrus lead to an inability to understand metaphor (Ramachandran and Hubbard, 2001, 5).[33]

What this suggests is that at the locus of shape, sound, and semantics, various proprioceptive mechanisms arise. Humans understand shapes within their bodies; sound-shape associations have been found in many cultures.[34] Sound-shapes pairs are also not arbitrary because they arise from repetitive activity: spoken muscle memory like song's scar on the trachea. Our tongues and breath passageways have memorized how to create specific sets of sounds; and thus, the morphemes that comprise language are cross-referenced as volumetric forms. Children inherit these morpheme-shape pairs as they learn words. As they say something, they feel it (i.e., Put the tip of your tongue behind the teeth, and say sssssss … do you see the snake?).

In the poetic realm, sound poetry obviously investigates the acoustics of the body. Kurt Schwitter's merz performances recognized the mouth as a sculptural form, a tunnel for a torrent of morphemes.[35] The Four Horsemen performances in the 1960s and '70s (continued on by Paul Dutton) explored breath and sound, scream and guttural glottal, as means for poetic expression.

In summary, based on these precedents, it is safe to assume that volumetric text is interpreted at a visceral embodied level. Poets are uniquely adapted to explore this terrain of embodied language. Furthermore, volumetric text will be accepted or rejected on the basis of widely distributed shape-sound archetypes. And these sound-shape archetypes (that may correspond to the shapes our bodies make when speaking, the physiological constraints of our internal tubings vibrating as sound waves pass through them) will be modeled by digital media.

Synopsis of Volumetric Shape-Sound Argument

- The human body is composed of cavities that operate as sonic resonators (mouth, tongue, palate, larynx, and so on).
- These resonators take specific shapes when speech occurs.
- Over millennia, shape-sound associations have developed that link morphemes (morsels of sound) with structural forms. This is known as the Bouba/Kiki effect. It is cross-cultural.
- More specific and fine-grained shape-sound associations probably exist. These embodied shapes associated with sounds and speech are latent sculptures. Specifically, these shapes are the latent shape of letters, or the appropriate geometry of clusters of letters.

- Prior to digital media, no inscription tools existed capable of depicting these sculptural archetypes (of the resonating body cavities) as letterforms.
- Future digital letterforms may adopt characteristics of these internal innate shapes.
- As these innate shape letterforms emerge, writing with them will become an intuitive art. Cadenced and nuanced use of formal weight and texture may be idiosyncratic and suggestive of character. For instance, the speech of one character might express its subjectivity (or conceal it) through surface tensions. Another voice might be characterized by its refractory index.
- In short, as text-audio-visual (*TAVs*) emerge, proprioceptive and interior aspects of our physiognomy may find means of expression through the descendants of technology such as VMRL and CAVEs in augmented reality on mobile phones and *avatart* (avatar-based art).

A Theory of Multimedia Synergy: In, Out, and Between

In order to understand how synergy works in multimedia, imagine assigning a vector or region of proficiency to each of the major components of a TAV. Let these vectors delineate the general directional influences exerted by sounds, images, and words in a TAV. Imagine, words are interior, sounds are in between, and images are primarily outward. That is to say, a typical reader will take in words, and the dominant strength of words (in comparison to audio or image) is descriptive of psychological interiority, subjectivity, and thought processes. Words convey thoughts and concepts that are extremely difficult to convey with a camera or sound. Exactly the opposite is true of images, particularly video; these provide a quick, instant sense of exterior space, and navigational feedback is comprehensive, detailed, and simultaneous. And sounds operate in between, nonlocally, moving between objects and subjects, expressing both external orientations and internal processes, emotively resonant.[36]

Under this (admittedly overgeneral) proposed schema, it's not difficult to conceive how TAVs function as a synergetic system: amplifying interior subject (word), relational space (audio), and exterior environment (video).

The cyberneticist W. Ross Ashby, echoing ideas proposed by Norbert Weiner in 1948, described how the environment informed the brain: "Coordination between parts can take place through the environment, communication within the nervous system is not always necessary" (Ashby 1960,

222). In their work Autopoiesis and Cognition, Humbert Maturana and Francisco Varela (1980) postulated a model of the brain extended outward in cyclic connectivity with its environment, with the inward cell assemblies of neurons receiving stimulus and provoking external responses that alter stimulus to feedback. Clearly, outwardness and inwardness are aspects of a conjoined system. As in TAVs, vision, hearing and language intersect. Each has a clear region of strength that overlaps with, but is nonreplicable by, the others. Meaning emerges.

Digital technology fuses communicative modes in a way only previously offered in representational media by films. Films only rarely included text as part of their central media. Film credits, although key to a history of motion graphics and digital poetics, are exiles that exist outside the body of the film; they are appendages or labels, not aesthetic ends self-complete in themselves. What they clearly convey, however, is that words, visuals, and sounds are not antithetical; there is capacity for their integration.

TAVs challenge readers to absorb semantic concepts and visceral, visual sensuality simultaneously.

Presentation as Predator Impact

The yelp of an animal caught in the teeth of a predator impacts physiognomy differently than the cry of orgasm or religious ecstasy. Even using rudimentary 2-D typesetting tools, it is possible to represent the rudiments of voice. "**HELP!!**" is different than *"Help?"* and "Help." Hearing a cry for "**HELP!!**" might activate a cascade of fear-flight hormones. *"Help?"* might initiate seduction. "Help." might be in a brochure. Graphic novels and comic books have well understood the synesthetic potentiality of visual words. In each case, adopting Maturana and Varela's view, contextualized, sonic appeal evokes a distinct transient cell assembly, a neurological hypergraph, an ad hoc neural network. It is my feeling that there is a deep correlation at the neurological level that can be leveraged between the affective volume of an acoustic cry, the ensuing waveform or neurochemical cascade, and the letterforms used to represent such an incident. Letterforms effect cognition as they mirror its processes.

Cadence expressible by letterform influences the architecture of cognition. In each case, geometric forms in the inscription technology evoke geometry at the physical level that our surface personalities interpret as feelings. It is these feelings that living language, augmented digitally, enhances by directly speaking to archetypal forms inherent within the body. The rudimentary 2-D tools of italic, bold, and underline are being superseded by an enriched set of expressive utilities: morphs, tweens, kinematics, and so forth. These devices bring voice and temporality, cadence and intonation, emotive structure and animated ambiguity onto the page-screen-skin. The screen is the page by another game.

Esoteric Infinities at the Core of Interiority

You become what you hear so listen closely.

—Charles Bernstein, 2005

Strong proposals about future, general collective beliefs based on a nebulous marginal subject like digital poetry are not candidates for verifiability. The structure of human attitudes toward matter—what we conceive of as alive, to what we attribute the status of life—are diverse. Generalizations are generalizations. Yet the society we exist in has characteristics that define it; these defining characteristics modulate as technology modulates. There is a depth to our being that is not plumbed or known by news account or even a psychologist's report. It is to that depth that poetry speaks, or it is that depth that poetry speaks. And as poetry's formal tools increase into volumetric, kinetic metadata, it seems appropriate to consider how esoteric infinities at the core of interiority have been classified by various thinkers.

Lumps, Logarithms, and Julia Kristeva's Chora

The experience which I am attempting to describe by one tentative approach after another is very precise and is immediately recognizable. But it exists at a level of perception and feeling which is probably preverbal—hence, very much, the difficulty of writing about it. … The experience in one form or another is, I believe, a common one. It is seldom referred to because it is nameless.

—John Berger, 1980

With the concept of aesthetic animism, what I am searching to express is a nameless, preverbal apprehension of the otherness of something. How can language reach that nonother, pre-I otherness? How is an apprehension of otherness made available to us at the confluence of digital tech and poetry?

Kristeva distinguishes the semiotic trace from the term chora (derived from Plato's Timaeus); chora is "an essentially mobile and extremely provisional articulation" (Kristeva 1984, 35). In other words, it describes somewhere deep in the psyche: nebulous, prearticulate, and preverbal. Perhaps Eduardo Kac's "A Syntactical Carbogram (Biopoetry Proposal #17)" (Kac 2007, 191) for letters created with carbon nanotubes is floating nearby. But the chora that Kristeva portrays is basically without dimension. It is in that dimensionless space that esoteric, topological intersections of sonic forms and letterforms are born.

For Kristeva, chora is antecedent to semiotics; it is an interiority that might be shapeless. It is "not yet a position that represents something for someone (i.e., it is not a sign); nor is it a position that represents someone for another position (i.e., it is not yet a signifier either); it is, however, generated in order to attain this signifying position" (Kristeva 1984, 35).

Generated by what? By whom? As an experience, chora evades categorization. In a similarly enigmatic way, I use the term aesthetic to denote experience antecedent to language, to induce instability at the core of how we perceive words as banal servants, to reintroduce them to their roots as invocation. Embodied but somehow nonaccessible to consciousness, aesthetic experiences rupture subjectivity before it emerges. Primordial, concealed beneath and within language, beauty pierces the enclosure necessary for self-formation; it delivers perception over to reception, and evokes an indeterminate situation. This delivery occurs regardless of media.

One of the tasks of poetry is to speak chora, to convey a direct jolt of existence without negating nonexistence. At the digital interface between audiovisuals and language, in the malleable, palpitating presence of reactive words that emit sound, an opportunity emerges for chora to refine its expression.

Before body delimited itself, amputated off the other, and arrived as an identity, the world existed as proximal ooze; this ooze is the chora that digital technology sometimes provokes. This is why digital culture is a returning, recycling, and refusioning of literate sensibilities onto visceral apprehensions. And it is the textural verisimilitude and tactile irrefutability (conveyed empathically by mirror neurons) of digital typography that accesses both chora and literate consciousness simultaneously.

Eyes read as enteric viscera absorb. The cumulative whoompf of this knot evokes aesthetic animism. This mode of experience expands text into flesh, equalizes the gap between viewers and viewed, and resituates reading as a primal act. And if this process is dependent on technology, then probably it will mimic technium's entropic change and occur at a logarithmically accelerating rate.

We are on the curve toward a cusp. At the cusp, a letter is contorting in mouth's eye.

The Expanded Field

Kac's work is not about biotech, but instead about a kind of "biopoetics" in which language, form, and life intersect.

—Eugene Thacker, 2007

In 1979, Rosalind Krauss influentially diagnosed the logic of modernist sculpture as monument, established why that logic was failing, and then suggested an expanded field for sculptural practice. Poetry is in the same position today as sculpture was in Krauss's era. Iconic poems are bastion-like monuments—inscrutable, sturdy, pompous edifices etched with innumerable critiques by self-perpetuating cliques. The logic and inspiration that raised them to esteem falters; critics repair the myths, but their infrastructures are crumbling.

Poetry now needs, more than ever, in this epoch of inexorable technological change, an expanded field. This call for an expanded field occurs regularly within the poetics community. One can see it in Gomringer, Drucker, Glazier, Kac, Bense, Philippe Bootz, Friedrich W. Block, Rui Torres, Bernstein, Hayles, Seaman, Jeremy Douglass, Pressman, Cayley, Rita Raley, Strickland, George Landow, Ricardo, and many, many other prescient, prophetic minds lost in the mists of marginality.

Eugene Thacker (2007), reviewing Kac's Telepresence and Bio-Art, states, "The very notion of poetics implies a congruence of some sort between language and life."

Expand poetics to include the aesthetic wherever it overlaps with language. Like food into the stomach, all seen or heard words hurtle inward, ricochet off the lateral geniculate, on a trajectory toward amygdala and hippocampus. There the words nestle down; they burrow and are stored and breed together, like with like. Some words eat others. Cliffs and forest are covered in them, writhing like sticky bees. Words inside the mind do not obey the categorical imperatives of reasoned thought that dictate what words in what contexts can and/or will be considered poetry.

Just for a moment, invert the anthropocentric view, and imagine that words speak to each other through poems. They are not spoken by us; they are speaking to each other. They don't care whether they have to use papyri, digital networks, poets, cell phones, holograms, sculptures, videos, CGIs, or billboards. Words want to speak. They use us to make them. They made computers be born so they could begin to develop faster networks for communication. Perched on our lips, they leap toward each other as sound.

Four Approaches to Aesthetic Animism (Steps on the Path)

The four arguments/approaches for aesthetic animism are:

1. An argument from Evolution

a. The separation between language and nature as methods for aesthetic experience (a separation that emerged with inscription and was mass disseminated by the printing press) will be resolved when digital language adopts features of organic life, and is perceived as natural and natured.

b. Related software case study: Mudbox.

2. An argument from Prosthesis

a. Languaged media is technology, and therefore (following McLuhan) it is an extension of our body. Our bodies are perceived as alive. Thus the more mediated language becomes, the more it will seem alive. Eventually its abstract foundation may be forgotten or overshadowed by the dominant perception of living text.

b. Related software case study: Mr. Softie.

3. An argument from Assimilation

a. Language is slowly adopting features of a real object in a real world. The assimilation of language into audiovisual interactive environments occurs in stages. The assimilation of text by image requires a new terminology. I propose the term TAVIT: text inhabiting an interactive audiovisual environment.

b. Related software case study: AfterFX.

4. An argument from Networks

a. Network (or graph) theory is often used as an explicative model for neurology, language, the Internet, culture, and computer code. Poetry can be defined as the perturbation of congealed semantic networks through the use of ambiguity, ellipsis, tropes, rhythmic allusions, and so on. This ubiquity of networks points to a fundamental structural continuity between systems that are considered living and those that are considered abstract or mechanical. Network paradigms suggest that language is already alive; digital media permits us to perceive it as alive.

b. Related software case study: Python.

Evolutionary Approach

For me (on my traditional days), a poem is an event that enchants through language; it eclipses reason and restores being into resonance with arriving. Let's assume that the aesthetic experience (activated by poems) precedes all language and all symbolic written records. Interim conclusion: the first object of aesthetic awareness was not language (as we know it) but instead phenomena. Entities felt beauty and meaning (Gendlin 1962) before writing about it.

Then, sometime long ago, came language: words were born, sprouting from sounds, small phrases formed colonies, sentences made walls with grammar, and linguistic structures became semiotic. Eventually poetry leaped from the mouth into symbols: petroglyphs, hieroglyphs, and scripts. Then poetry lay down on the page (in eleventh-century China, and then because of Johannes Gutenberg), inert and evocative; invocation encoded itself in letters, and letters were printed.

After print, the tree of meaning (Bringhurst 2009b) sprouts a new major branch—a literary branch.[37] In the old physical trunk, organic aesthetic experiences of nature remain audible-ocular-tactile sensorial and immersive. In the literary branch, written language (leveraging imagination and empathy to activate simulations of sensorial data) evokes aesthetic experiences. Evoked literary experiences may be rich and immersive inside the reader, yet the means of their production are symbols: letterforms that do not bear any resemblance to their semantic content. The word "wet" does not yet appear moist. The word "heavy" does not visually have weight.

In contrast, contemporary mediated language is already capable of displaying complex semantic levels visually in the appearance and behavior of letterforms and words. Digital technology is mutating literature into many synesthetic hybrid species. In the same way that literary critics might have spoken of style or genre before, the prevalent use of motion graphic presets constitutes a transfer of stylistic parameters that are quasi-organic, as if the text is injected with DNA. In motion graphic environments, poems flock, stalk, reflect light, cast shadows, bounce, collide, react, and vanish. Reading the attributes as a whole, the reader-viewer may experience digital poems (or the words within them) as entities inhabiting a natural domain. Does a word that moves as if alive express only its dictionary meaning? Specular depth, polygon density, inverse kinematics, and other terminology from 3-D modeling may prove useful as digital semiotic indexes—as may easing equations, matrix transformations and word co-location splices. Many critics have recognized this hybridity necessitated by digital literature.

Aesthetic animism is that moment in the evolution of language (its integration of attributions associated with living things) when an enactive feedback cycle occurs between literate viewer and renaturalized, technologically enhanced word-object-organism. Digital language is once again perceived as innately natural. Renatured letterforms entail an augmented semantics. Letterforms, imbued with organic qualities by digital media, become situated critters, leveraging evolutionary reflexes not literate responses. The aesthetic experience evoked (that is simultaneously reading, viewing, using, and experiencing relationally) becomes a fulcrum where ontologies about life and attitudes toward language converge.

Prosthetic Approach

McLuhan described all media as extensions of our bodies, and technology as prosthetic. Hayles also notes that "anthropologist Edwin Hutchins and neuro-philosopher Andy Clark have pointed to the ways in which cognition is enhanced and extended beyond body boundaries by everyday artifacts, from pencils to computers, that interact with bodily capacities to create extended cognitive systems" (quoted in Ricardo 2009, 39). If McLuhan and others are correct and media is an extension of our bodies (or even perceived as such), then language (or more precisely letterforms, which are increasingly mediated) may become a palpable reactive prosthetic of our bodies. I am not talking of the cursory projective identification that authors have with their words: *those are mine*. Our bodies are alive, and thus language may (in some circumstances) be seen as alive: a phantom limb of letters. This will occur due to the synergy of McLuhan's recognition that media is perceived as the body of its user (with language as media, and hence an extension of ourselves) in conjunction with letterforms exhibiting behaviors and adopting representations that emulate bodies.

Unlike material objects that when rendered by a computer do not gain dimensional qualities they did not previously possess, it is possible to point to a chair in a virtual space and say, "That is a chair."[38] Chairs existed before virtual worlds. Drucker points to a similar distinction comparing letters to chairs: "The functional life of letters is obviously different from that of chairs, if only because letters' significance depends on their being recognized" (Drucker 2009, 150). She relates this distinction to Donald Knuth's struggle to program the essence of letterforms. The distinction I am trying to make has nothing to do with the functional life or essence of letters, but with their perceived ontology—in other words, their being or existence.

Prior to the digital expression (what could be termed the embodiment) of language, it was not possible to point to language and say, "That is language." Or perhaps more correctly, language could not point to itself or contain data pertaining to itself. Prior to digital mediation, language as a self-reflexive physical entity existed only in recursive conveyed meanings resonating in readers. There was speech, audible reverberation, synaptic tingles, jolts of lucid grace, newspapers, books, and lead type, but language itself did not possess a physical body capable of retaining knowledge of its form and location in a network of other words. Language was printed and its ink seeped into paper, but it had no skin or skeleton of inverse kinematics capable of dynamic reactivity. It acted as an extension of our minds, imperceptibly like air, but it did not extend beyond itself.

Digital technology may nudge collective perceptions of language, so that letterforms are perceived more as autonomous tribes, clusters cohering in the service of an ideology, clouds capable of developing and delivering communication.

The more that language is entangled with kinetic, intelligent, embodied, and responsive letterforms extruded onto screens, the more likely it is that we may forget, collectively, a time when language did not swerve to avoid us, try to serve us, and dance to capture attention. Its presence may still be largely (in daily life) transparent, but its transparency will be as the earth underfoot, a massive living organism that supports and guides. Imagine a mountain getting up and walking toward a horizon. That is the situation now. A mountain is walking off. Living language is a nontrivial development in the history of communication.

Assimilation Approach

Before language can be seen to be alive, it must at some level belong to the environment in which it is perceived. How does belonging occur? It occurs slowly in steps that recoil and meander. Like the symbiosis between mitochondrion and cell, text and image have evolved cohabitation patterns over centuries. Digital media is accelerating the process of their interrelation. The ecosystem is culture; the fauna they inhabit is networked media. Belonging is a historical process of slow assimilation. It is not a unidirectional flow. Human language is adopting the capacity to disguise itself as imagery; it is becoming capable of merging within images; it is being assimilated into a physically representative system.

I am not using the sense of belonging that refers to a lack of incongruity. Language that belongs to a scene can be incongruous and in revolt as long as it seems to live there. The word "mutation" can perch on my shoulder as long as it seems physically appropriate, obedient of basic laws like conservation of momentum, gravity, collision detection, receiving light, casting shadows, and occupying space. If the basic physical appearance of belonging is satisfied, then the automatic presupposition is that it has a life; it must experience its space. Perhaps as a plant experiences space, perhaps as a stone, but innately it is of its environment. This sense of text belonging to the language scape is crucial.

Think of how we see worms. We know they are living. We don't expect conversations from them. But we know that they function beneath soil, they are tubular hermaphrodites, and so on. And each of us has used the word to refer to computer code. What I am suggesting is that mediated words, the words we read in ads and kinetic typography, increasingly share that sort of status. Their interactivity and code endows them with quasi-autonomy. Sometimes small, mediated augmentations to the data structures that make these words also change them considerably. For example, in 2009 I built a simple application that made words sensitive to sound; the equation is rudimentary: if the device hears a sound above a threshold occurring after a set time since the last loud sound, it changes. This sort of "hearing" has been around for decades in DJ/VJ beat-matching application. Now it is proliferating. With handheld distributed devices that are capable of sensing locally (microphones and cameras) and globally (satellite, cell coverage, and wireless), the sophistication with which devices, images, and words merge is shifting.

Network Approach

Virtually all complex systems, regardless of whether they are composed of molecules, neurons, or people, can be meaningfully described as networks.

—Olaf Sporns, 2010

The question of life, or what is living, is a question of ontological status. In prescientific eras, answers arrived intuitively and subjectively through sacred texts that granted humans status as the creator's favored children, freewilled organisms. In the traditional scientific view, living things somehow have self-organizational properties; they have metabolisms (internal modular structures), and are capable of autonomous homeostatic action. Both these paradigms (which insulate humanity from considering matter equal with itself) are less tenable in light of multidisciplinary insights from graph theory. It is possible to reorient the question of life into a question of networks. Networks from a sociological poet's perspective are sets of relationships that transfer meaning along trust channels.

Increasingly from ethnology to primatology, animate beings are considered as rule-based creatures (and human industry applies these insights into flocking algorithms, predictive consumption, AdSense, etc.); inversely, it has long been recognized that inanimate objects synchronize and communicate through mechanical forces. The line between life and mechanism never existed except as a theory. Humanity's sacred and scientific reinforced perch on humanist notions of freewill is unstable.

Albert Barabasi in *Bursts* contends that human actions are potentially computational; his view is not on the fringe; as a mathematician, his research introduced the idea of analyzing networks as scale-free power-law structures. In his seminal 1999 paper, he outlines how network structures emerge from the preferential attachment of new vertices to extant vertices that are already well linked. His research suggests that power-law distribution applies to networks as diverse as genetics and the Internet. Sporns applies similar analysis to neurological evolution. His research shows that neurological structures developmentally self-organize in ways explicable by network theory. Network connectivity in brains follows power laws. So do the size of cities, popularity of artists, distribution of wealth, solar flares, and so forth.

Power Laws Bridge the Inanimate and Animate   What are power laws? Power laws express the relationship between two quantities where one value changes at a rate derived from a "power" (as in two to the power two is equal to four) of the other. The Zipf law in language is a power law that states the word frequency of a word is inversely related to the power of its frequency rank (example: "the"—the most frequent word in English—occurs 7 percent of the time; "of'"—the second most frequent word—occurs approximately 3.5 percent of the time). So power laws control distribution. This distributional network is scale invariant (like a fractal, looking at the curve at any degree of resolution does not change the relation).

So why is it relevant to digital poetry and the claim that animation in computation implies animism? Because words, neurons, and Internet servers are currently kept separate in ontologically sealed categories. Words are aspects of an abstract symbolic system; neurons are biological structures; Internet servers are machines. This is the commonsense view, a Newtonian ontology. But the shared structural aspect of these divergent things suggests a deeper poetic continuity, a quasi-quantum leap toward a space where humanity surrenders its preciously guarded autonomy and dissolves again into the sea of all that is: language, Internet, meanings, and emergent things. And this transformation points toward a crucial dilemma or choice. Either all items that share structure as power-law networks are mechanisms, governed by the imperturbable rigor of defined laws, or all of them somehow partake of life.

In my view, to accept either view as a totality is to succumb to a fallacy of incompleteness. It seems preferable to conceive of a nondualist viewpoint where both views coexist, parallel and simultaneous (oscillating in a form of binocular-concept rivalry). Words, neurons, and servers are both living and machines. Digital poetry amplifies and problematizes this nondual bridging of categories. It brings passion into contact with reason and suggests that the words themselves may want to speak, to breed with the ambient fullness of images, contort on the writhing waveforms of sound, and react as responsive creatures: resilient, incomplete, and evolving.

Summary

Aesthetic animism is a subjective attribution of life or livingness based on a perception of credible autonomous motion or systemic beauty. Poetry (as I define it) is both an aesthetic and ontological act; it challenges our conception of what is living. Digital media introduces a dynamic change into poetry, aesthetics, and ontologies by creating letterforms that engage shape-sound archetypes etched into our anatomies by millennia of speaking, and by offering letterforms the opportunity to appear to be alive. Enhanced by digital media, this appearance of living language heals the split that separated the written from the spoken: words are renatured, given visual voice. As an extension or prosthetic of our bodies and minds, language—once it assumes a body (of skinned, kinematic, reflective 3-D) and mind (of networked metadata memory and protocols)—seeps across an ontological boundary. Physically appropriate and obedient of basic laws like conservation of momentum, gravity, collision detection, receiving light, casting shadows, and occupying space, digital letterforms appear as tangible real-world objects. The introduction of metadata structures into volumetric digital text introduces memory and metabolism into language. This transition is not some hallucinatory revelation that transfigures society; it is a subtle, gradual, osmotic shift in our subconscious apprehension of language. The ubiquity of power-law network dynamics suggests from a different perspective that this metamorphosis of language is at another level a coming into focus of what was already there. The partial dissipation of ontologically sealed categories evidences a poetic continuity: digital systems, living organisms, and language conjoined.

3 Practices

Cultural ecosystems influence literature. Modernity deified creative genius; postmodernity elevated collaboration and appropriation; net-art celebrated independence and vision; and the postinternet proclaims an uncertain blend of platform and process. As these diverse, often-contrary threads encounter technology, literary practice leaps beyond its incarnation on the page and screen through a quantum convulsion that fuses image, text and code on a trajectory toward object and agency.

Pioneers (Late Twentieth-Century Digital)

Chris Funkhouser's (2007) book *Prehistoric Digital Poetry: An Archaeology of Forms, 1959–1995* includes: exhibits such as the 1968 Cybernetic Serendipity, which featured Nanni Balestrini's 1961 *Tape Mark* poems; conceptual poets who used code and algorithms like Jackson MacLow; poet-physicists like Philippe Bootz, who cofounded LAIRE (an algorithmic writing group in France); the collage kinetics of Geof Huth (1986–); South American software scientist and concrete-extension poet Silvestre Pestana's 1988 *Povo-Ove*; eccentric Alan Sondheim, whose prodigious output includes videotapes made in 1972, extensive outpourings on listservs and social networks, Second Life virtual reality (VR) psychedelia, and dance-poetry performances marked by an irreverent disregard for longevity or protocol; and Jim Andrews's many experiments, among them his 1992 *The Collected Sayings of Time*.[1] In the same epoch, the hypertext publishers Eastgate Systems, started by Marc Bernstein in 1982, published a long list of clickable, astute gravitas, including renowned classics of the genre like Michael Joyce's 1990 *Afternoon, a Story* and 1996 *Twelve Blue*; Deena Larsen's 1993 *Marble Springs*, which maps the history of a fictionalized mining town with hyperlinked images; and Shelley Jackson's 1995 *Patchwork Girl*. The list also includes the first electronic networked journal, *Swift Current*, established in 1984 by Frank Davey and Fred Wah; an iconic physical interactive installation in 1988: Jeffrey Shaw's *Legible City*; Jim Rosenberg's 1993 *Intergrams* with graphic programming pipes between illegible blocks of text; and Bill Seaman's installations such as *Passage Sets* in 1995. Instead of redoing or reviewing that prehistory of digital poetic pioneers (pre-1995), which Funkhouser more than capably covers, I have selected only a few works from prior to 2000 that contribute to an emergent gestalt, the seed of an idea that typography, design, linguistics, and programming irrigate each other in an interdependent, emergent synergy.

Key Premillennial Events

1995: Electronic Poetry Center founded by Loss Pequeño Glazier and Charles Bernstein. The center's biannual conference-performance-exhibit festivals, initiated in 2000, highlight and nourish an eclectic community.

1995: *Electronic Book Review* launched.

1996: *Media Poetry: An International Anthology*, edited by Eduardo Kac. Originally released in a special issue of the journal *Visible Language* (vol. 30, no. 2). The contributors to the *Media Poetry* anthology constitute a pioneer pantheon.

1996: Ubuweb.com.

1999: Electronic Literature Organization, founded by Scott Rettberg, Robert Coover, and Jeff Ballowe. Currently housing a directory, publishing *Electronic Literature Collection*, and hosting biannual conferences where elite critics and practitioners blend.

Media Archaeology and Modernism (Jessica Pressman and Lori Emerson)

Honey Dear

My sympathetic affection beautifully attracts your affectionate enthusiasm. You are my loving adoration: my breathless adoration. My fellow feeling breathlessly hopes for your dear eagerness. My lovesick adoration cherishes your avid ardour.

Yours wistfully,

M.U.C.

—Noah Wardrip-Fruin, 2011

Erkki Huhtamo and Jussi Parikka's (2011) *Media Archaeology* suggests that history is preserved, remade, reconfigured, reincarnated, and remediated (not eradicated). Innovations in poetry production (that begin with personal computing and then burst in a flurry onto the Internet) inherit poetic traditions. And it's not just tech that gets reconstituted; it's often the approaches, passion, aesthetics, and concerns of poets (Pressman 2014). In 1952 Christopher Strachey, a researcher working on the foundations of denotational logic, programmed a computer to write love letters.[2] In 2009, David Link built a replica of the original computer on which Strachey worked, a Ferranti Mark I console with an emulation of the original code, allowing viewer-readers to attempt to write their signatures onto the letters (Link 2009). Link's *LoveLetters_1.0* resurrects love and letters (ancient roots of writing) in digital form. Other examples include William Poundstone's (2005) *Project for Tachistoscope* and Young-Hae Chang Heavy Industries' (1999) *Dakota*, both identified by Pressman as exemplars of a continuation of modernist influences, principles, cadences, and preoccupations. In the case of *Dakota*, it is a reverential rewriting of Ezra Pound's *Cantos* (Pressman 2014). Pressman (as previously noted) also details the debt that media art criticism owes to literary criticism, as Marshall McLuhan imported his foundational training into media. So the influence of what preceded computation inhabits the content of contemporary work and criticism.

At the level of the device or tool, streams and threads of influence also emerge. Lori Emerson's *Reading Writing Interfaces* delivers a critical perspective informed by media archaeology. Her examination of the effect of digital media on play reveal how early interactive media art (such as Myron Krueger's 1989 *Videoplace*) or computer science initiatives like Alan Kay's (1971) *Smalltalk* belong to, borrow, and share the same gestalt aesthetics as bpNichol's *First Screening* kinetic poems (programmed in 1983 in Apple Basic). In 2007, Jim Andrews (whose website vispo—a neologism for "visual poetry"—an archive began in 1996) reverse-engineered bpNichol's pioneering work (in a team involving Geof Huth, Dan Waber, Jason Pimble, and Lionel Kearns), built an Apple IIe emulator and launched it online, proclaiming, "O ye digital poets: the past of the art is in your hands and it is you who must recover and maintain it" (Andrews et al. 2007). The case studies that follow attempt to perform a similar service.

Jean Baudot: *La machine à écrire* (1964)

In 1964, Baudot, a pioneering engineer-linguist, created the first French machine-generated published poetry. Published by the Editions du Jour in Montreal, *La Machine à écrire: Mise en marche et programmée par Jean A. Baudot* (A Writing Machine created and programmed by Jean A. Baudot) is still circa 2008 available (mildewed and seemingly unread since 1976) in the Concordia University library. A rough translation below (by myself) of Baudot's introduction reveals his language and concerns as strikingly contemporary and lucidly clear. Either time has stood still or it seems that new media evoked unresolved concerns early in its evolution. In his preface, Baudot (1964, 2), who was an engineer by training and became a linguist writing on formal grammars, writes about the ubiquity of computers, their capacity to emulate human tasks, and his elation at the power elicited by automated poetry:

> Humans have always been attracted to automation. From the beginning of time, humans have invented devices to imitate and surpass human capacities. Most often these machines have reassured humans of some control over the material world.
>
> Certainly a sense of domination is elicited when contemplating a machine performing a task previously only possible through labor. We find ourselves stronger and above all conscious of our privileged nature.[3]

But what of the poetry created by Baudot's machine? Baudot warns us to consider it as examples of a process not a literary exercise. And that is an appropriate warning because the text only occasionally illuminates. It's a bit like a randomized Scrabble board played by semiliterate spiders: the verses are stiff formal aphorisms that rarely congeal into sustained impact. It possesses astonishingly readable basic grammar, but is lacking in the subtle contours of emotional play and contextual taste of life. These are machine words. They are fragments that suggest a state space of potentialities that marches and meanders toward automated plot generators and Ray Kurzweil's *Cybernetic Poet*.

I showed these poems to a friend using the pretense that they were poems by a human.[4] For her, the language of the machine-generated poems immediately evoked Charles-Pierre Baudelaire and Alain Robbe-Grillet: "I don't understand the juxtaposition of words. ... Other poetry has a flow that I can feel and understand. This I can't."

These alienated responses resonate with experiments done by linguists in natural language: humans cannot learn artificial languages without extreme effort. Generative grammar suggests a neurological foundation etched into synaptic circuitry that predisposes us to syntactic conjunctions and organic morphemes. Extrapolating, perhaps there is a neurological parser for art, a dendrite module for meaning, a cluster coiled into a knot experienced as soul.[5]

In one of the appendixes to *La Machine à écrire*, the Quebec poet-troubadour Felix Leclerc points out a crucial ongoing, often-repeated, unresolved challenge to computational creativity: "Ask it [the computer] to be numbers, that's reasoning, it will be it, but to be heart, I don't believe it" (Demandez-lui d'être chiffre, c'est-à-dire raison, elle le sera, mais d'être coeur, je ne le crois pas) (Baudot 1964, 15).

Muriel Cooper: Visual Language Workshop (1975–)

Subtle contextual connectivity, the sinew of heart's narrative, the twisting truth of lived emotional reality, the ache and ebb of tidal hormonal moods —the microscopic parts of our biological bodies are not concerned with such macroscopic experiential perspectives. Organisms are clusters of processes, many of them mundane, functional, rudimentary, and mechanistic. One could argue that decades of artists following in the footsteps of John Cage have elaborated complex conceptual strategies for including ordinary processes (breathing, digesting, and so on) and contingency into art making. These interventions filter, explicate, and enrich approaches to accidents, and they circumvent or sublimate deficiencies of macroscopic meaning by instigating complex performative events where excess invites audience/viewers/readers to interpret curated chaos.[6]

Alternatively, other artists control for chaos, consider language as interface, simplify and clarify design through control for function, and investigate the dense, rich, lived sense of literature using analysis and visualizations. This is the path of designers, architects of experience, and engineers of encounters. The Visual Language Workshop started in 1975 by Cooper was not primarily a poetic space but instead a space of technological exploration of the graphic design opportunities of computation. It preceded the *Aesthetics + Computation Group* and the *Physical Language Workshop* in prototyping systems that often involved language, code, interactivity, and large data sets. The landscapes of informational relationships that Cooper developed (prior to 1994) in conjunction with her teams utilized

3-D infinite zoom, layering, transparency, multiperspectives, maps, and data visualization. Technically, they anticipate the virtual reality modeling language (VRML) literature of Matthew Kirschenbaum, Ollivier Dyens, and many others; they also anticipate the contemporary *Distant Reading* of Franco Moretti. And Cooper's emphasis on design mechanisms implies an ontological approach: her design engages multiple units into an emergent process analogous to a landscape or ecosystem. Cooper's tradition continues in information visualizations such as *Poem Viewer* out of the Oxford e-Research lab, which uses statistical techniques to provide a (static 2-D) graphic representation of poems that resembles a genetic map

for observing many different attributes of a poem along its textual structure, and for comparing a poem with other poems or texts in such a multi-dimensional attribute space. In the sciences, this is often referred to as multivariate data analysis, while in poetry, such an observational and comparative study is commonly conducted in closing reading, typically with little help from any digital technologies. (Coles and Chen 2014)

Tom Konyves, Robert Ashley, and Gary Hill: Videopoetry (1978 and 1981)

If design explorations of spatialized language suggest an organism's map/grid neurons (as in the preceding examples), then video suggests an organism's sensory orientation: seeing and hearing. Video is not necessarily digital, but the rise of video-text amalgamations (inspired in part by the prevalence of film credits and masters such as Saul Bass) constitutes an ancestor of contemporary e-poetry. *Videopoetry*, a term coined by Konyves to describe his 1978 video *Sympathies of War*, is a genre utilizing the affordances of film/video to investigate the written/spoken word. According to Konyves (2010), what distinguishes videopoetry (from traditional film/video) is incongruous, dissonant, technology-assisted writing. In *Sympathies of War*, breath punctuates or parallels montage cutaways to on-screen text ("STOP" fragment) that amplifies a reading by Konyves in profile. The effect blends oral performance and theater tropes with Sergey Eisenstein's cut.

Gliding in from an unperturbed postmodern music-composer identity, Ashley's (1978) opera for television (commissioned by the Kitchen and composed in parallel with "Blue" Gene Tyranny), *PERFECT LIVES*, constitutes a masterwork of interdisciplinary amalgamation. Incorporating overlay text, spoken word, live performances, video of video, and effect wipes, all edited together with an implacable sonic sense and indubitable sereneness, *PERFECT LIVES* is a soft sardonic whisper, ode, memoir homage to the midwest arcana of America—its parks, bars, supermarkets, backyards, churches, and living rooms intoned and desecrated with a self-reflexive, subtly reverent irreverence. In many ways, Ashley's poem is an elegy to banal life among the apparitions and eradications of market forces. It is also one of the first sustained text audiovisual voice (TAVV) that in symmetry with Ashley's hypnotic droning delivery, assumes a flat ontology between media: privileging none.

PERFECT LIVES shares resonance with Hill, an avant-garde video artist whose videos over the last forty years often used discontinuity and process to render linguistic and psychological principles palpable. Notable here is *Primarily Speaking* (Hill 1981), where background video of manipulated television-test color strips and two panels with writing (often found signage) are

accompanied by Hill's recitation of a long text, whose syllabic sequence determines the rhythm of the images (the screen changes with each uttered syllable). His voice comes alternately out of the left and right stereo channels functioning like a dialogue. This is broken into sections by a singing, but electronically altered, voice. The text, constructed for the most part from idiomatic expressions, extends the themes seen in *Around & About* (1980). In both works, Hill is concerned with disclosing and deciphering the codes of human relations. The desire for a community through language comes very much to the fore, while the constantly changing images attempt to compete. (Hill, Holger, and Iles 2002)[7]

In Konyves, Ashley, and Hill, a concern with transducing writing and language into the syntax of cinema creates a precursor for digital poetry.[8] It establishes the beginning of what might be termed *reciprocal reactivity* in video between word and eye, breath and edit, specific to the reading of texts that are nonnarrative. This is one of the birth nodes of the exchange of flow and information, symptom of an organic network—an animist language fetus twitching in a pluripotent audiovisual womb.

Eduardo Kac: Holopoetry and BioArt (1980s–)

In the 1980s, prescient observers prophesied holographic poetry competing in the mainstream of poetic evolution. In 1986, Kac claimed that *Holopoetry* provides

an extreme, pluridimensional level of complexity. This new holistic perception, source of the fruition of real immaterial objects, volumes without mass, requires a response in the structure of language: the possibility to transform the instrument of intellectualization—the word—into a sign as fluid and elastic as thought. ... [H]olopoetry launches a perceptual syntax, relativizing the cognitive process according to the different points of observation in space. (Kac 2007, 129)

Kac's discourse revolves around dimensions; it follows the classic manifesto formula of establishing a necessity ("requires a response") and then providing a cure ("revitalizing the cognitive process"); and if viewed from the perspective of his current preoccupations with BioArt and manipulated life-forms, holopoetry can be seen as the precipitating site where his ideas of volume (body) and code (poem) gestated.

In his more recent BioArt works, the activity of writing is biological, the poem is embodied by bacterial DNA, and the technology is nature; in holopoetry, Kac attempted to write text as bodies of light. Bodies in cities are read; we read each other using fragmented codes. Similarly, in the 1980s, Kac viewed his holopoems as discontinuous, multiple perspective spaces where reading proceeds by ruptures. Words fracture into shards of light, and signs "change or dissolve into thin air" (ibid., 130). It is this multiplexed stability that is shared with bodies: temporal ephemeral units extruded from evolutionary imperatives, bodies die as do holopoems when the power goes out.

Kac's *OCO*, 1985 and 1990, is a rough set of doughnut-style letterforms: the letters O-C-O form a cylindrical worm. No textures, no phong or ray tracing, or not much by contemporary CGI standards, but a step toward the development of a dimensional body for letterforms in the literary milieu. In later work, Kac links DNA to code and the corporeal tablets of tribal edicts as in his 2001 work *Encryption Stones*, a laser-etched black granite diptych that translates the canonical passage from Genesis ("Let man have dominion") into Morse code and codon sequences. These are cultural transcriptions that operate authoritatively at the membrane between archaeology, chemistry, and information processing. These are poems that visually assert and literally subvert the force of authority by decomposing *the Book* into stone that is a mere cipher for a much richer living code. Dimensional poetry is politicized by referencing distinct domains of expression to "critically reveal the intersemiotic operations that lie at the heart of our current understanding of life processes" (Kac 2001). If life is understood as semiotic structure, perhaps semiotic structure is life, the word made data flesh.

Donald Knuth: Punk Font (1988)

Like a poet has to write poetry, I wake up in the morning and I have to write a computer program.

—Donald Knuth, in Platoni 2006

Knuth, a computer scientist and mathematician, was among the first to experiment with converting letterforms into mathematical notations. As such, he is a technical contributor to the structural substrate of every single poem displayed on a screen. Knuth's skill and tenacity at carving out immaculate digital replicas of ancient typographic masters (down to nicks in a bowl) is present in the words you are reading now. He loved type, he loved the tradition of its forms, he carried it over, he connected those worlds, and his efforts partially brought you here. He also wrote a historical programming textbook, titled *Digital Typography*, and developed the curve-point model for digital fonts.

The parametric creation of font shapes for aesthetic purposes originated with Knuth's Punk font produced using his software Metafont. Originally published in 1988, these fonts were inspired in 1985 when Knuth (1999, 391) heard that "typography tends to lag behind other kinds of stylistic changes by about ten years." He immediately set about perturbing some control points by random amounts: "I had my first proof output 20 minutes later" (ibid., 395). Thus the practice of programmatically creating digital typography for aesthetic purposes was born swiftly, intuitively, and without much fanfare. And with this Knuth earns his title as the first hacker of visual poetics.

André Vallias, *Nous n'avons pas compris Descartes* (1991)

The concept of poem as an open diagram, when it incorporates the notions of plurality, interrelationship and reciprocity of codes, not only guarantees the viability of poetry in a society subject to constant technological revolutions, but places it in a privileged position -> that of an universal progressive poetry (as Schlegel foresaw) or simply: poiesis (from greek = creation, making).

—André Vallias, 2003

The minimalist experiments in visual poetics conducted by pioneer Vallias—including *Nous n`avons pas compris Descartes*, conceived in 1990—do something he perhaps had not intended: they translate Charles Olson's *open field open line* theory into 3-D form, and give visual form to the topological dimension of cadence. Vallias's 1991 *The Verse* looks like an information visualization of a poet's breath, a spoken-word oscilloscope. So the body and territory (the TAV and TAVIT) converge at the point where the body produces the form on which the words rest, so even in their absence something is spoken.

Google the word "Love" and then look under "Images" tab. Do the same for "Death." Unsurprisingly the common color tone and style of the images in each case is distinct and consistent. Love is predominantly red and curved. Death is black and jagged. On both pages, text incorporated in the images conforms to those criteria.

So is this evidence of an assimilation of text by image? Or are both being colonized by instinctual-emotional preconceptions? Or does the consistent style serve a functional necessity: dampening the oscillatory fluctuations between reading and viewing until they are quantitatively imperceptible (merging into apparent concurrency)? What happens when the impact of visual and verbal wash up on the shore of consciousness simultaneously in harmony? Is it analogous to an epileptic synchronous wave that precipitates an epiphany? Metaphors are necessitated but ineffective because there is no neurological lab or equipment capable of measuring the subtle flux and flow of meanings that arise and subside as the eyes wander, saccade, and absorb focally and peripherally, both text and imagistic data.

What is apparent is that synergetic enhancement of semantic processes occur when the naturalistic aspect of the text (color tones, light, shadows, textures) match that of the image. On the path to equal potency, text needs a body and substrate to rest on. In 1990, Vallias produced an ultrasound of that substrate twitching.

Robert Kendall: *It All Comes Down to* _____ (1990)

Lo·go·zo·a *n* [fr. Gk *logos* word + *zoia* animals] (2005) 1: word animals: textual organisms 2: a phylum or subkingdom of linguistic entities that are represented in almost every kind of habitat and include aphorisms, anti-aphorisms, maxims, minims, unapologetic apothegms, neokoans, sayings, left-unsaids, shamelessly proverbialist word-grabs, epigrammatological disquisitions, lapidary confections, poemlets, gnomic microtales, instant fables, and other varieties of conceptual riffs.

—Robert Kendall, 2005

Kendall's early DOS work *It All Comes Down* _____ is still, circa 2008, downloadable from his website, with the caveat that *"the program will not run at speeds above 33Mhz; sorry, it was written a long time ago."* In this contemporary era of dual core 2G laptops, Moore's law has effectively sealed off Kendall's creation inside a vault guarded by emulators. Funkhouser, who evidently went to the trouble of seeing these works on an emulator, writes: "Kendall was exploring textual experimentation in a manner similar to Bootz, Dutey, and Maillard and Papp by using a hypermedia narrative that combines linear words and phrases in various fonts, sizes and colours" (Funkhouser 2007, 137–138). Funkhouser also cites Kendall's readme file: "Soft Poetry is an update to the ancient traditions of the word as art object—the tradition of calligraphy, illuminated manuscripts, visual and pattern poetry. ... [B]y making serious poetry more tangible and just plain fun it can serve as a great introduction for students. Again and again it has captured the imagination of young people and those who don't like poetry" (quoted in Funkhouser ibid., 137–138).

Twenty years after Kendall wrote these words, in a mediated ecosystem filled with frenetic-kinetic text, where slick television information bars and motion graphics (think CNN transitions with 3-D audio-synched, glow-strobed ribbons of DNA-style headlines) and advertisements (for soap, toilet paper, cosmetics, or cars—racing over a desert of letters, chased by a swirl of gracefully chaotic logos) feature the aesthetics of a film's credits, it seems probable that the awe and wonder effect of kinetic text might face a steep threshold of boredom in a media-saturated consumer. The wow-wow moment of a student introduced to poetry requires greater and greater labor and budget to compete with the coalesced output of Hollywood and ad agencies. Independent poet-designers (the contemporary equivalent of the small press of yore) cannot really compete against big-budget team efforts.

But Kendall continues, and in *Logozoa* (2005) he places words into public spaces as stickers and then photographs them. It is a nonanimated, simple intervention process that occasionally transcends all the hype and fixation on effect of mass media. Here the words—stoic like bugs, static as stickers, ponderous as dormant beetles—decorate statues and road signs. These are quiet, simple, nontechnical aphoristic probes appropriate to their space. Lo-tech augmented reality (AR) is delivered by sticking paper onto objects and then photographing the result from a distance and up close. The result is a website that celebrates raw conjunctions, and anticipates a literature of place that is reactive and pure, configured just well enough to seem as if the objects are speaking. It's the maxims of François duc de La Rochefoucauld (1678) reconfigured for camera phones with PHP: "Neither the sun nor death can be looked at without winking."

David Rokeby: The Giver of Names (1991)

Part of poetry's power is that it names things; the act of naming is knowing, and naming precipitates a shift in ontological opportunities for the named thing and the namer. Objects become identities after naming, identities provide opportunities for emotional connectivity, and the human cognitive system often names things so it can project attachments/aversion onto them. Naming may be just the necessary administrative step that conceals the larger purpose of emotional grounding in a subconscious trinity of *name-known-need*.

Rokeby (1991), a media artist, implicitly explores parallel questions with his installation *The Giver of Names*, which "is quite simply, a computer system that gives objects names." Users choose an object to put on a pedestal, a watching computer analyses the object visually, and then it constructs a phrase-name from an associational database. "One aim is to highlight the tight conspiracy between perception and language, bringing into focus the assumptions that make perception viable, but also biased and fallible, and the way language inhibits (or alternately enhances) our ability to see" (ibid.).

The Giver of Names is not directed by accuracy; it does not attempt to identify the objects but instead bestows on ensembles of objects strange triplets that reflect a psychic symmetry, an autopsy of introjected relations, patterns intuited by algorithms. For example:

At a newly extramarital dinnertime,
the robustness refracts the emerald dunce cap
that is sprucing up this phone.
(ibid.)

Poets or writers acting in this mode arbitrate the imagination. They speak for contours and undulations; they extrapolate logic until it is illogical. Computers for now excel at appearing to emulate this style of excessive derangement. But (as I wrote this paragraph) a team from Google announced "a generative model based on a deep recurrent architecture that combines recent advances in computer vision and machine translation and that can be used to generate natural sentences describing an image" (Vinyals et al.

2014). *Ekphrasis* (the ancient art of describing what is seen, using appropriate names and words) is an art that for millennium was indelibly associated with intelligence, memory, and capacity—for those who could recount tales were the repositories of oral history; and those who could write the news down were journalists and reporters; and those who could see distant patterns were poets. This task is now computationally tractable.

What will remain intractable (for a while) is the giving of names to the contours of *interior* states, dimensions of thought, and processes of experience. In order to be able to do so, one of the steps might involve having a model of affect and experiences.[9] And that is a subject many morbid melancholy poets have contemplated over millennia, and one that is dealt with in chapter 5 in the section "Reverse Engineering Intimacy."

Mez Breeze: Mezangelle (1994–) (and Natchka Nezvanova)

One of the capacities of humans is to identify and play with words: deformations, truncations, modulations, resonances, ricochets, and other spasms of intricate, respectful, gracious mutations. If computers are to write and live poetry, fuzzy, soft, variational spaces must open in the texture of how they treat (eat, read, and rite) words. The brittle must be made soft. Poets excel at suggesting such fluid limits.

Idiosyncratic Breeze aka Mez aka Netwurker is a poet whose language stretches poetry into code; her idiom incorporates machinic tropes into an idiosyncratic, virtuosic tangle. She often writes in her own language-system, mezangelle, which incorporates computer programming language syntax. Her work is social; it began in 1994 on Telnet/Unix virtual networks and has led to Netprov, character-driven performance-narratives conducted in chat spaces and social network streams.[10]

In her defiance of conventions, adherence to severe language play, and exuberance, Mez belongs to a poetic tradition that includes practitioners like bill bissett. Yet Mez's practice shares much more with renegade Listserv provocateurs like the infamous Netochka Nezvanova, a programmer who coded the early NATO video plugins for MaxMSP. Here is a sample email I received from Nezvanova (quoted in Johnston 2002):

gender - 0 | null pointer
location—copenhagen.denmark.europe.
dayjob - 0 | null pointertzzt. antiorp.
[last phaze of beauty = beauty due2 error]

When asked in 2014 what digital writing will be in ten years' time, Mez responded, "In 10 years' time digital writing will have escaped contemporary constraints [e-books, EPUB, Kindles, personal computers, tablets, phones, etc.] and will instead have manifested in a sophisticated merge of Wearables, Robotics, Artificial Intelligence and Virtual Reality [such as working AR devices that take audience involvement to a completely different participatory level, with biofeedback and telemetry/locative data integrated in a much more granular fashion]. Think: *Emotiv, Oculus Rift, LEAP Motion,* or *Project Morpheus* tech married with *Jawbone, Fitbit* and/or *Kinect*-type gadgetry to create stories that bypass many of the standard ebook or interactive story conventions we encounter today" (quoted in Pope 2014).

This bypass may (assuming Mez's hypothesis is accurate) involve significant interplay between objects and biometric processes, leading to a blurring between the structural forms of being and bling. According to the neuroscientist Jaak Panksepp (1998), play is one of the core key modules shared across all mammalian brain structures. Poetic play will be integral to the blurring bypass that gives birth to *new formalisms* aka *worms in flames.*

J. Abbott Miller: *Dimensional Typography* (1997)

Bulbous, rooted, twisted, woven extrusions proliferate in landscapes; yet the binary eight-bit geometry of computer graphics often lacks the rough sensual chaos that signifies the organic. One classic that explores how typographic forms can delineate psychic states, how shape creates identity, is Miller's (1997) *Dimensional Typography.* Miller's work exists at the threshold between a predominantly computational culture and a typographic tradition based on print. As research, it bridges the two cultures; in practice, it playfully and astutely probes the gap between page and screen—proposing experimental forms based on 3-D rendering techniques, probing volumetric-language concepts, and proposing a taxonomy of volumetric letterforms.

Miller's taxonomy of typographic forms revolves around the simple block-capitalized categories of SPATIAL and TEMPORAL. The SPATIAL includes extrusion (along nontraditional axes), rotation (around the font), sewing (as in cursive scripts and handwriting stitches), molecular construction (as in pixels), modular construction (as in geometric primitives), and bloating. These terms (native to 3-D modeling) enter design discourse and migrate toward literary theory.

Miller explores what happens when these simple 3-D modeling techniques are procedurally applied to letterforms. They *extrude*: letterforms suction into space, logos protrude, and poems are enacted around massive monumental letters. There is *rotation*, which conceals legibility; if the object exists at all angles, it becomes like a vase on a lathe, and concealment becomes gestural. Cursive *handwriting* scripts flow into visibility in a multitude of examples; these have become a cliché of branding, and evoke the path of nostalgia. *Molecular* fonts, where pixels flow and swarm along field lines, are particle system exercises, establishing flow patterns where letterforms interstice math. *Modular* construction (popularized as Miller notes by Matthew Carter's font for the Walker Art Center) is a typographic Tetris: innumerable logo fonts in 3-D environments composed from clumps of cubes.

With advances in graphics processing, thick protuberant or thin flexible fonts proposed in *Dimensional Typography* have spawned many undulant, sinuous, morphing, malleable motion graphic descendants. No longer stoically transfixed by the notion of the page as reading device, dimensional typographic is now fully filmic. The gestalt of typography has shifted from single state into multiple, from single frame into 4K (soon to be 8M? 16R?). And it is among this multiplicity of formats and metamorphic jolts that semantic meaning and interpretation arrive. It is in the fluctuations and vibratory transformations that readers become viewers. In time-based animation, the temporal becomes aesthetic as well as navigational.

All the formal qualities of dimensional typography labeled as SPATIAL by Miller have a corollary in contemporary digital malleable typography, a corollary augmented by tactile response; all the TEMPORAL aspects have a corollary in digital timeline animation and interactive change. So Miller's primary theoretical role bridges media and contributes to a hybridized fusion of computer modeling with typographic design. It also regrounds bits and byte letters in the choppy, swollen, tumescent, unpredictable lands of life.

Peter Cho: TYPOTOPO (1998) and Takeluma (2005)

They rise from the ground like a mountain range, shard flanks cut rough by the tempo of their growth; they flock into configurations during the night, each item of their vast bodies made of a tiny letter; they flow on paths that merge with the sound of their own speaking.

Contemporaneously with Miller's *Dimensional Typography*, Cho (an award-winning designer who later received a master of fine arts from the University of California at Los Angeles and a masters of science from the Massachusetts Institute of Technology) began to release typographic experiments—TYPOTOPO—that stretched conceptions of type as a carrier for meaning; the boundaries were stretched digitally with a Zen-like precision using programming and rendering. His concerns place him at the membrane between an artist, a poet, and a designer, but his consistent focus has been fonts, glyphs, and the squirming squiggles of the semantic word. In 1998, Cho developed Forefont type. "These letterforms stemmed from dissatisfaction with flat, texture-mapped type that disappears when rotated in a virtual three-dimensional environment. Forefont type pushes up against a grid and retains its bumpy profile when tilted towards the viewer" (Cho 1998a).

In the same year, Cho (1998b) developed a storm swarm 3-D algorithmic text, *Nutexts*: "*Nutexts* is a series of experiments exploring three-dimensional space through typography. In each experiment, the text of a short or medium-length written work is laid out in a virtual three-dimensional environment according to a set of simple metrics or rules." Spatially configured layouts correspond to virtual architecture, precursors of presence.

Cho's (2008) work *Wordscapes* continues the process of exploring dynamic force and participatory 3-D typography. Interactive, thoughtful, and brief, one word for each letter of the alphabet is mapped onto a set of mouse sensitivities. The interactivity amplifies the semantics; it is animation in the classic sense. This is Warner Brothers not Fyodor Dostoyevsky; behaviors do not change over time, but each in its succinctness satisfies and nourishes expectation.

Cho's work that reaches the deepest (for me) is *Takeluma*, a speech-sensitive installation completed in 2005. *Takeluma* reminds me of Kurt Schwitters if he had been exposed to shape-memory alloy. It is in essence a project that directly explores synesthesia (between the sound of words and the forms we associate with them) and develops a speculative visual idiom. Cho's (2005) description reaffirms my contention that visual language can heal the gap between sign and signifier as it evolves into a new synesthetic presence:

Takeluma is an invented writing system for representing speech sounds and the visceral responses they can evoke. Takeluma explores the complex relationships between speech, meaning, and writing. While modern linguistics suggests that the relationship between signifier and signified has no discernible pattern, poets and marketing experts alike know that the sounds of words can evoke images which elicit an emotional impact. The project explores the ways that speech sounds can give rise to a kinesthetic response. The Takeluma project comprises several animated and print works and a reactive installation.

By loosening language from the straitjacket of definition, *Takeluma* explores a tentative hybrid between linguistics, abstract art, and sound poetry; this occurs formally, intellectually, and physically. Speech acoustics bind to letterforms. *Takeluma's* audio waveforms are ribbons, worms that extrude into space. These are precursors to letterforms that directly correspond to the body's internal resonant cavities, letterforms capable of expressing archetypal congruences between acoustic forms and felt semantics.

Installations: Stream of Consciousness (1998) and Text Rain (1999)
The surface of writing is and always has been complex. It is a liminal symbolically interpenetrated membrane, a fractal coast- or borderline, a chaotic and complex structure with depth and history.

—John Cayley, 2005

David Small and Tom White's interactive text installation *Stream of Consciousness* is an obvious precursor to Cayley's (2005) notion of "Writing on Complex Surfaces." Cayley wraps the page around the reader in an immersive CAVE space; in Small and White's (1998) work,

a six foot square garden sits in the middle of an otherwise ordinary computer lab. Water briskly flows down a series of cascades into a glowing pool. Projected on the surface of the pool and flowing as if they were caught in the water's grasp are a tangle of words. You can reach out and touch the flow, blocking it or stirring up the words causing them to grow and divide, morphing into new words that are pulled into the drain and pumped back to the head of the stream to tumble down again.

Fluid language that follows contours and reacts to touch constitutes physical metaphor. Letterforms, freed from the page and released according to the dynamics of an algorithmic gravity path, changing as the reader reaches out to touch, become dynamic structures, evolutionary creatures, and quasi-organisms. *Stream of Consciousness* is literal nature, as is *Text Rain*.

It is intriguing to note how the literary critic Francisco Ricardo opens his treatment of *Text Rain* (Achituv and Utterback 1999) defensively by examining how the advocates of "pure literature" exiled images from literary texts; the expulsion used a litany of doctrinal objections against the integration of imagistic content perceived as hostile to literature's essence. Against such critiques, Ricardo explores how the effect of *Text Rain* is "transmodal, a recursive amalgam of filmic, literary, performative and near-sculptural conditions" (Ricardo 2009, 60). It is within the ideologically hostile environment outlined by Ricardo that text and image establish illicit yet fertile contact.

Romy Achituv and Camille Utterback chose to use the body as obstruction; but the body also then becomes the letters. Letters collect on the surface of the body; they become its fur. It's a simple metaphor that has been reused and adapted many times within multiple contexts (from snowflakes to ashes collecting on the tongue). The body in this space operates as the book, an interactive obstruction, a metaphor for memory, embodied coagulation. Letters cover the body, text and texture combine, the line between language as an exterior inert inanimate abstraction dissolves.

The preceding outlines a few late twentieth-century pioneers in the transition from the printing press era to the screen. The next section dives into the networked transcription processes of the twenty-first century: the embryo elongates into the first suggestion of a living reactive form.[11]

Twenty-First-Century Digital Practice

As language practice evolved over the period between 1995 and 2014, visceral aesthetic technical and philosophical tendrils unknotted. Works defied simple categorization, and of necessity, flexible taxonomies emerged: cyborg, networked, tactile mashups of discourse terminology navigated fertile chaos. Variable criteria and a diversity of formal constraints arose as critical components and creative modules contributing toward many (often-divergent) goals: psychological, interactive, conceptual, and social.

The lens of a potential emergent animist art-language form is the interpretative tool selected here for viewing this complex, contradictory, mediated-poetic evolution. It is a contingent choice validated by the insights it allows. The language-organism, animism-ecosystem lens allows wide focus—given the highly differentiated modular forms of existing bodies (our own) situated in ecosystems (the earth). The analogy of animism allows for casual interpretations of creative practice (as if on an aesthetic hike) or critical investigations (as if analyzing phenomena for formal laws). Aspiring to breadth, the following section explores simultaneous paths up from the microscopic to human and social scales, conjecturing toward an emergent moment when independent poetic trajectories culminate in emergence.

The question "why?" is ancient; why invokes the mysterious autopoietic (self-assembling) origins of humanity's apparent and constrained agency, and somewhere near those origins, poetic agency rewires and rewrites biological codes (at microscopic scales: as Christian Bök, Zuzana Husárová, Joe Davis, Eduardo Kac, and S. S. Prasad demonstrate). At a scale larger than the microscopic, both skin and body arise, currently as screens, mobiles, tablets, motion graphics, projection surfaces, and interfaces (explored by Jason Lewis, Erik Loyer, Andy Campbell, Ben Fry, and Amaranth Borsuk, among many others). Beneath the skin, active connections examine premises: digital poetic practitioners detonate assumptions, satirize ridiculous aspirations (as Christophe Bruno, Talan Memmott, Jaap Blonk, Daniel Howe, Karsten Schmidt, Brad Troemel, TRAUMAWIEN, etc.). And in the marrow of a potential computational poet lurks a machine that generates poems, drawing on diverse insights from linguistics and big data (as Darius Kazemi, Ray Kurzweil, John Cayley, Nick Montfort and Stephanie Strickland, Antonio Roque, Håkan Jonson and Johannes Heldén, and others investigate).

Supporting a claim that poetry is coalescing into a nascent organism involves showing how some poems act like creatures.

Organisms navigate, mark, and organize terrain, as do the map anecdote-poems (with their lithe demented logic and internal calibrations) of J. R. Carpenter. Carpenter's poems are tenderly ironic articulate reservoirs of intimacy, and also formal explorations of identity as a cartographic space; a virtual space that utilizes interactivity as an analog for anecdotal quests. Set within a browser, these whimsical creations delineate stories that are proximal to landscapes populated by personalities that are isometric, quirky, and contorted by their communities. The dynamic overlaps between language-interactivity-and-image distort space and place identity into sets of flow.

Organisms react to touch enigmatically: Serge Bouchardon's *Loss of Grasp* is a synesthetic and eerily alienating descent into a computationally modulated environment where mild gestures evoke major effects, touch cannot grasp anything because slick words escape and synthetic voices reassure; as they evolve, his works invite the reader to revise expectations and provoke paradoxical relations to text that operates as if it were skin.

Organisms babble, cry, and exhort: the quirky, metabolic programming prowess of Jörg Piringer deflects categorization; he exerts a Merz-like presence, exploring the lineage of Schwitters's *Ursonate* using iPhone apps and conceptualized vocal interventions to instigate conceptual interventions that dissolve linear narratives. Piringer (2011) describes his performance work (and iOS app) *abcdefghijklmnopqrstuvwxyz* as custom software that analyzes "voice to create animated abstract visual text/sound-compositions. The autonomous movement and behaviour of visual element on the screen again influence the sound which creates an audiovisual feedback loop or an autopoetic live performance system."

Organisms dream and think: Brian Kim Stefans (2000), after the quirky delight of *The Dreamlife of Letters*, has emerged as a formidable theorist-practitioner-poet, whose sinuous, pragmatic, codified language reflects a programmer steeped in continental philosophy and conceptual language play. Stefans's writing appears with many others in the seminal critical compilation edited by Adalaide Morris and Thomas Swiss (2006), *New Media Poetics: Contexts, Technotexts, and Theories*.

Organisms appropriate material to build nests: Natalie Bookchin's (2007) *Zorns Lemma2* re-creates Hollis Frampton's structuralist film with security footage and webcam: "In each subsequent set, one letter of the alphabet is replaced by a web cam recording representing a visual language of surveillance cameras, continuing until all letters are replaced." As mentioned previously, today's poems also forage and die: Darren Wershler-Henry and Bill Kennedy's (2006) *Apostrophe* creates illuminated strophes from Net scruff (in other words, it constructs an infinite poem based on web searches; an original poem operates as template); although currently dormant, its five-year life span of active searches constitutes a form of pseudoinfinite burrowing and harvest writing based on network foraging.

One of the evolutionary destinations of digital poems is that they become tangible structures that incorporate enough intelligence and sensors to detect and generate poetry appropriate for each viewer. Eitan Mendelowitz's (2002–2006) *Drafting Poems: Inverted Potentialities* prototypes such a system: presenting users with a glass surface on which a dry-erase marker can draw, a soup of letters respond to the input, and an AI system generates a poem. Another paradigm is the ongoing installation-performance, data-driven amalgamation of Mark Jeffrey and Judd Morrissey's (2009) *The Precession*, which "makes use of original writing and real-time data collection to create visual-poetic arrangements based on inquiries into architecture and the night sky. The piece mixes databased sources, real-time interruptions, and algorithmic composition in an evolving ecology." The result is an unsettling physical hybrid of many media: Net art, postmodern glee club, architectural installation, data center, poem.

Agency, Action, and Scale

One way of perceiving an object is as a system of encoded physics, absolute predictability inserted into a modular ontological niche, agency denied. Space materializes hives of these hierarchical niches—each with limits, parameters, permissions, and positions. In *Vibrant Matter: A Political Ecology of Things*, Jane Bennett promotes objects into the continuum of agency formerly reserved for entities. This is an example of what is termed a *flat ontology*. "A lot happens to the concept of agency once nonhuman things are figured less as social constructions and more as actors, and once humans themselves are assessed not as autonomous but as vital materialities" (Bennett 2010, 21). Her conceptual gesture simultaneously elevates things and grounds human thinking in its material instantiation.

Extending Bennett's notion of agency to language (as it erupts into objective coded forms) is the core idea of this book. The following section explores case studies of viral code poems, interactive installations, distributed tattoos, icon narratives, physical event poems, poetic inscriptions on integrated circuits and genomes, 3-D printed conceptual sculpture poems, and game-poem architectures that all contribute to this shifting gestalt. Things embedded with sensors and code (spimes) and poems that operate as things (spoems) are interim opportunities in a cascade of opportunistic infections by language of ontological categories previously reserved for entities.

In Patricia Piccinini's (2006) *The Nest*, a sculpted moped mother twists her handlebar-neck, responding solicitously to her infant moped. Imagine their expressive robotic bodies in the future written by code, their behaviors controlled by AI, language physicalized into form. This coded architecture (anticipated in the affective robotic models of Rosalind Picard, Cynthia Breazeal, and Aaron Sloman) suggests that writing occurs at many levels of scale in devices and bodies. The dichotomy of a page-screen expands to become a continuum of page-screen-human(viewer)-object-thing-organism.

Product specialists call it 4-D; synthetic biologists practice it as reverse transcription; poets wait for the intuited core cadence, the extrusion of the virtual into existence. Michael Joyce (2012) references (perhaps inadvertently) similar potential when he insists that "if writing is to be anything, it must first be an action in this world." To act is to exist.[12] The following poems do just that: they act.

Viruses
Language is a virus.

—William Burroughs

If poetry is a language virus that destabilizes pretentious perceptions or congealed opinions, then the notion of a poem as a computer virus is a natural fit. *Biennale.py* (created by Eva Mattes and Franco Mattes [2001] with the assistance of hackers group Epidemic for the forty-ninth Venice Biennale) was a Python virus that replicated and wrote itself into the "body" of text files on host computers. The code itself is poetry of a kind; allegorical code-poetry with erotic twists:

```
"soul = open (guest,
body = soul.read()"
```

Even here in what is essentially a provocateur art-joke, the implicit analogy used refers to the body reading a soul—a terminological system that would have satisfied Saint Augustine. The implication being that computers are the metaphoric site of resurrection; the trembling, inert host wavers (a thin and somewhat-inconspicuous transubstantiation) distributed by the Catholic Church are in this schizophrenic parable seeded with a computer virus that overwhelms biological autonomy. *The second coming of Christ is an articulate AI virus.*

Parables generated by *Biennale.py* reflect the uncertainty and paranoia behind embodiment: How did evolution inscribe us with code that allows us to be conscious? The evolutionary biologist Lynn Margulis (1980) conceptualizes the mitochondria at the center of our cellular machinery as a viral form that took symbiotic refuge. Mammals are the progeny of invasive cellular "poems": machinery devoted to reordering and rhythmically regenerating the world.

In 2000, Jason Lewis programmed an executable poem that reads the hard-drives of its host computer and displays a shifting textual animation based on the contents it has scanned. *"I Know What You're Thinking* is a 'stream of consciousness' poetry generator that reanimates the bored and restless texts residing on your hard drive" (Lewis 2000). Just as insight into human nature allows authors to parasite the secrets of their subjects (revealing through concrete details the intricate mechanisms of hatred, greed, fear, lusts, sorrow, vulnerability, etc.), *I Know What You're Thinking* functions as a mirror, refractory and disruptive, dispersing familiarity and linearity; presenting the user to themselves as a data narcotic, as it activates a procedural subconscious scavenging. In this case, the reader self-infects (inoculates) their own machine in order to experience the narcotic disruption of the poem-virus.

As pure action, these pieces of writing, written as code, operate in ways analogous to classical poems. They collect, disperse, fragment, corrupt, and reinvigorate the integrity of existing forms and phenomena in order to reveal the world as a new process. Reconfigured, reoriented, infected. The muse both mad and made, poetry as a contamination, a sickness that does not heal, a horizon that curves. From these preliminary experiments, in the post-Stuxnet era, it is possible to conceive of poetic-viruses released by gray-hat hackers that splice debris at the bottom of our collective unconscious, our networked mobile memory—anamnesis hacks.

Viral poems can be simple organisms that follow a simple rule such as "Find all phrases containing phrase __Y_, in social network _X_." *We Feel Fine* (Harris and Kamvar 2005) and the playful accumulation project *The Dumpster* (Levin, Nigam, and Feinberg 2006) both use variations of this naive premise to create dynamic, insightful archives of texts harvested from online and represented as particles that reveal words when touched.

Part of the intimacy of poetry is its implicit surveillance of us before we read it. *How did the poet know just that secret thought?* It's a psychological trick: we all often think similar. And at another level, it's an aspect of the project underlying poetics to suggest a primordial unity, and hence intimacy, joining all beings into a single unified field of awareness. Ultimate awareness implies both nurturance and paranoia. The perfect eye of the all-seeing Google, the helpful search engine, the government surveillance that knows all, the mystical trance of schizophrenia, panopticon Mother. Digital poetry tinkers with the fragments that arise as ultimate knowledge explodes into emotional insights in the network, and it does this by invading us as a virus.

Microscopes and Nanopoems (Prasad and Husárová)
There's Plenty of Room at the Bottom.

—Richard Feynman, 1959

Under the narrow beams of metals, in the labyrinths through which our thoughts flow, is a tiny scar, legible by accident, a minimonument. It is a poem. Its author S.S. Prasad, an engineer, lives and works in Bangalore, distant from the core of Western poetry, yet in *Rampike*—a journal of experimental poetry with a history of showcasing the avant-garde—Prasad published several images and wrote, "Nanopoems are poems written inside the microchip to surprise an engineer while examining the integrated circuit under a microscope" (Prasad 2008, 24) His intervention reorients the discussion of the page away from screen to the microchip, where writing first occurs in the process of computation. Subtly disruptive, mildly heretical, a folly, these poems exist to question preoccupations with surface, invert scale, nudge the mind into exoteric wiggles.

Zuzana Husárová also employed scientific techniques to write at levels of scale that are illegible to the naked eye. Husárová's (2011) work *Any Vision* "was created by scanning electron microscopy. The lines of the gradually self-reducing anagram poem were printed on a semiconductor device sample of Germanium and Silicon dioxide. The lines of the poem were written by a focus Ga ion beam into the sample. Placed into the microscope, the sequences of images were scanned by electrons at ranges from 400x all the way to 10000x. The first line was taken from the manual of the focused ion beam imaging system." Her gesture of using the manual as the first line is a postmodern reflex that forms a metareflection on the process, but it is also interpretable as a bootstrap process.[13] A poem informing other poems how-to be-born; an act of mechanical gestation, silicon fertilization, a muse in less than a micron.

Why are these poems important? The labyrinth on Crete at Minoan forms a palimpsest visible from space as faint tremblings. Our greatest cities

are mere luminous undulations beside mountain ranges. Humans are proficient at forgetting how tiny within the vast precipice of time and space our
most ambitious projects are. These poems touch to that core, implicate us in
evidence of oblivion. And they also suggest physically how writing permeates space at all levels (not just the human), constituting it, molding every
making. Molecular resonances write poems at levels of physical materiality
only perceptible with instrumentalized vision. They reflect the numerical
future that N. Katherine Hayles presciently anticipated (and resisted) where
"physicality is also data made flesh, another flickering signifier in a chain
of signification that extends through many levels, from the DNA that in-
formats her body to the binary code that is the computer's first language"
(Hayles 1999, 47).

Genomic Poetics (Davis, Kac, Venter, and Bök)
As far as I know, there have been four primary interventions that involve
directly writing poetry into genes.

The first was renegade BioArtist Joe Davis's *Microvenus* project. He wrote
an ancient fertility glyph into an E. Coli bacterium in 1996 and exhibited it
at *Ars Electronica* 2000. For this he invented his own coding structure (Davis
1996).

The second (as mentioned in *Kac: Holo and Bio Poetry*) was Kac's (2001)
insertion of a biblical verse into a strand of DNA for his 1998 *Genesis* exhibit.
In this exhibit, networked viewers control an ultraviolet light that effects
the rate of bacterial propagation (in other words, alters cellular *publishing*).

The third was Craig Venter (2010), who on May 20, 2010, announced
that his team had *created and watermarked the first self-replicating artificial
organism* with a codified puzzle, the names of the organism's authors, and
three citations, including one from James Joyce: "TO LIVE, TO ERR, TO
FALL, TO TRIUMPH, TO RECREATE LIFE OUT OF LIFE." Ominous? Perhaps. Trivial? Not at all. This shifts the definition of self-publishing.

The fourth poetic-genetic intervention, Christian Bök's (2008) *Xenotext
Experiment*, was *proposed* in 2007 and almost *implemented* in 2011; in this
arduous cryptographic experiment, an extremophile bacteria is modified
so its DNA contains a poem that also expresses poetic proteins (proteins
encrypted in ways that once decrypted are readable as poems).

Each of these preceding interventions is far from creating a living language that will persist without complicated life support (as in computers

and humans), or function as viable technology for reading that will challenge the book or screen. Davis inserts, Kac intervenes, Bök expresses, and Venter's replicates, yet each relies on an extensive substrate of molecular syntax. And even though Bök intends his durable verse-critter (extremophile: radiodurans) to potentially outlive humanity, there is the problem of user interface developments: How exactly do we read these texts except as interventions that challenge our conception of memory substrates?

Each project is more akin to a microbe making a tattoo on an elephant than a sustained treatise on molecular poetry. Yet these tiny revolutionary, incremental splices interject imagination onto molecular substrates, intertwine the context of text with molecular biology, and anticipate a radical shift in the materiality of reading.

How does this connect to digital poetry? Rapid sequencing and subsequent manipulation of the genome emerge in parallel with computation. The genome for the first self-replicating synthetic cell was "designed in the computer" (Venter 2010). Binary encoding processes convey the word into flesh.

Body Echoes (Kallir, Nadeau & Lewis, and Jackson)
Crisp and tight. Dust-wrapper a little age-darkened but internally seemingly unused.

—Online antiquarian description of first edition of Alfred Kallir, *Sign and Design*, 1961

In 1961, Kallir wrote one of the strangest books in the history of linguistic analysis: *Sign and Design: The Psychogenetic Origins of the Alphabet*.[14] It is a treatise on the symmetry between the physical world and the shape of letters. According to Kallir, letterforms inherit synesthetic archaeological and genetic features from mythology, history, and sexuality. A inverted is a bull's head, a standing man, a call to sacrifice, and the raised legs of a female and her sex. B is a pregnant woman. C is the womb. Each letter carries its own symbolic genome; implicit encodings of primordial meaning inform the daily semantic level.

As Kallir's alphabet reflects the body, so in some digital poetry installations, the reverse is true: the body carries the impact of letterforms. In *Still Standing*, a kinetic and interactive installation (Nadeau and Lewis 2005), the body's contours enclose letters, and skin becomes a container to hold a tumbling set of words, but it is only when the viewer is still and motionless that the TAVIT (interactive text) arrives at legibility; letters endowed with gravity and physical parameters do not rest until they find a vacant, viable viewer-outline (womb) to inhabit. Contemplation, that ancient mode of poetic awareness, inverts interactive reading; passivity becomes key. *Still Standing* invites readers to perceive embodiment as a reservoir, an empty vessel activating a silent process of linguistic accumulation.

Tattoos are an accumulation of ink pigment particles too large to be eaten by white blood cells; it is a technical invasion designed to exceed the body's defenses. Under the skin, injected, tattoo ink merges with the body, becomes part of it. Shelley Jackson's (2003) *Skin*, "a story published on the skin of 2095 volunteers," began with a published call for volunteers to agree to merge with a story, to tattoo one word each on their body; the conditions:

The text will be published nowhere else. ... The full text will be known only to participants. ... From this time on, participants will be known as "words." They are not understood as carriers or agents of the texts they bear, but as its embodiments. ... Only the death of words effaces them from the text. As words die the story will change; when the last word dies the story will also have died. The author will make every effort to attend the funerals of her words.

Skin forms a distributed network story, a collective meme viral archive of intimate ink injected into social psyche; the Internet enabled it.[15] Jackson's work as an Internet hypertext writer was seminal. *Patchwork Girl*, released by Eastgate Systems in 1995, was a branching narrative, retelling the story of Frankenstein, the word made flesh in cybernetic form available on a USB stick for Macintosh at $24.95 (Jackson 1995). Her work now extends that branching, linked structure into the flesh of lived lives, the skin of bodies (that will over time wrinkle, distort, and eventually decay) releasing one by one the text they hold. As she visits each funeral, the writing and erasure of the text constitute a story only she is told.[16]

Even as in our pockets, tiny rectangular gleaming screens display news, alerts, science, love letters, spam, dating sites, games, porn, and shopping lists; a bull runs toward upraised antennae legs in the mall, a womb of wires swells with infrared sensors, and cascading through the flesh of letters, new encoding evolves new metaphors for the physicalized flesh of language.

Disruptions (Zelinskie, Bing, and Simon)

People all say I am a practitioner of contemporary art; in fact, what I have polished and refined are mostly obsolete things. These "obsoletes" contain within them the most fundamental things, core things.

—Xu Bing, 2013

It is generally agreed that animism is obsolete, and that formal systems (physics, computation, linguistic recursion, genomics, etc.) intervene in layers between the origin and emergence of symbols, objects, and organisms. In our era, things are understood as reflections of language, information, and process. Manifestations rely on invisible transcriptions for display. Since transcription processes create entities, unstable transcription processes contain potential disruptions, poetic energy. It is in this disruptive energy that animism is reborn.

With her homage sculpture *One and One Chair*, Ashley Zelinskie played with notions of destabilized transcription by creating a 3-D model of the chair used in Joseph Kosuth's conceptual installation *One and Three Chairs*. Zelinskie (2011) then converted her 3-D chair model to hexadecimal code, and used the hex code to construct a real chair from what appears to be glued, 3-D printed models of that code. The rebuilt chair is literally language printed into the shape that it encodes. It is a poem that wears its code as skin.

When a poet (as many others before and after them) opens a JPG as a text file and throws a quotation into it, they perform a distortion of the informational stream; it is a juggling in the order of scale. The poet is a surgeon transplanting a brain into the cavity reserved for the pancreas. Mutations in the display, glitches in the skin, emerge from such deliberate and accidental disruptions. It is as if the interpreter (in this case, the JPG code) thinks it is reading Latin but the text is actually part Hindi—and stutters of meaning emerge. Glitch coding a low-fi magic trick: it causes the thing itself to disappear as the process of its construction surfaces.

For *Book from the Sky*, visual artist Xu Bing (1987) created twelve hundred imaginary Chinese characters, hand carved them into wooden letterpress, and printed unintelligible books and scrolls. His gesture highlights the strangeness of the received world, and the arbitrary nests of our language. Poetry (in the sense of poetics as a destabilizing tendency designed not to provoke insecurity but instead to reawaken wonder) has often been considered unintelligible or simply wrong. In this case, Xu Bing modified the code of language so culture could not compile it; his gesture was the equivalent of disrupting a network of self-reinforced meanings; it was a protest against the propagandistic use of language that stabilized the Cultural Revolution. In 2013, Xu Bing published and exhibited *Landscape Landscripts: Nature as Language in the Art of Xu Bing*—the culmination of drawings that began in 1999—where the Chinese character literally represents what it is in a painting. Language and landscape, poetry and painting, the thing and its term conjoin.[17] In Xu Bing's ongoing project *Book from the Ground*, the process is similarly disruptive. Icons (fastidiously collected from diverse sources, signage, digital sources, etc.) repurposed as language, in comic-book-style panels, evoke ambiguous narratives (Xu Bing 2003). Human, computer, and symbol intertwine (the book is entirely icons: cat-clock-cab-ampersand-smiley-stop-arrow-plane-kiss …); this hybrid grid of semaphores both encourages nonlinear guesses and obstructs a decoding into linear sequences.

Icons are contingent apparatuses, liminal symbols: part language and part depiction. Ideogrammatic and visual, they are images that substitute for letterforms. In John F. Simon's durational computer drawing, software art project *Every Icon*, a Java applet is slowly trying all the potential monochrome variations of a thirty-two by thirty-two grid. Code displays for a moment each icon. It has been running since 1997. In *Every Icon*, there is not enough time to read anything; most of the icons are nontenable (unreadable), yet the project highlights how arbitrary the finite set of alphabet is, how fragile are the circumstances that give birth to culture, how vulnerable is the process of shared reception to disintegration.[18]

The thing is what we project into it. Context conceived in circumstance. Poems are what things project out of themselves. Poetry reflects this awareness that sinuous streams connect across levels of scale. Digital poetry must in its perpetual quest for relevance contemplate the code inside chairs, look beyond the book, behind, beneath, or within the screen to the thing itself, the ripe suchness that perpetuates not just media but also medial states, processes of mind where borders eradicate and blur predominates.

Labyrinth Games (Baldwin, Benayoun, and Jhave)

What did emerge from these researches apart from the immense diversity and range of picture poems was the archetypal quality of some of the imagery which occurred and reoccurred in so many different cultures. Closely wrought mandelas, and endless labyrinths were common; mythological merged animals—winged serpents, eagle horses, man-beasts, griffins, unicorns, the ladder, the tree of life. The fleurs-de-lis were discovered in texts ranging from Malay magic and ancient Greek Papyri to Hebrew massoretic texts giving one the sense that the global village existed long before the twentieth century.

—Berjouhi Bowler, 1970

At the roots of language is the labyrinth, a space of danger and ultimately liberation from ignorance. The Minotaur who lurks at the center of labyrinths devours minds; paradoxically there in the center, ultimate knowledge is death, sacrifice, and unjust loss. Icarus retraces his path with a thread: literacy is a memory technology. The architecture of how we arrive at language arises from myth. It does not die; it migrates.

French multimedia artist Maurice Benayoun, in collaboration with poet Jean-Pierre Balpe, created an interactive labyrinth for real-time dialogue in 2000 called *Labylogue*. Participants in four cities (Brussels, Lyon, Dakar, and Quebec) search a space where words (generated in real time based on dialogues between participants) cover all the walls. The conceptual gesture implicates words as union and separation: what divides us is what we have to know each other. The encyclopedic excess of the written knowledge in which all are lost or meander becomes the space we explore.

Most contemporary games occur in labyrinths; we are the hunted-hunters, warrior-shooters. Antagonistic to the mode of reverie associated with the classic notion of poet, games and their labyrinth locations have attracted language arts mods. Sandy Baldwin (2003) says of his first-person-shooter poem: "*Basra [New World Order]* is a mod for the game Half-Life. … When you enter the map you see words hanging in the air. You can jump and climb on them, you can run along the tops, you can keep playing and wandering in the space. You soon attack the words. You use the broken words as a reduced and processed writing. Break the words, destroy the letters. NWO, along with every game and every image, is about the recirculation of bodies and interpretive agendas."

In 2013, I converted the default games that shipped with Unity3D (versions 3 and 4) into two art-poem-game spaces. In one game, the player is always alone, weaponless in a labyrinth of words. The next level is reached by leaping off, going down. In the other game, the player is a gun—only a gun, bobbing in the air as it runs. Flowers are everywhere. Words are woven into barbed wire and walls (Jhave 2013). Poems extrapolate the impact of endemic violence toward an imminent anthropocene.

The precursor to the walled labyrinth was the forest. In the fourteenth century, Dante finds himself in a dark forest having lost his way. That metaphor would have been a familiar situation to many of his readers. As urbanization flourished so did the references to concrete jungle, urban forest, and city as a maze. Now metaphors proliferate around the network, the Internet incomprehensibly vast, convulsive, and bifurcating. The disembodied body of desire, the forest of our words and images, the labyrinth of end user license agreements (EULAs) and status updates, our click demographic speech, the Internet as a poem collectively written in packets, assembled and read only by machines—a disorientation at the heart of eternity sifted by logic gates.

Skin and Body

As media-specific materiality ascended, engorged on an analysis of the denser substrate of digital technology that underlies written language's creation and diffusion, words were also paradoxically becoming objects (things that stood for things). In advertisements, emotional words were given animate form, physical muscles, data flesh—the word *fear* shivered, the word *moist* was wet, *antibacterial* words hunted down animated pathogens. Parallel to the increasingly analytic tone of literary criticism, animated words adopted shapes that approximated beings designed to evoke affect. And the codes that drove these animations became comparable to metabolisms (code that ran in rudimentary ways through conditional if-then gates reacting as if decisions—evasion/attraction—were being made). These systems invite biological metaphors: algorithms *grow* letterforms, equations motion *flock* (Reynolds 1986). Biological metaphors lead to a consideration of letterforms as things and more than things—material inscriptions transformed into precursors of life.[19]

Jason Edward Lewis: *It's Alive* (1996) to *P.o.E.M.M.s* (2008–2014)

New media technologies reintroduce an animism and dynamism that re-engage the movement and gestures of the body in the scenes of writing and reading, rendering these processes explicitly performative in a way that is intimately involved in the generation of meaning.

—Maria Angel and Anna Gibbs, 2013

The animism referred to above by Angel and Gibbs is gestural: the body invoked in the production of meaning. Jason E. Lewis's career spans the trajectory from the definition of animism (used in this book) as recognition of life, to the animism (defined by Angel and Gibbs) as gesture or touch. Among Lewis's (1999) first works was a custom-built typographic animation software called *It's Alive*; it referenced the ancient tendency of human minds to see the earth as living matter. Among Lewis's (2009) more recent works are *P.o.E.M.M.s*, 2008–2014, which are multitouch apps for exhibition and iOS; the animism they reference is tactile and gestural.

Poets for millennium have self-published; with the arrival of the Internet, this practice proliferated and intensified to become the homepage. Yet few poets had the skill, tenacity, or inclination to dive deep into the modes of production and develop their own software, build their own press, and redesign Gutenberg from the ground up. There is a significant steep difference in effort required between using code inside a proprietary application and developing your own software for making apps. One is a cake mix, and the other involves growing and then grinding your own flour before developing your own recipe. *P.o.E.M.M.s* represent the culmination/continuation of a consistent, arduous software-poet development practice that includes *It's Alive* in 1996, *NextText* in 2003, and *Mr. Softie* in 2005.[20]

In addition, it requires extreme perseverance and technical acuity to convert vision into a tactile mobile app, and then in its next incarnation leap from virtual back to physical and become "visual art." The *P.o.E.M.M.s* deploy across a full spectrum of material and immaterial forms: app, posters, book, exhibits, and performance. Their context echoes and amplifies their content: a consistent concern with defiance and belonging. They invite an interpretative filter based on recognition of what they entail as organizational events. They speak of diffusion and union at a psychological and material level, and they enact a tenuous, graceful traverse across modes of publishing and being. They are both natives and refugees; the heredity they carry (poetic and technic) is integrated not eradicated. They uncategorize themselves.[21]

The visual-tactile interactivity of the *P.o.E.M.M.s* demands a different category of cognitive effort than reading lineated verse; touch redefines relations to reading into intimate action. *P.o.E.M.M.s* are loud and boisterous, bright colored beings. And to read one must touch, which is to be among, immersed in coherent chaos, risking the awakened word.

Eric Loyer: *Lair of the Marrow Monkey* (1998) and *Strange Rain* (2011)   Loyer is one of the pioneers of narrative-based, poetic, and elliptical, programmer-savvy electronic literature; his techno-trajectory encapsulates the evolutionary shifts occurring rapidly in industry and media art. In 1996, Loyer created "an interactive CD-ROM in which users experience a poem from the 'inside out,' by exploring a cyclic web of links between the images, sounds, symbols, and themes the poem evokes"; Loyer's (1998) iconic Web-interactive-sci-fi story *The Lair of the Marrow Monkey* magnetized words and phrases to mouse motion. At the time of its release, it was astonishingly new, yet now it's interactive tricks are widely replicated (in ads, kids' games, and innumerable installations), and its authoring software Director has been mothballed (obsolete and semifossilized). So it is with evolution: features subsumed, new forms emerging, ecosystems annihilated, tectonic overlap.

Loyer (2011) built one of the first iOS apps to creatively utilize the affordances of mobile device for e-lit: *Strange Rain*. In *Strange Rain*, orientation of the device alters the viewpoint, touch triggers the narrator's individual thoughts to fade-in, and drag provokes sequences of thought to emerge. As reading continues, features modulates; Loyer (2011) describes this as "going deeper into the experience," where readers earn "game-center achievements," and the app remembers who they are and their level. Loyer's (2013) *Freedom's Ring* provides an interactive timeline archaeology of Martin Luther King Jr.'s iconic "I Have a Dream" speech: part cartoon, oral history, animation, temporal scroll, and revisioning. He programmed the interface for Sharon Daniel's *Public Secrets* (Daniels and Loyer 2007), which adopts cells and cages as its interface design (tiled) to explore the supermax experience of California's woman prisoners, the business of imprisoning and release repeated by the viewer-reader who visits, listens, moving from cell to cell, anecdote to anecdote, which expand and contract reactively.

So in a decade, Loyer's interactive tropes evolved (in conjunction with the affordances of software and emergence of mobile hardware) from the swish and click of a mouse, to the sway of the body, the orientation of the hand, a memory of place, sets of levels, and atmospheric cameras that float like raptors on an updraft. They offer ecological integration, embodiment, and sense of a book as an eye perched in a scene where touch of different kinds and degrees triggers texts of different kinds, where the direction is clear; the complex nuanced expansion of the domain of interaction constitutes expansion in poetic potential.[22]

Andy Campbell: *Dreaming Methods* (1999–)   Campbell is a programmer whose dexterity with design, extensive practice dating back to 1999 (that epoch when so many of us leaped onto the web using Flash), and dark visions place him into a lineage congruent with Edgar Allan Poe's Gothic perambulations. Like the tentacles or root system of a macabre plant, on his website *Dreaming Methods*, Campbell (often with primary collaborator/ partner videographer Judi Alston) distributes audacious and sensual digital fiction through multiple media: browsers, apps, and PDFs. Its vision is disturbing: conspiracy theories, incest, suicides, rape, dreams, runaways, and amnesiacs. Brooding soundscapes and destabilizing (frequently impeccable) interactivity provoke a gliding psychotic trance. The reader's body is a body threatened by memories embedded into objects that leak words when touched.

Info dribbles through the stale air of decaying flats, the polluted breezes of derelict rail lands, infected with casual malice, ripe with stories. Each work sutures vignettes of eerie tranquillity with implied violence and trauma scenes. It's like being paralyzed and a bit stoned. There is always a story about someone who might have done something, but no one is ever seen. No faces appear. Time shatters into melancholic shards. Psychosis is just offscreen.

Words seep out of furniture—their meanings as fragmentary and ephemeral as dust. Chapter readings often require fulfillment of goals. Readers become players as they are played (sustained and engaged, drawn in and drawn on). Scale shifts frequently; rooms zoom into details. The edge of a decaying mattress. An old calculator. Text is swimming everywhere. Memories saturate space, as if molecules were tongues. The system is permeated with stories all the way down. Yet even proximity cannot resolve the palpable abiding sense of alienation.

Dreaming Methods is a creepy excursion into the hypnagogic trenches: part waking, part wonder, part abyss. It is also an exercise in sustained stylistic grace and a profound engagement with digital literature. Over a decade's work, Campbell has succeeded in developing a signature that combines sophisticated coding, narrative torque, and aesthetic fastidiousness. It has a bit of the glitch of hi-res.net during its *Donnie Darko* days before it got totally branded. On *Dreaming Methods*, the work aims not to sell or shock but rather to shelter in homage, lost memories, latent dreams, bits and bandwidth, esoteric audiovisuals, and intricate code. Swaying between being lost and feeling loss, it iterates (and exits) loops both computationally and emotionally.

Ben Fry: *Tendril* (2000)   In the domain of dimensional typography with ontological implications for digital poetry, there are some prescient pioneers. Fry's alternative web browser called *Tendril* sets precedents aesthetically and technically. In Fry's (2000) words, "*Tendril* is a web browser that constructs typographic sculptures from the text content of web pages. The first page of a site is rendered as a column of text. Links in the text are colored, and when clicked, the text for the linked page grows from the location of the link."

As *Tendril*'s text dynamically grows, it is woven into bulbous 3-D threads that evolve over time into spinning, bloated rhizomatic tubers. The surface of these structures is visually composed of text. These are now visual objects, hybrids, or chimeras: data-mining refuse (conceptual probes into knowledge and reading), modulated geometric primitives (abstract visual art), and animated organisms (information visualization of biological memes). *Tendril* is a quasi-organism and hybrid cultural entity; it feeds on text, digesting it into rhizomatic skin. *Tendril* automates appropriation; it is like Flarf exponential: reconfiguring what it retrieves into a format that is readable as tumescent infinities.

Obviously, legibility is not the key pleasure involved in most typographic sculptures. These redolent forms, undulant in black space, swollen with language, are unreadable. The reading machine process programmed by Fry operates unseen behind the screen, engorging itself on texts that stretch into curves that ripple as they excrete networks. This is sculptural animation that occurs in an on-screen ecosystem. The residue of *Tendril* is a few movies and JPGs, and probably a snarl of code rendered inoperative by shifts in network protocols—a fossilized excretion. So what the documentation provides is evidence (but not the actuality) of the passage of an incipient text-eating network-organism, a progenitor of creatures that will roam the Net eating words and shitting pulsating rhizomes.

For me, *Tendril* is a canonical example of time-based, language-driven digital art that simultaneously satisfies aesthetic and conceptual criteria. Naive viewing derives satisfaction from the organic suppleness of its form unraveling from nothingness; informed viewers derive additional stimuli by contemplating the interaction of networks at an abstract level.

What's also interesting about Fry's *Tendril* is how amenable it is to both cinematic and computational critiques. The archetypal story of cinema is the chase scene (hunt or seduction); *Tendril*'s morphology can be read as extruded paths, tunnels of words through which we seek each other. Perhaps these are the vibrant paths of preening literary culture, excess verbiage of reporters, infinite roots of a forest of bloggers, frying dendrites of epiphany-prone poets. Or perhaps these tubes are spaces of latent intent, topologies where words seek each other.

Let's push the metaphor into embodiment: curvaceous and plush *Tendril* evokes language's guts, the throats of oral storytellers, and the fallopian tubes of Orphic oracles. In the trembling of its languaged surfaces, it is possible to read culture as a single tongue. At the same time as it seems to invite metaphoric transplants and poetic close readings, *Tendril* denies this possibility; its river of words pass by in fragments of texture-mapped polygons rotating away from the eye like whales breaching in oil. Any oscillatory rivalry between legibility and pictorial subsides quickly into pure pectoral awe; watching *Tendril* flex its form takes precedence. Aesthetic instinct trumps contemplative text.

Thus, *Tendril* stripped of its semantics remains capable of conveying thoughts viscerally; it speaks to the articulate muscles in us. It is the writhing hollow intestines of poetry itself articulating a challenge to both authorial intent and flat page, offering a generative leviathan inflated into kinematic writhing. *Tendril* is the ancestor of language that will feed off network content and reconfigure phrases into its own volumetric flesh.

Born Magazine (1996–2011)   *Born Magazine* is an example of digital poetry emerging from Silicon Valley collaborations, outside the university context, external to the central materiality dogma. A website operative between 1996 and 2011, *Born Magazine* commissioned and published collaborations between published poets and professional interaction designers. Consider the notion of a poem that is "born" from the union of opposites: poet and interaction designer, feminine and masculine, anima and animus, text and its audiovisual-interactions, literature and code. The poets arrived bemused by technology but saturated with insight. The designers arrived from industry and advertising—fresh, accessible, clever, accomplished, and often slickly seductive. They were trained to make interfaces transparent, clean, accessible, and proficient.[23]

Born Magazine was efficiently productive, over the course of 15 years, 417 TAVITs, 900 collaborators, and 10,000 to 30,000 visitors per month. Yet the impact of *Born Magazine* (proportional to the size of its body of work) on the academic electronic literature community in critical discourse is negligible. Materiality theorists (in general) distrust polished surface aesthetics; formal rigor considers cosmetic interfaces as mere play, distractions from serious intellectual investigations of deeper substrates of language and technology.[24] The almost-total exclusion of the (sensual and emotional) *Born Magazine* archive from serious critical analysis in academic discourse arises (I believe) from materiality as central dogma.[25] One exception is the critical theorist Giovanna Di Rosario who applies a close reading to Rebecca Given and Monica Ong's nostalgic classic *Fallow* (it's a withered picture-album of blunt phrases and evocative transitions). Rosario reads not just the words of the poem, but the structure of interactivity, the montage of audiovisuals and the interactivity in a way that uses traditional methods for multimedia insights.

Here are a few of my favorite *Born Magazine* works: *Watching a Young Mother Walk with Her Infant through a Cemetery on the Day before My Funeral* by poet Joshua Stuart designer Nitrocorpz (2006)—an effective silent conversion of page-turning into an infinite-zoom triggered by the user.[26] *The Blank Missives* by poet Esther Lee and designer Chris Erickson (2007)—participatory echo of the typewriter, the Elizabethan reading room shuffled. *Beautiful Portrait* by poet Thomas Swiss and animator Motomichi Nakamura (2005)—not what the title suggests, this brief noninteractive microanimation with computer voice-over suggests that the network juggles narcissism.

Walking Together What Remains by poet Chris Green and artist Erik Natzke (2001)—a virtuoso demonstration of code tinkering by the master of ActionScript, Natzke, shreds the page flip, includes a noninteractive mode, and contains hidden footnotes that are part of the poem.

The quality of the *Born Magazine* design work almost invariably exceeds the design work emerging from intelligentsia circles. A final example is *Two Blinds and a Bittern* by poet Michele Glazer and interaction designer Zoltan Lehoczki (2004), which entertains visually (across multilayered, shifting fields), sonically (with bells that erupt as segments unfurl), linguistically (tangentially encoded), and conceptually (symmetry, synesthesia, and symbiosis between design, audio, and poem). Words inhabit an ecosystem populated with dream and psychic debris. The page becomes a slice of the hippocampus, the earth of its neurons shifting with an eerie shattering cry as new lines emerge. It is imagination made manifest, and it functions unequivocally as something more than its print-based incarnation: it is an ecosystem, tiny and unequivocal, an unsettling amalgamated TAVIT.

Billy Collins, FAD, and Head Gear: *Action Poems* **(2006)**   In 2006, Sundance commissioned a series of motion graphic videos based on poems by Collins. Advertising creatives skilled in animation and special effects adapted eleven poems into brief video vignettes. A few of these explore ways of working with visual words that (although not unprecedented) are often virtuosic, sensitive, and revelatory. As noted previously in the *Born Magazine* section, the professional skill level and attention to craft they display diametrically opposes the resistance to surface effects that sometimes permeates the conceptual and academic poetic communities. In these videos, attentive delicacy enhances the accessibility of the spoken word through visual synergy. These are masterful, consensual symbiotic mergers.

It has been suggested that linear videos are not digital poems; they are merely echoes of film, animation, stop-motion. Yet without computer graphics and motion graphic software like *After Effects*, these video-poems would not exist. Words would not cling to a wall with perfect perspectival geometry leaking a form of milk; or lie across barren concrete blocks, bent and folded in the bright sun; or slide wistful down a gritty stairwell wall—as they do in *Hunger* animated by Samuel Christopher from FAD agency. The spines of books would not shudder and lose their titles and covers; nor would a map of Paraguay reveal a word (alluded to but not spoken) before it too is erased and folded away; and a toy chemistry model of planets would not rotate in stuttering eight millimeter footage beside handwritten names scratched out by invisible charcoal—as they do in *Forgetfulness* animated by Julian Grey of Head Gear agency.

These are digital poems that exemplify interdisciplinary potential; duets where eye and ear churn word and audiovisual into experience; and they anticipate a next generation of writers who work collaboratively or write within motion graphics software, building their poems line by line to accompany sound and image. They also metaphorically extend the poet's reach into the abyss of the body, and place the metaphors found there into the world as actualized elements, releasing inscription from the book.

David Clark: *88 Constellations for Wittgenstein* (2007)   As a metamonument, a monolith to the confluence of philosophy and poetry, and an extended meditation on the convergence of thought in multimedia, Clark's *88 Constellations for Wittgenstein* is a rapturous, virtuosic, sprawling labyrinth that confounds, nourishes, and provokes. It is (in my view) a consummate example of hybrid interactivity, future cinema, Net art, and scholarship. It is in effect a poem.

Written, directed, and animated by Clark with a team of collaborative assistance, *88 Constellations* establishes learning as an aesthetic act, philosophy as path based, and trivia as profound. Without conflict it merges the dichotomies of abstraction/figuration, analytic/affect, and materiality/ontology. It does this by weaving biography with philosophy, conceptual concerns with stories, and an interactive map with text animations and voice-overs. This TAVIT reveals an attention to both materiality of media and expressive details.

Each of the *88 Constellations* is a microfilm woven around ricochet facts. Facts: Ludwig Wittgenstein didn't talk until he was four years old, gave away a fortune, went into exile, read pulp novels, and published one thin book. Simplicity become thick with synchronicity. Why is *88* poetry? Here's a morsel of the voice-over: "Constellations and piano keys, two upright infinities, two fat ladies, 1, 8, 8, 9, Chaplin, Hitler and Wittgenstein, star-crossed sons of fate, born to love and born to hate, one would last to 88" (Clark 2007). In my view, Clark is constructing epigrammatic riddles just as the ancient oral poets regurgitated the news of their time in convulsive, memorable, writhing heaps of enigmas. Clark investigates coincidences until we "connect the dots." Probing the paradox of superstition's roots in fact, parables grow out of perturbed patterns. For Clark, thought (in conversation with culture) exudes a quasi-schizophrenic overconnectivity that traverses tangents in circuitous semantic networks. *King Kong*'s 1976 finale on the Twin Towers evokes the Petronia Towers: "Two tall twins side by side, 88 lights, a ghost in the sky, 88 floors, 88 floors, 88 floors in Kuala Lumpur, the world's tallest building has 88 floors, 2 Islamic stars, 8 sides a door" (ibid.). Eighty-eight lights echoes Albert Speer's cathedral of light for Adolf Hitler's Nuremberg rally. In Clark's words, these lights look outside ourselves to look in, in an act of reverse astronomy. Culture becomes a catastrophe, a mutating shape we impose meanings on.

As virtuosic as it is sinuous, in *88 Constellations* enigmas sprout from collisions and connections erupt from hidden symmetries. "Infinity is the number 8 lying down." Jean-Luc Goddard filming cities and woman: to get laid; to lie; to lie down. Language too lies down, and lies and gives up at its limit, which is love. As lovers discuss Wittgenstein and Jacques Derrida in a café, concepts become corporeal and eventually confound; we become the cream in their coffee, harvesting the crushed, whirling, suctional effervescent force of spoons. Wittgenstein wrote: "Our words will only express facts" (quoted in Clark 2007). Wittgenstein also said, "Nothing is hidden" (ibid.). Yet here in the *88 Constellations* everything through surplus seems obscure, making less sense as it makes more. Loos: "Design purged of ornamentation" (ibid.) in the style of the Tractatus, effortless computation.

Moving sideways through such a ripe evanescent turmoil of excess facticity, Clark repeats certain themes like fugue motifs (repetition, logic, 88, repressions, and twins), weaving toward an idiosyncratic reservoir where innate ideas absorb and integrate their opposites. Similarly, the soundscape (designed by Clark) operates contrapuntally, as a generative modular entity: sparse, elegant, and effective. It is appropriate for an architecture of "more is less." And the question for us is: What is David Clark? A poet? Animator? Musician? Scholar? Philosopher? Culture junkie? Provocateur? Pulp media maker? Wittgenstein loved mystery novels. But here there is no mystery: this poet is interdisciplinary. The poem itself is a TAVIT. The content is aesthetic and formal, embodied and conceptual, media specific and emotional.

Sasha West and Ernesto Lavandera: *Zoology* (2009)   Consider the word *dog*; it is not the Wikipedia definition that is evoked, nor is it a zoologist's conception or a veterinarian textbook that arises, but it is an archetype of dogs or a dog-we-have-known (or touched or smelled or held or been bitten by) that emerges. Words do not mean one thing. And it is perhaps this divergent nature of meaning that makes many people (especially poets and traditional critics of poetry) hesitate before accepting multimedia representations of intimate poems. Perhaps this is why many poets cling to the sanctity of words alone on the page. The austerity of their presence betrays no memory, complexifies no situation.

Conversely, imagine that I invite you to the cinema, and once seated (instead of starting the film) you are given the screenplay and asked to read it. Quietly reading, you enter into a world envisioned by your own mind. Visions erupt because writing (in a poem or screenplay) touches unique experiences in the reader. All words trigger universal or shared meanings, but the particulars of each experienced meaning are different.

But it is obvious that screenplays require significant cognitive effort to convert into a streaming, vivid, complete immersive world like a film. The absence of a cineaste impoverishes; the existence of auteurs nourishes, as do multimedia poems: they can operate as translate-transport systems. *Zoology* by West with visuals by Lavandera is a case in point proving that archetypes of a literary experience can be enhanced by appropriate interactive audiovisuals. It is an exemplary TAVIT.

The poem itself alone is quiet, almost nondescript.

The dog loves the moon for being homely & the widow
loves the flowers for having no earthly scent. They swim
like small fishes round the coffin.
(West and Lavandera 2009)

In its interactive format, *Zoology* is lithe and sinuously revelatory; its particle systems create visual representations of animals that are vague enough to not trespass on particular memories. Tweening algorithms (that control the elasticity or bounce of particles as they transition between animals) connect line to line; the poem breaths. The audio clarifies tension, like a pulse or metronome, scuffing mild distortion as the poem's theme shifts from the organic realm to industrial consuming. Interactivity is minimal yet sufficient: the reader reads at their own pace, disrupting these forms with touch. From a historical perspective, it is possible to imagine Ovid pleased with the evolutionary capacity of computation to transfigure metamorphosis.

Zuzana Husárová and Ľubomír Panák: *Enter:in' Wodies* **(2012)**   Husárová's strength as a digital poet is in a versatile exploration of diverse technologies. Since 2011, she has etched a poem using electrons (see segment on *Microscope and Nanopoems*), made a spoken-word mashup using audio triggered from a Launchpad, performed with dancers accompanied by generative visuals, and with her partner Ľubomír Panák, built several Kinect-based interactive poem systems.

One of those Kinect-based interactive poem systems, Husárová and Panák's (2012) *Enter:in' Wodies*, leverages the Kinect's capacity to create an infrared depth-field map of viewer's motion; this permits a classic *Minority Report*–style flexible interactivity: gesture, response. Touching the air in front of a whirling ball of threaded lights, it pauses, retracts, and a body silhouette emerges. The body silhouette is generic, standing, with palms out; there are seven circles on its body (a little reminiscent of the kid's game, Operation). Gesture to touch a center on the body and a poem emerges. Gesture more and a typographically intricate weave of words follow the path of your hands.

Between 1988 and 2000, David Daniels published over 350 visual poems online titled *The Gates of Paradise*. Stanzas sculpted into tentacles, balls, bulbs, clots, horns, threads, chimeras, bones, pillars, fractures, continents, houses, vulvas, insects, fluids, fields, spikes, stars, mutants, vases—each fastidiously made on a typewriter or computer (one would hope). The gesture-path-drawing word-stream interactivity of *Enter:in' Wodies* places that fastidious power into the hands of casual viewers. The typographic effect is similar to Daniels's work, yet the mode in the digital is instantaneous. Technically, *Enter:in' Wodies* reacts when the reader waves their hand (and it is registered by the Kinect infrared sensors) and the path of the viewer's hands erases a mask in front of a text layer, allowing the gesture to sculpt the text layout. This echoes the stencil technique used in *Carnival* by Steve McCaffery (1975–1976), who used masks applied over paper fed into the typewriter.[27]

In *Enter:in' Wodies*, each segment of the poem is thematically linked to the body center activated—internal monologues about the storms, worries, confidence, concerns, concepts, displacements, pleasures, and explorations of the body are written as intangible pressure from the viewer-reader to activate the interface. Instead of page turning or scrolling, there is simply a gesture in space, a caress that causes text to flow beneath the fingers. Body explores body; an authorial inner monologue erupts.

Amaranth Borsuk and Brad Bouse: *Between Page and Screen* (2012) and *Whispering Galleries* (2014)   The title of poet Amaranth Borsuk and programmer Bouse's (2012) AR project *Between Page and Screen* might give the impression that something is moving between the page *to* the screen, as if there is a trajectory moving social reading and writing habits from book to electronic display. In fact, this piece exists exactly where it says it does *between* page and screen. Yet it almost exists as a hypothetical proof of how textual reality will eventually operate *beyond* both page and screen when language leaves behind print and digital instantiations and merges again with environment, the lived ecosystem, the space in between bodies.

Between Page and Screen is both software and book. The prowess of Bouse's programming anneals and animates a conceptual erasure: "The pages of this artist's book contain no text—only abstract geometric patterns and a web address leading to this site [betweenpageandscreen.com], where the book may be read using any browser and a webcam.[28] The poems that appear, a series of letters written by two lovers struggling to map the boundaries of their relationship, do not exist on either page or screen, but in the augmented space between them opened up by the reader" (Borsuk and Bouse 2012).

Borsuk is a fiercely refined, crafted, careful, and sophisticated poet. Her words resonate with meditated, mediated intensity, and her style and conceptual austerity reflect extensive reading. She contains mountain ranges of pages as she moves beyond the screen. And as with many other digital poetry practitioners (notably Strickland, Cayley, Glazier, and Ian Hatcher), Borsuk rejuvenates tradition as she exceeds it. Residual etymological genomes skirmish heart's shard arias; the entire book is a pole that travels a palindrome passage as if to prove that all media is traveling, the page works between people, and the screen shields us from and reveals us being the wor(l)d.

The Borsuk and Bouse duet between code and literature provokes and sustains a multiplicity of interpretations. Bök claims their work "heralds the virtual reality of our own poetic future, when everyone can read a book while watching it play on television, each hologram standing in its cone of light, hovering above the open page."[29] The prolific critic Leonardo Flores

(2013) identifies "a blurring of the boundaries between media and in the concept of the reader. As people trying to read this book with an iOS tablet may discover, the implied reader is no longer just a human being but also a machine, both integrated in their configuration and behavior to perform the work: a cyborg." And I see the words leaping off the page, off the in-between, somewhere articulate, tenacious, ephemeral, and brocaded, where page and screen merge, the shallows adjacent to the depths, subduction trenches falling away under semantic ships as code begins to breathe, and language learns to live.

This process of physicalized letterforms continues to evolve in Borsuk and Bouse's (2014) AR Leap-Motion-controlled *Whispering Galleries*, where the viewer's hand wipes away a blurred field of dust, to reveal erasure poems constructed from archival shopkeeper diaries in the region of New Haven, Connecticut (which commissioned this site-specific installation).[30] Archaeological and intimate, reader-witnesses explore how poetry resides within normal speech, and can reach it through simple motions. In an inversion of the process in *Between Page and Screen*, where text floats above the book, in *Whispering Galleries* the viewer floats above the screen, and without touching it, influences it. In each case, the reader is part of the text, seen and apprehended, implicated and informed. As words pop out of the screen, and gesture enters into the flow of words, new interim ontological states for text emerge.

Danny Cannizzaro and Samantha Gorman: *Tender Claws* **(2014)** *Pry*, an interactive multimedia fiction—an iOS app by Tender Claws, the duo Cannizzaro and Gorman (2014)—solves some fundamental problems of multitouch storytelling, and evokes a complex, unprecedented coherence between custom interactive gestures, audiovisuals, and psychological insights. Ironically, *Pry*'s interactive gestures advance plot psychology in a way that is so clever, sophisticated, impressive, and prescient, this virtuosity overshadows simple engagement, and even erodes it. The first chapter opens with a video sequence from a classic remorse point of view, the camera descending from ceiling onto the figure staring up from a bed, and then (without knowing if this occurs before or after the prologue) the first sentence appears: "Awake, but not full. What time is it? Check." And beneath it, "Spread and hold open to see through James' eyes." So we are given the character name in a didactic, after a brief word-free intro video vignette.

On entering *Pry*, engagement blooms not because of character development or plot suspense; it blooms because the transition effects are gracious,
the didactics are sufficient and minimal, and the writing sophisticated,
ambiguous, and personal. A pinch-open touch spreading gesture flicks the
screen open like an eye, a brief shot of ceiling—ink jelly blooming stain—
and then it's gone. The screen has sealed itself, and in its place the second
written phrase of the novella appears, and beneath it the second didactic
"pinch and hold closed to enter James' subconscious."

There are only two unrequested didactic panels displayed in *Pry* (*pinch
open to see outside/memories*, and *pinch closed to see inside/subconscious*), and
on release the screen returns to its previous state.[31] Based on this austerity
of interface design, the reader progresses: reading the surface, peeking out,
and peeking in. Solely for this gestural precision and serene minimalism,
Pry deserves to be experienced. It distills user effort down to relevant essen-
tials. The two gestures reflect a nascent syntax, a minimal set, for how to
navigate between three layers of text.

Yet this simplicity is a ruse, in fact. In chapters 1, 2, and 6, the pinch
gesture works (with mildly different effects in each), then for chapter 3
there is a new (unannounced!) gesture to learn, and this is part of the joy
and trouble with *Pry*. The gestures are so elegant that experiencing them
generates a pleasure that eclipses the story. The effect is often proximal to
wonder; it's playful, giddy, and strange. A disjunct arises between the heavy
themes of eroticism, violence, and loss expressed in the content, and the
joy felt pinching mediated text into innovative transitions. Ironically, the
writing must swim against the tide of joy generated by the interface's success; it is difficult to allow entry into darkness if the door is a playground.
And if you fail to understand the gestures (as I did on first entering the third
chapter), the effect is frustrating, a bit like wandering into a television store
in search of coffee.

The electronic book desperately needs conventions; after the printing
press the novel emerged, and along with it narrative techniques for how to
handle first-person narration; film adopted montage, but on the commercial multitouch screen—first launched in 2007 with the iPhone, its current
parents (Android and Apple's iOS) divorced, its growing pains evident—and
the new syntax has not emerged. Kindle, Nook, and other e-books are literally only books; the paradigm of flipping pages prevails. One of the values
of *Pry* is the alternative expanded hybrid-media page it proposes; these are

not pages or texts but rather TAVITs. The *Pry* pinch gestures are strong candidates to consider for general adoption. They "meaningfuly relate to the reading process," as the *Pry* web page puts it. Pinch-open-eye (see), pinch-close-eye (think or dream), and release (narrate).

In chapter 6 of *Pry* (as of this writing, currently only 1, 2, 3, and 6 are released), the pinch gesture modulates and begins to trigger the appearance or disappearance of blocks of text within existing paragraphs. It's tough to describe, but the animation is slick, and the effect sinuous and addictive. It induces a sense of the text as a Pandora's box capable of infinite expansion or contraction. There is no exact precedent for this particular interactive animated insertion, but inserting more text-within-text has many precedents; word replacement has been at the core of e-lit techniques for decades. A couple prominent examples: Cayley's work since the mid-1990s consistently used word or letter replacements to morph texts; Cayley directs the Digital Language Arts program at Brown University (where Gorman studied). In 2000, Judd Morrissey's *The Jew's Daughter* used rollovers to replace sentences and words within paragraphs; his text transformed as it was touched.

The one dilemma of the active-replacement technique is that it requires the reader to read sentences that are modulations of previous ones; as new phrases are inserted between sentences already read, continuity issues arise; formally it has merit, but for populist engagement it's problematic. Sent back to read again, I often ask why? It takes a rare writer to operate like a linguistic Phillip Glass, looping phrases. Humans are relentless and remorseless in rejecting narratives that do not reward our time. *Pry* risks alienating readers who lack a taste for variational disclosure.

The dilemma for the e-lit hybrid-media writing discipline is that the kind of clever custom transitions *Pry* and other projects use might become next season's stock filters. Eventually, the novelty wears off. Apply with one click: audio as a structural aspect of narrative, flickering one-word-at-a-time RSVP stream of consciousness, and video vignette sinews. Few reviews of contemporary novels marvel over paragraph size or book binding or layout; unless you are a materiality-specific critic, what matters is not matter but the immaterial aspects: the writing, psychological acuity, structure, and impact. But no credible review of an interactive e-lit work can ignore the materiality of the media or the innovations established that demarcate its space within the turbulent, evolving field.

Pry accomplishes what no prior e-lit work has done so far: credibly blend competent video, text animations, and literature with custom interactivity specific to iOS multitouch that contributes psychological insights into character.

"The Poetics of Such a Situation"   Future reading devices will read their readers in ways that allow subtle reciprocal sensitivity. Writing will involve feedback sensitized to the emotional state of the user. Skins will respond.

Who as a reader has not been exhausted to the point of boredom and indifference by a text? Contemporary sensor-technologies (like Kinect, Wii, Xbox, and Leap Motion) suggest a literature where the body of the reader is ultimately implicated in the rhythm and structure of the poem, where writing is no longer an activity without any feedback from the body and mind of the reader. The works in the preceding section are entry points into the poetics of the peculiar potentials of twenty-first-century interface-animation-skin. As Charles Olson (1960) stated in "A Later Note on Letter #15" (from *Maximus Poems*): "The poetics of such a situation are yet to be found out."[32]

Thought & Things

We spend our lives in front of screens, mostly wasting time: checking social media, watching cat videos, chatting, and shopping. What if these activities—clicking, SMSing, status-updating, and random surfing—were used as raw material for creating compelling and emotional works of literature?

—Kenneth Goldsmith, 2014

Poets (or those who explicitly demarcate themselves as such) are not the only folks to be concerned with language at material and ontological levels. Since the ancients, fusions of art, literature, and science have occurred (see Cramer 2004; Higgins 1987). From the alchemists to OULIPO, the GTR Toolkit (Klobucar and Ayre 2003) and Flarf, procedural techniques have immigrated from science into poetry.[33] In parallel, hieroglyphs, concrete text, mail art, conceptual language, and visual glyphs have migrated from design/art.

Andrew Klobucar, speaking of the effect of networks on identity and writing practices, details how the ubiquity of network technology ruptures the subjectivity, elitism, and language referentiality associated with modernism. Instead, according to Klobucar (2012), networks have instigated a diffused open system that culminates in a seizure of absolute openness whose excess challenges the capacity of identity to configure itself: "Modernism was not ready for the network. ... [I]t was built to provide a refuge." Now media increases the porosity of processes and investigations open to artists; archives and repositories replace dictionaries and libraries, and fusions challenge tight disciplinary categorizations; the refuge dissipates.

An example of an artist who does not publish but instead exhibits poems is the sculptor and anthropological installation artist Camille Henrot (2013), who says of her video work *Grosse Fatigue*, "It doesn't work like a logical story, that's why it is actually a poem." The video's sound track is a long spoken-word, cosmological poem, appropriated from ancient creation myths, constructed by her and Jacob Bromberg (editor of the poetry journal the *White Review*), and performed by Akwetey Orraca-Tetteh in the style of the Last Poets. The visuals show digital "shufflings" of Smithsonian archival footage, personal computer desktop windows moved within and overlapping each other, with the video frame and digital materiality of our epoch foregrounded. *Grosse Fatigue* is an analytic, ontological artwork that questions myths and stories from the origins of being, using poetry as one of its media, with a style that foregrounds diffracted consciousness, multitasking, and the numb archaeology of hard drives.

Another example of a nonpoet poem is R. Luke DuBois's information visualization *A More Perfect Union*, which explores a terrain parallel to poetics. DuBois (2011) explicitly analyses data from dating site idioms in order to establish how "we accumulate a vocabulary to describe ourselves and where that comes from." He then traces a map of the United States by hand and replaces all the town names with keywords extracted from the database during the text mining. The resulting artifacts (exhibited at Bitforms gallery in 2011) are literal maps of the psyche of networked desire; poetry without prepositions presented as a topology; handwriting mingling with data science investigations into love; networks translated into physical matter.

The infamous Vanessa Place (poet-lawyer and reader of transcripts from sex-offender trials) has emigrated in the opposite direction, going from publishing physically as a poet to opening an online corporation for the sale of conceptual objects at VanessaPlace Inc. From that networked habitat, Place

(2014) sells limited edition found objects: "Poetry no longer confined to the page, the screen, the tongue or the text, but conceived as sheer object."

The object is (as I say elsewhere) a precursor to an organism on the ontological hierarchy. Combined with computation and code, dynamic objects (spimes/spoems) exist in between object and organisms. Language sculptures that inhabit that interstitial space display a remarkable range of adaptations: some static and dense; others interactive and expansive. Some examples are: Airan Kang's (2010) *Hyper Open Book (Lord Byron)*, an installation that displays classic poetry in Day-Glo streaming LED lights, resin encasement, and custom electronics; Janet Zweig's (2010) *Lipstick Enigma*, a software-driven sculpture that generates short new phrases and then displays them using "1200 resin lipsticks powered by 1200 stepper motors, controlled by 60 circuit boards"; the ironic single-print edition of Adam James's (2007) *Lord*, the King James Bible reduced to 0.0001% using Microsoft Word's AutoSummarize—a residual excretion of a massive corporate algorithm, tuned to anarchic anorexia; the extension of that same technique to a book, Jason Huff's (2010) *AutoSummarize*: "The top 100 most downloaded copyright free books summarized using Microsoft Word 2008's AutoSummarize 10-sentence function and organized alphabetically"; and the interactive installation *TEXTile* by Jean Shin (2006) made of "22,528 recycled computer keycaps and 192 custom keycaps, fabric, customized active keyboard and interactive software, video projection and painted aluminum armatures," a continuous textile transcript of email correspondences between the artist and exhibit organizers, permitting users to input their own lines into video display.

Talan Memmott: *Lexia to Perplexia* (2000)   Memmott (2000) describes his poetic work *Lexia to Perplexia* as "a deconstructive/grammatological examination of the 'delivery machine.' The text of the work falls into the gaps between theory and fiction. The work makes wide use of DHTML and JavaScript. At times its interactive features override the source text, leading to a fragmentary reading experience. In essence, the text does what it says: in that, certain theoretical attributes are not displayed as text but are incorporated into the functionality of the work." *Lexia to Perplexia* on its surface appears to repel—the repulsion is playful and insidious—but beneath allures with a set of unresolved self-referential conundrums, a network of neatly synchronized chaos that reveres and mocks the incestuous recursion of discourse (that insular subset of language).

This difficult work represents an apogee of a particular mode of inquiry: the core of the user's poetic experience is hollowed out and the DNA of theoretical inquiry is injected into the cellular bioplasm; code extrudes onto the surface of the work to become the work (the gestures of the reader refined into algorithms of repetitive inquiry). Philosophy morphs into interface design; poetry devolves into perplexity; and wonder is replaced by the raw release of a river of irony, a cascade of devious architectures constructed to induce awareness of context: reader-organism struggling to navigate the new machine.

Christophe Bruno: *Iterature* (2001–2010), and John Cayley: *Pentameters* (2012)

The Web has often been compared to our own memory, or to consciousness. There are indeed some similarities, simply because they share the same raw material: language.

—Christophe Bruno, 2004

From 2001 to 2010, the artist (and ex-physicist, ex-mathematician) Bruno had a website called iterature.com. L-iterature lacking the *L*. L-istening? As a performance installation, Bruno exhibited a *human browser* who wears wireless headphones, hears a transcription of a web page, and then speaks it for the viewers. "Depending on the context in which the actor is, keywords are sent to the program and used as search strings in Google (thanks to a Wi-Fi PDA) so that the content of the textual flow is always related to the context" (Bruno 2001). It was a short-circuit in communication made by the long circuit of an intervening human speaker—orality as slow information; a return to literature as listening: an *iteraturer*.

Do ads use words to move us? This is obvious terrain for poetic investigation. So in 2003, Bruno (2005) intervened in "the commodification of speech." He bought Google ads and wrote poems in them. Bruno's (2002) first purchased ad-poem was triggered to display every time someone searched for the word *symptom* and read,

Words aren't free anymore.

Capitalist value and linguistic slaves recombine. Medium of distribution: the Internet. Mode: advertisement. Demographic: defined in advance by the author. Point of sale: search engine, in-box, and web page. Economies of scale: invert the paradigm of print publishing. The author buys space on a publication platform and pays the distributor a percentage of pennies for every word read *that inspires a click*. Semantic mouse-based measurement equals money. As Bruno (2002) explains,

During the fourth campaign, I kept receiving these emails from Google:

"We believe that the content of your ad does not accurately reflect the content of your website. We suggest that you edit your ad text to precisely indicate the nature of the products you offer. This will help to create a more effective campaign and to increase your conversion rate. We also recommend that you insert your specific keywords into the first line of your ad, as this tends to attract viewers to your website."

Then I got a last email:

"Hello.

I am the automated performance monitor for Google AdWords Select. My job is to keep average clickthrough rates at a high level, so that users can consistently count on AdWords ads to help them find products and services.

The last 1,000 ad impressions I served to your campaign(s) received fewer than five clicks. When I see results like this, I significantly reduce the rate at which I show the ads so you can make changes to improve performance. ...

Sincerely,

The Google AdWords Automated Performance Monitor"

My ads were then Disapproved and my campaigns were suspended.

L-istening? The word *listening* is often used (instead of *sensing*) to refer to the activity of networked sensors or servers; listening implies a self-registering consciousness rather than a mechanism. Bruno (2006) refers to the Google takeover of Blogger in 2003 while discussing Jeremy Bentham to suggest that corporations are the next panopticon, listening to us "to scientifically predict the behaviour of users, what they are going to think in any given circumstance (not as individuals but as a statistical set), in order to optimize the adwords/adsense machinery, on which Google IPO is based."

When Bruno (2005) in his Cosmolalia project refers to the role of words in "the circulation of information, desire and advertising," it raises a few hypothetical questions: If (just if) words are bought and sold, and if (just if) they are pseudoautonomous viral entities moving between us as hosts, then isn't it possible that words can be en*slaved*?

Cayley's *Pentameters: Toward the Dissolution of Certain* Vectoralist *Relations* (which examines the effect of Google on language and poetics, numeration as vectors, and the erosion by stats of the qualitative flux) expresses a parallel concern. In this incantatory poem, Cayley speculates about the impact of search engine technology on our own writing that is given to it *free of charge*. He continues the long tradition of bard as critic, polemically exposing the implicit assumptions that erupt from the infrastructural underbelly of culture. Cayley's (2012) poem opens as follows:

Language is a commons, and yet by contrast
With first nature's free resources, it is constitutive
Of culture while all at once incorporate within
Those cultures it enables. As language is a commons,
To use it, we need not agree to terms.
Now, counter to our expectations and our rights,
Agreements as to terms of language use
Are daily ratified by the vast majority
Of so-called users—you-and-I—by all of us
Who make and share our language on the Internet.

Pentameters is worth reading in its entirety, since it isolates clearly the intricate paradoxical permissions (in the implicit EULAs) that invoke our agreement in a power dynamic: the ownership of language (analogous to land or livestock) is an ownership of life and lived thought.[34] As *search* increases in its anticipatory power (its intelligence powered by our contributions), the dynamic may shift from one of service to bubbled guidance, linguistic kettling, co-opting modes of forbidden thought before they can occur; corporate computational autosuggestion capable of subconscious programming; poetry metapater.

Golan Levin and Jaap Blonk: *Ursonagraphy* (2005), and Levin, Kamal Nigam, and Jonathan Feinberg: *The Dumpster* (2006)   Since the physical language workshop at MIT, Levin has been at the forefront of programmatic explorations of typographic space. Interspersed with visual art interventions, he sporadically returns to typographic explorations that usually involve text generated and manipulated in real time. In *Ursonography*, Levin built an audiovisual interpretation of Schwitters's 1932 classic sound performance rant *Ursonate* with "an elegant new form of expressive, real-time, 'intelligent subtitles'" (Blonk and Levin 2005).

Volume and intonation activate physics emulators. The body becomes the source of an information visualization residue. It interacts with this history—gestures destabilizing avalanches. With "the help of computer-based speech recognition and score-following technologies, projected subtitles are tightly locked to the timing and timbre of Blonk's voice, and brought forth with a variety of dynamic typographic transformations that reveal new dimensions of the poem's structure" (Blonk and Levin 2005). Schwitters screaming at the top of his lungs probably imagined his gutteral morphemes spattered against clouds, strewn across buildings, diving through screens. Levin's *Ursonate* approximates chthonic hallucinations within pristine geometry and a physics engine. Cadence maps onto gravity and incoherence coheres.[35]

In Levin, Nigam, and Feinberg's (2006) *The Dumpster*, blog posts are dynamically searched, and the ones that refer to romantic breakups are injected into a visualization. Brokenhearted bloggers become collective authors in a speech mashup. Texts that were once announcements of isolation enter into a massive herd of blobs that fall in a sinuous heaps. *The Dumpster* exemplifies the uncategorizable object that lurks at the edge of poetic discourse: simultaneously infographic and crowdsourced, it is an immense reservoir of phrases orbiting love, and as such constitutes a dynamic, sprawling networked poem whose form echoes geology.

Stephanie Boluk and Patrick LeMieux: Dwarf Fortress (2013)
The history of the twentieth-first century will not be written by human hands alone.

—Stephanie Boluk and Patrick LeMieux, 2013

When Boluk and LeMieux analyze esoteric fan-cult text-game *Dwarf Fortress*, they explore not narrative or conventional poetics or writing but rather lived play, fan-fiction tendrils, and game mods (*modifications*). In spite of J.R.R. Tolkien, dwarfs are not what spring to mind when one thinks literature. And a geeky game that requires arduous devotion to intricate procedural choices, while providing glyphic instead of graphic feedback, seems an unlikely candidate for comparative literary insights. Boluk and LeMieux, however, argue that "Dwarf Fortress is not a game at all but rather an ontological experiment" (Boluk and LeMieux 2013, 139).

The computation needed to generate this *ontological experiment* can cripple ordinary computers, because *Dwarf Fortress* is attempting with fidelity to generate a living ecosystem. Yet the surface like an e. e. cummings poem appears naive and eight-bit; it refutes the graphics of Hollywood, the gloss of advertising, and the raw fetishization of the eye, and adopts a set of "437 (CP437) characters in sixteen different colors to represent its world" (ibid., 129). In other words, it looks like a flat grid of glyphs.

Boluk and LeMieux connect this contradictory sheen of simplicity that overlays a dense programmatic complexity to Manuel De Landa's (2013, 62) claim that "sedimentary rocks, species, and social classes (and other institutionalized hierarchies) are all historical constructions, the product of definite structure-generating processes." *Dwarf Fortress* combines structures (AI, architecture, tectonics, social engineering, and physics) without much outward show; it is a silent ontology, a nongloss agency, a surreptitious reminder that the semantic networks of ancient poetry (which cascaded through centuries gathering genomes of royalty, peasants, wars, and loves) coexist in a digitized mulch with worms and muttering bacteria quorums, amino acids, and discarded game controllers.

Organisms accumulate energy into habitats. Poetry will in the next decade experience its first massive epic digital poem; this poem will in all probability be a form of collective writing (or a harvest from the network), or as in the case of *Dwarf Fortress*, centered around a core team (brothers Tarn and Zach Adams) who build a platform/framework that enables/inspires a community of writers to create orbital commentaries and follies. Perhaps Facebook and other portals are such devices already: collective writing apparitions through which the next epic poems will be carved. Perhaps the epic will shrink (temporal compression) and become a micron delivering a similar gestalt jolt.

As I write these lines, the sleep agent on my phone autonomously activates *bedtime-silent mode*; behind me a dehumidifier hums in low-power mode, tasting the air for its turnoff signal, and the city facade shifts from orchestrated to dormant; on the harbor water, a tanker on cruise control; somewhere military aerial drones sift their memory for viruses, and certainly somewhere a high-frequency trading algorithm runs a classifier to identify tomorrow's target. Thought permeates the night; we live perched on an anthropocene precipice cradling semiautonomous machines that whisper to us. What is it they say? "Dwarf." "Fortress."

John Cayley and Daniel Howe: *The Readers Project* (2009)   Life and death are deeply symbiotic, as are writing and reading. The universe writes our bodies into space to read other bodies written into space. When death arrives, the structure of what we have been, our written essence, dissipates, as do eventually the traces of what we have written into space: poems, emails, grocery notes. Culture is an accumulation of writings saved temporarily from the dissipation of death, the erasure that writes the blank again.

Words that are displayed on-screen, written from memory to display, must be read and transferred, moved in-between, deleted from buffers as the next page loads. Life is read by time; deleted (or overwritten) by death. Words read by a human reader are *written* into short-term memory, shuffled through a labyrinth of associational ricochets, sifted, and then overwritten by the next batch or consolidated into long-term storage, nestling down to etch the hippocampus until the organism dies. This system of flows and patterns incessantly saturates consciousness with thoughts as it reads and sorts and assesses intricate surfaces.[36]

Language artists Cayley and Howe (2009) have engaged with this flow by creating *The Readers Project*; it is referred to by its creators as an "art system … [that] visualizes existing and alternative *vectors* of reading, vectors that are motivated by the properties and methods of language as such and linguistic aesthetics." Basically, it is a computational agent (a programmed entity, semiautonomous, endowed with code given by its programmers) that sifts through texts and displays paths through those oceans of words. In other words, it reads by navigating through text according to rules. Cayley and Howe (ibid.) acknowledge the symbiosis of read-write, "because the project's *readers* move within and are thus composed by the words within which they move, they also, effectively, write. They generate texts." This reciprocal activity of give–take echoes the core root activity of digital devices constantly burrowing through RAM and registers.

The Readers Project reflects the urgent necessity for creative literary authors to write the autonomous writers who will read for us. It does so formally and numinously, words drifting and vanishing in modernist cascade, as Cayley and Howe (ibid.) put it,

Of falling lines
That make headway
To Olson's open verse.

F.A.T. Lab: EyeWriter (2009)   In 2009, members of the Free Art and Technology (F.A.T.) Lab, Open Frameworks, the Graffiti Research Lab, and the Ebeling Group communities teamed up with a graffiti writer named Tempt One. Tempt is paralyzed due to amyotrophic lateral sclerosis. The team developed the prosthetic *EyeWriter* to allow him to tag using movements of his eyes. Prosthetic remote projectors wrote in real time his ocular gestures onto walls.

EyeWriter marks, as far as I know, one of the first remote signatures written with light onto a building using only eye gestures. With this, language escapes the box of its traditional inscription limits and moves more proximal to the mind, even as gaze becomes capable of entering into a more intimate, subtler relationship with letterform and etching: interiority as interactivity.

The F.A.T. Lab consciously distances itself from corporate platforms by moving hacker interventions into unconventional spaces like hospitals. Even as type design hurtles forward, much commercial and volumetric typography owes a lot to the past, to graffiti and tag styles (which in turn are indebted to illuminated manuscripts, Elizabethan burlesque ads, archaic snuff/cigarette boxes, and later Walt Disney). Letters that walk and roil with sinuous spines in thick, shadowed, acrobatic contortions exist somehow in between stasis and animation, legibility (legality) and illegibility (illegality). Graffiti operates as a frozen photo of a language in the process of morphing.

Graffiti nourishes contemporary dimensional text evolution. Because of the adversarial culture in which it evolved, many graffiti artists (i.e., visual poets of dimensional gestural type) have come and gone without any recognition at all, writing ephemeral works on alley walls, freight cars, secluded doorways, and under bridges. In those specific ecosystems, visual language has become a dense, delirious, hallucinatory rebellion: statement of identity, Sharpies' pee-point scrollwork, industrial interior deco, and toxic spray effluence of intricate creativity. This subculture mingles with the high-tech augmentation done using open-source tools to mark *EyeWriter* as a progenitor of computational brain-machine-interface writing tools of the future that will reduce the gap between imagination and expression, bringing mind closer to immediate distributed externalization.

Karsten Schmidt: Type and Form (2009)   PostSpectacular design studio, directed by Schmidt, in 2009 developed dimensional typography experiments that operate at the boundary between animation, code, and sculpture. The PostSpectacular *Type & Form* cover for *Print* magazine was grown generatively using a diffusion model. No typeface is involved. Pixels migrate into and populate rough letterform masks. Two-dimensional slices were combined to form a 3-D volume using techniques borrowed from MRI data scanning. The final result is output from a 3-D printer. This is incunabula of the digital age. By synthesizing the formal elements of his work into a singular object with extraordinary technical skill, Schmidt establishes a benchmark for generative digital typographic excellence.

But is that all it is? Is it only typography? If so, then why consider it as digital poetry? Eugen Gomringer prophetically worried that concrete poetry might someday degrade into "an empty entertainment for the typographer" (quoted in Solt 1969, 10). *Type & Form* might seem at first glance to be vulnerable to such a critique: lacking in direct references to either human experience or organic nature, it can be interpreted as a superficial design exercise, as superfluous technology applied without concern for deeper resonance. Yet I think an alternative interpretation is equally valid.

Type & Form operates at a physical level as the preliminary extrusion of a computational and poetic use of materials that forces us to question our relation to language as mediated entity. Granted, it is a static fossil for now, but future descendants will be kinetic. Borrowing algorithms of fluid diffusion that mimic the flow of blood or estuaries to develop its form (mathematics as meaning generation), superimposing complex layers (ambiguity and/or the classic striated onion of literary studies), extruding data into brittle stone (inverse Frankenstein), *Type & Form* contains within its developmental process all the crucial vectors of postdigital postmodernity. Linear, flat, paper poems become architectural nodes. A 3-D printed heart begins beating.

But a critic might point out accurately, "Karsten Schmidt does not even identify as a poet; he identifies as a programmer and designer. Perhaps as often happens in ideological tug of wars he is being used to make a point." This is true: he does probably not even conceive of his work as a poem.

Yet in 1953, one of the founding members of the Noigandres movement, Décio Pignatari, was a designer; he did not identify as a poet. *Type & Form* (perhaps inadvertently) echoes numerous concrete manifestos that repeatedly stress that *form = content / content = form* (Solt 1969). The links between this block of minimalist type and visual minimalist structural and semiotic poems are far from tenuous.

Type & Form may well be the preliminary fingernail of what will eventually become a body of work—poems made out of matter, machinic-molded poems carved on computers that will eventually contain actuators and metabolisms.[37] *Type & Form* connects the clay-finger-stick origins of language to the tradition of concrete poetry. Similar to a fossil, it emanates latent aesthetic animism—the body of language squeezed through 3-D printers into palpable physical form. Publication notices of the future might read: *Download and print this poem; it feeds off your network and responds to touch.*

Brad Troemel: BSTJ (2009–2013)

dean & deluca low calorie snack inside Marlboro box w/ Cerebral Palsy Tissue/Organ Kidney Cancer Green Ribbon Glittery Sticker (Ethical) 1/2.

—Brad Troemel, 2008

The thing about things is that some things seem to be vibrant talismans, while others appear to be stillborn trinkets. Merchandise, popularly known as *merch*, carries (or is be*smirch*ed with) the stigma of being dead before it arrives. Ironically, the *most* hyped language often accompanies merch. And in contemporary usage, merch is literally imprinted with language, its surface and semantics contiguous.

Box labels, brand idents, and public service announcement stickers all claim a larger readership than most poetry. And linked to cross-modal multimedia campaigns (YouTube, television ads, billboards, animations, pop-ups, touchscreens in washrooms/restaurants/elevators, sneeze guards, trinkets, etc.), they are usually far more widely distributed than most poetry.[38] They are certainly more desired than poetry. Yet the form of experience commercialized-language objects evoke is a nonexperience poetically—by activating glands of greed, brand identification breeds bland nonidentification, or circular comatose contusions in the corporality of conviviality.

Troemel (2008) harvests vilified mental toxins seeping into the ground-water of the psyche, preserves the objects in sculptural shrink-wrap, converts slogan collisions into incantations, and then sells these modified marketing and pitch-speak surreal collages on his Etsy online store: *BSTJ*. If there is a deranged Warhol Ubu Tzara Catellan of contemporary poetics (with no interest in the myth of genius artist nor in being associated with anything as pretentious as digital poetics), Troemel is the candidate.[39] He deconstructs deconstruction to disclose the vacancy inside the vacant. He dreams of vomit, and then sorts it for edible food. The result is capitalist compost: concise, incisive nourishment direct from the network maw.

LIVE STRONG yellow Hotdog, Pen, and Q-Tip HOLDER / The Exquisite Design You Trust & The Phenomenal Tastes You Grew Up With (Quite Limited) (Troemel 2008)

TRAUMAWIEN (2014), Mimi Cabell and Jason Huff: *American Psycho* (2010), and Carla Gannis: *In Search of* (2013)

Computer systems produce an unprecedented wealth of text, only the smallest part of which is contributed by users. Protocols, listings, algorithms, programmes, source codes, universal binary codes—the background operations of the systems themselves write a massively larger share.

These text units—produced, read and transmitted by computers—internalize trans-codability and transliterality as the computer system's basic underlying operating principle. The emerging forms of text take place between writing systems and text generators.

—Luc Gross, 2014

Since September 2014, the TRAUMAWIEN Product Store uses the TRAU-MAWIEN Product Algorithm to select and repurpose (without authorization) Tweets and Facebook status updates through print-on-demand portals like CafePress, Zazzle, Pikistore, or Printalloverme. "*Post Digital* is the conscious decision to dispense a final, physical product with respect to integrate latest conditions of digital media. Just like the printed book, the product (or object) is a freezing of time and information as a means and way to consider reflection" (TRAUMAWIEN 2014). As Carpenter (2011) intuits, TRAUMAWIEN "conceive[s] of the print books they publish as narrative snapshots of computer generated literary processes."

A "traditional-media book" published by TRAUMAWIEN is Cabell and Huff's (2010) rendition of *American Psycho*, a book written "by sending the entire text of Bret Easton Ellis' *American Psycho* between two Gmail accounts page by page. We saved the relational ads for each page and added them back into the text as footnotes. In total, we collected over 800 relevant ads for the book. The constellations of footnoted ads throughout these pages retell the story of *American Psycho* in absence of the original text." The authors speak of this as a *blurry portrait of an algorithm*. It repurposes serial killing as ubiquitous corporate power, and networks as identity evisceration.

Network evisceration of identity, coding death, and defining entities through algorithms, haunts Gannis's (2013) existential *In Search of (Self Portrait Study 01 for \'gü-gəl\e Results Project)*, a video made by "searching string phrases on Google and publishing them on social networks, primarily twitter, as a way to share a textual *snapshot* of my thoughts relative to the hive mind that exists within my *Googlesphere*." The leviathan rising from Milton's lake, subconscious bearer of light and darkness, is now the network-platform AI, drenched in our identities, bearing both scandals and a smear of erased relevance.[40] It comes with a warranty, demanding we sign a EULA before we read ourselves.

Generative Organs

There's a glimmer in *Issue 1* of what poetry written without consciousness might be—but just a glimmer, luckily, because were it entirely so, we flesh-and-blood poets might not stand a chance any more than the chess players do. For now, it's a good reminder that we really ought to try and write better than a computer, while we still can.

—Barry Schwabsky, 2008

One of the ultimate goals of digital poetry (poetry in part generated by or dependent on digital machines) is for machines to consistently write high-quality, meaningful poetic language. This goal includes algorithmic devices assisting humans to write meaningful poetry that would not have been possible without it, or to advance literature instead of simply replicating traditional patterns.

If a living language is to emerge (somehow written into the cells, animated on its surface, and contextually sensitive to culture), then it will need to self-replicate; there will need to be some volatile robust encoding process that can write. Generative methods are that potential incarnate; they are the research strand concerned with giving computation and rules a fundamental role in creative process.

While past efforts at poetry generation have yielded little *readable* results, there are many indications (consistent advances in the capacity of deep learning to analyze complex data sets; massive increases in the cloud data scale) that poetry and real language generation may advance significantly in the next few years. The impact of this imminent shift extends the postmodern, avant-garde poetic emphasis on context over identity, language over self-expressivity, and combinatorial process over writing. Deep-learning techniques share an affinity with remix or mashup culture, but extend the granularity and level of precision of those techniques by orders of magnitude. In brief, data science will potentially alter our relation to poetic creativity.

Prehistory (From Zuse to Serendipity)

Poetry generation provides NLP/CL/AI researchers with testbeds to investigate ideas, on tasks that are near-term achievable but AI-complete in depth.

—Antonio Roque, 2011

Generative poetry has been around since early in the history of computation. It's been mentioned often in preceding sections of this book.

To reiterate (as already noted in the "Media Archaeology and Modernism" section), in 1952, working on the Ferranti Mark I, Strachey wrote a program to generate love letters (Wardrip-Fruin 2005). In 1954, the avant-garde interdisciplinary poet Jackson Mac Low wrote his first poems using dice, chance, and other nondeterminate procedures, which eventually included (in the 1990s) software for procedural writing created by the programmer-poet Charles Hartman (Roque 2011). In 1959, on a Zuse Z22 computer, Theo Lutz inserted sixteen chapter titles and subjects from Franz Kafka's *The Castle* into a database, and programmed them to recombine into phrases joined by grammatical glue; Lutz is potentially the first-known practitioner of contemporary digital poetry (Funkhouser 2007). As already noted in *La Machine à écrire* section, Baudot (1964), a pioneering engineer-linguist, created the first French machine-generated published poetry; he left the machine running overnight and was surprised at the size of the pile of poems printed in the morning. In the 1968 *Cybernetic Serendipity* exhibit, the Cambridge Language Research Unit's Margaret Masterman and Robin McKinnon Wood, Balestrini, Alison Knowles, and James Tenney, Edwin Morgan, Baudot, and E. Mendoza all produced poems generatively.[41] There was only one text animation in the exhibit (Reichardt and Institute of Contemporary Arts 1969).

These early examples all utilized combinatorial methods: array of words, and random select rules. The methods that follow suggest more intelligence, and culminate in probabilistic methods which aspire to induce machine learning.

History (from Hartman to Moretti)

Talking about computer poetry is almost like talking about extraterrestrials: great speculation, no examples.

—Charles O. Hartman, 1996

From the 1980s onward, Hartman (1996) created softwares for his own symbiotic human–machine writing that replicated meter and rhyming schemata; he documented this process in his book-length work *Virtual Muse*. Hartman's technique as a poet involved the enhancement of his personal capacity with the output of an algorithm.[42] His identity as a poet reflected the algorithms he wrote as a programmer.[43] The merger of poet-programmer (silicon-soul) suggests "the question isn't exactly whether a poet or a computer writes the poem but what kinds of collaboration might be interesting" (Hartman 1996).[44]

In 1984, the literary critic Hugh Kenner and Joseph O'Rourke (1984) tried to go in an orthogonal direction (from Hartman) and implement an algorithm to replicate authorial identity; their coauthored essay "A Travesty Generator for Micros," published in Byte magazine, detailed the software process and autopsied the code. *Travesty* is a word-frequency text generator.[45] The sardonic name they gave it perhaps reflects either the low hopes they had for its output or the reception they expected from traditional literature critics. But the questions they asked were serious: "To what degree can personal 'style' be described as a manifestation of letter frequencies?" (Kenner and O'Rourke 1984).

The futurist Kurzweil (2001) incorporated a similar insight about "style" into his *Cybernetic Poet*, which from the 1980s to 2000, used Markov models to replicate the meter-rhyme-vocabulary of poets; poets could be melted together to form hybrids; poetry was ostensibly a game of numbers and frequencies. More recent software initiatives include: *Issue 1*, a 3,785-page PDF posted online in that claimed to be 3,164 poems by established poets edited by Stephen McLaughlin and Jim Carpenter (2008); in actuality, it was a computer-generated text, causing a scandal. As mentioned in a previous section, Cayley and Howe's (2009) *The Readers Project* manipulates source texts so that algorithms discover reading paths based on rules through source texts; their algorithmic readers generate new animated visual rivers of intensity that erode the source to reveal a rule-based text.

None of these previous projects, however, utilizes deep-learning data science methodologies. The primary uses of data science in literature search for new critical insights using visualizations as in Scott Rettberg's (2014) information visualizations of Electronic Literature as a Model of Creativity and Innovation in Practice (ELMCIP) or Moretti's (2005) work at the Stanford Literary Lab from 2000 onward.

Short-Form Flourishes (tweets & ppg) In terms of contemporary generation projects, there are numerous active Twitter bots, which generate conceptual or micropoetry capably.[46] Between 2007 and 2014, the Twitter account *everyword* tweeted 109,000 times; it tweeted *every word* in the English language. At its peak it had over a hundred thousand followers. Allison Parrish (2014), programmer-poet, states her motivation for the work in traditional terms: "I just wanted to express an idea I was working through as a writer myself." This simple gesture of a single word, in lineage with Goldsmith's uncreative writing, also ironically operates as its opposite: an expressive computational chant—monotonous transcendence driving ritual toward routine (or occasionally driving the other way).

Short-form bots also have short-form lives: they disappear. The algorithmic incantation and procedural writing that drove *The Longest Poem in the World*, which was "composed by aggregating real-time public twitter updates and selecting those that rhyme. It is [*sic*] constantly growing at

~4000 verses / day," is currently off-line; it exists as a residue on Facebook after a flourish of couplets in 2009.

With mechanical regularity, *Metaphor-a-Minute* tweets a metaphor every two minutes; it was written "in response to the third chapter of Ian Bogost's *Alien Phenomenology*" (Kazemi 2012). Sometimes the metaphors generated seem good, as prescient as jazz sandwiches. In this case, is the code speaking or is the audience projecting? Questions of relevance arise: Are metaphors poems? Or is the entire feed a poem?[47] Can an algorithm evoke an experience that it will never know? Kazemi (2012), the creator of *Metaphor-a-Minute*, feels "skeptical that we can ever have good metaphors for anything; or rather, anything can be a good or a bad metaphor. I think metaphorism requires someone to take the stance of a poet, to have confidence in metaphor. And a poet I am not." That said, the metaphors produced by Kazemi's *Metaphor-a-Minute* often have a freshness that human-authored metaphors cannot attain; its depth of vocabulary and indifference to precedents create occasional audacious, irreverent combinatorial collisions.

As does Mark Sample's *This is Just to Say* Twitterbot that replicates William Carlos Williams's iconic *This Is Just to Say* plum poem, with ironic ludicrous results and serious implications: print canons are based on a single variation that survives editing process; digital canons provoke effortless variants that open a state space of serendipity.

I have cancelled
the fists
that were in
the dogma
Forgive me
They were unbridled
so firm
and so planned
(Sample 2012)

Creating convincing granules and sparks occurs often, as in Montfort's (2013) submission to (Kazemi's initiated) NaNoGenMo novel-generating competition, *World Clock*, which begins:

It is now exactly 12:05 in Funafuti. In some typical location a person named Kenny, who is of completely average stature, reads a well-preserved note. He looks away, then back.

Montfort (2009) is even more succinct in his *ppg256* series: Perl poetry generators that are precisely 256 characters long. The output as might be surmised reflects the restricted state-space source code; while the commented instructions for *ppg256–1* are 883 characters long, the poems composed are a bit like e.e. cummings after a severe concussion; 1-word titles with 3-word lines that are surprisingly rich DNA unraveling variation without apparent repetition.

The success of each of the Twitter projects and Montfort's NaNoGenMo *World Clock* reflect adherence to what search engine optimization marketers refer to as three principles for success: simple, deep, and social. The challenge for traditional poetry is that it is often complex, deep, and antisocial. When the machine makes friends better than the human, what habitat for the head-heart remains?

Nick Montfort and Stephanie Strickland: *Sea and Spar Between* (2010)
Montfort and Strickland's (2010b) *Sea and Spar Between*—although not strictly a 'big data science' project (it does not use unsupervised learning or classifiers)—is a 'big data' project: the source seed texts are large, the process involves quantified reasoning, and the purpose is to create a hybrid author; from two dead beings one computational being arises. As Montfort and Strickland (2010a) explain,

The words in *Sea and Spar Between* come from Emily Dickinson's poems and Herman Melville's *Moby-Dick*. Certain compound words (kennings) are assembled from words used frequently by one or both. *Sea and Spar Between* was composed using the basic digital technique of counting, which allows for the quantitative analysis of literary texts. We considered, for instance, words that were used by only one of the two authors. We also looked at certain easily enumerated, characteristic categories of words, such as those ending in "less."

The result is an ocean of almost-infinite stanzas; yet even though the amount of stanzas is combinatorially large, the stanzas attain identity—succinct and intimate among the overwhelming waves.

While the *Sea and Spar Between* code process reflects Montfort, the navigation and scale of the work reflects Strickland and echoes a project she made in collaboration with Cynthia Lawson Jaramillo, *Vniverse* (Strickland and Jaramillo 2002). Specifically, *Sea and Spar Between* echoes the *Vniverse* mode of navigating a massive ocean of text by entering a number. In *Vniverse*, poems emerge from an ocean of stars, written across constellations, and it is this sense of an infinite writing and reading that flows from *Sea and Spar Between*.[48]

Surely there were scribes or archivists who groaned at the idea of page numbers, then line numbers, folios, and Dewey decimals, and now the name too disappears in that vastness, and we know the poems by their numbers, coordinates within a system, our cursor-avatar a tiny shim on that wild.

Software: JanusNode, Gnoetry, McGonagall, and *Evolution*   A few contemporary software projects generate longer-format poems ostensibly to assist in the writing process. Programmers-linguists often write these softwares. The most common technique is to use source texts as seeds, quantitatively analyze that text for word collocations, and then generate new text with the same/similar collocations as the source.

Chris Westbury's *JanusNode* is the descendant of the 'McPoet' software he wrote in the mid-1980s. As he writes on his web page, "*JanusNode* is a user-configurable dynamic textual projective surface. It can create original texts using a rule-based system or can morph your texts using Markov chaining and various other techniques. It has been described (albeit generously) as 'Photoshop for text'" (Westbury 2000).

Gnoetry (a collaboration between programmer Jon Trowbridge and poet Eric Elshtain [2004]) "is an interactive word n-gram generator." Eddie Addad (aka Antonio Roque [2012]) ported it to JavaScript as *jGnoetry*, which generates poems into default templates (couplet, quatrain, sonnet, free verse, haiku, tenka, and renga); users can create their own templates. Users can also assign the corpora source texts and modulate weights. One of the most flexible aspects of it is the capacity to interactively select some words to remain while others are regenerated. This permits an iterative human-selection, machine-generation process allowing incremental improvements in the verse.

McGonagall, a genetic-algorithm system for deriving well-formed poetry, applies a *restricted definition* of poetry to "render *falsifiable* the claim that a program successfully generates poetry. Our proposed definition is: a poem is a natural language artefact that simultaneously satisfies the constraints of *grammaticality, meaningfulness,* and *poeticness*" (Manurung, Richie, and Thompson 2012, 48). In my opinion, the falsifiable process (while laudable in its rigor and replicability) confines the *successful* poem to a classical ghetto of harmonious regulated order, thus amputating the potential of radical, tangential, esoteric, marginal, and even perverse manipulations of language.

Evolution, a collaboration between the poet Heldén and programmer Jonson, utilizes scientific data as randomization seeds in software built specifically to emulate the style of Heldén. (This software is discussed in more depth below.) The publication produced to document their work contains an amalgamation of generated poetry, theory, and code (Heldén and Jonson 2014). Heldén's style softly deflects and evolves over time as it absorbs meteorologic and astronomical data.

Of the preceding projects, only McGonagall uses statistical methods that partially align it with data science, yet it does so within a formal conservative and ultimately restrictive notion of poetry. By utilizing big data sets, it will be possible to avoid using any definition of poetry, and instead allow the poetic field itself to reveal its norms and deviations, thus providing a range of templates of definitions.

Heldén and Jonson: *Evolution* (2014)

Evolution is an online artwork designed to emulate the texts and music of poet and artist Johannes Heldén, with the ultimate goal of passing "The Imitation Game Test" as proposed by Alan Turing in 1951.[49]

In 2013, the Swedish poet Johannes Heldén stops writing poetry. He has been eliminated from his own creative process; ruled out by *Evolution*[,] … by the ontology—the problematic *being*—of linguistic artefacts that are generated by computational process.[50]

A poet once told me that the most autobiographical writing there is, is procedural writing that introduces constraints and rules governing the outcome. … Perhaps poetry, if not literature in general, is inherently algorithmic. Even automatic writing is regulated, dictated. Moreover, the algorithmic imagination is a crucial trait in modern and modernist writing—from Mallarmé to Cage to concrete to digital poetry, etcetera.[51]

Tielhard de Chardin claims "Interiority, the rudiment of consciousness, exists everywhere; it is only that if the particle is extremely simple, the consciousness is so small that we cannot perceive it; if there is an increase in complexity, this consciousness comes out into the open and we have the world of life." … The stone is pregnant with the mind. Matter thinks.[52]

For a reader familiar with Heldén's poetry something strange takes place on the screen. It is almost an uncanny feeling of having read the words that appear in front of you before, and probably you have, but not in this order. ... In the fragments of *Evolution* that appear on the screen a vegetative setting slowly emerges: "woven grass, rising trees, treehouse a rain, weed, sprout, plant, moss luminous, oak tree, night blooming."[53]

text 144 - _ evolution: generation: 58 _____

text 145 - sequence: northern hemisphere land-ocean temperature index in 001 degrees celsius, 1951

text 146 - roll in: 9

text 16 - method: REPLACE

text 17 - pivotal: __[1] INDEX: 81

text 42 - predecessor: __[1] INDEX: 80

text 43 - sucessor: __[1] INDEX: 81

text 44 - result: "__ __" => "__ __"[54]

almost, or

all

and

unfamiliar region on

GENERATION: 696

SEQUENCE: { IMAGE SERIALIZATION } STORM[55]

From a mathematical and computational perspective *Evolution* utilises the theories developed by mathematician Andrei Markov and computer scientist Ingo Rechenberg. In *Evolution*, new permutations of poetry are generated by applying strategies from evolutionary algorithms over a stochastic model of the text. ... Linguistic progression is achieved using word and white-space frequency analysis combined with a decision model continuously influenced by a semi-deterministic random seed ... derived from atmospheric data, visual imagery, space observations and popular culture.[56]

source material;

works by by Johannes Heldén[57]

java/

  net

    evolution

      drone

        domain

      DroneRepository

      DroneService[58]

Data, Machine Learning, and Neural Networks Big data, cloud computing, data science, and neural net deep-learning techniques present extraordinary, viable, unprecedented computationally-tractable opportunities for radical poetry generation; ensemble techniques (which use a weighted ensemble of many classifiers algorithms) might do what Big Blue did for chess: topple or at least wobble the master poets. This vulnerability of human creativity to computational engineering might seem threatening; a reflex might be to retreat. Yet the cybernetic intelligence that emerges from big data might enhance creativity, adjunct it, and extend "augmented imagination" (Wilberg, 2014). And retreating from a storm does not negate the presence of wind; data science will increasingly be applied across all domains of language to ensure that computers both speak and write competently.

Contemporary technology radically challenges the creative process of poetry authorship. It is important that poets (and not technologists/linguists) interrogate what the practice of poetry is in a big data/cloud world. Under what conditions do poets or audiences engage with machine-generated poetry? What are the sociological/cultural barriers to thinking mechanic poetry—both in production and consumption? Data science generative poetry problematizes the exorbitant claims made by advocates of big data. Poetry as an edge case illuminates the contradictions and strengths of big data methods.

It is already possible to augment writing with autosuggestions derived from machine learning and big data (i.e., Google or Swype), and it may eventually be possible to generate plausible poems in specific styles independently: contextually sensitive, metrically and visually sophisticated, using parametrically defined vocabularies and authorial models. As stated earlier, Kurzweil (2001) implemented models of poets in the 1990s. But the real hard terrain is an algorithm which emulates poetry without being told what poetry is, merely by reading lots of it: machine learning lyricism. As of 2015, there are few projects utilising data science methods such as ensemble learning and deep neural nets to generate poetry. Dekai Wu and Karteek Addanki in *Learning to Rap Battle with Bilingual Recursive Neural Networks* "teach machines how to rap battle by improvising lyrics on the fly, in which a novel recursive bilingual neural network implicitly learns soft, context-sensitive generalizations over the structural relationships between associated parts of challenge and response raps, while avoiding the exponential complexity costs that symbolic models would require" (Wu and

Addanki 2015, 2524). Their approach is unsupervised: the machine learning algorithm finds salient features without any human intervention.

Admittedly, data science seems distant from poetry, but the arts and culture and literature will not remain immune to exponential growth in computational power and shifts in the capacity of algorithms to produce credible emulations of cultural products. If we accept that poetry (permit me to gloss a definition) is *the act of intuitively or conceptually building meaningful (emotional, conceptual, spiritual, or perceptual) patterns with words*, then since at a profound and pragmatic level both art and science share an affinity for patterns, there is a role that computation can play here. The future equivalent of being *well-read* may mean having examined statistical evidence and generated output from literary corpora in order to discern sets of overused phrases, memes nearing death, and young, fresh nodes of language just dawning into relevance.

Data Science Glossary   For those readers from a literary background who may be unfamiliar with the terminology, I offer the following rudimentary definitions. *Data science* is a set of techniques that statistically analyzes large data sets for patterns. *Natural language processing* (NLP) combines data science and linguistics into a single discipline in order for machines to try and interpret naturally occurring statements in a human written or spoken language. NLP includes techniques like n-grams (words that occur together) and Markov chains (a statistical model of word co-occurrence or semantic proximity based on analysis of corpora). *Unsupervised learning* extracts features from data without predefinition of those features by the programmer. Typically, a training set of data is fed to the algorithms; on a second pass, the capacity of the trained algorithm is then checked with a test set of data. *Distributed Stochastic Neighbor Embedding* is an unsupervised dimensionality-reduction algorithm; it classifies by *discovering* the most relevant features of a big data set. *Deep learning* refers to machine-learning processes that use neural nets that recently have demonstrated unprecedented unsupervised accuracy at identifying subtle features in language.[59] *Ensemble methods* involve clusters of techniques applied simultaneously, and then a meta-algorithm analyzes the effectiveness of each member of the ensemble relative to the others. *Cloud clusters* are Web-based services that offer (super) computing power for rental. *To spin up a cluster* means to rent time on a cloud service to crunch big data; the power of supercomputing is rentable.

Jhave: *BDP* (2014) In summer 2014, I took an intensive eleven-week course in data science.[60] Based on this theoretical and preliminary practical coding introduction to Python and statistical reasoning, I produced a set of generative experiments called *BDP: Big Data Poetry* (Jhava 2015). In *BDP*, I apply a combination of data visualization, language analytics, classification algorithms, entity recognition, and part-of-speech replacement techniques to a corpus of 10,557 poems from the Poetry Foundation, 57,000+ hip-hop songs from Ohhla.com, and over 7,000 pop lyrics. The poems currently generated lack thematic structure. Occasional glimmers of cleverness emerge; yet narrative and coherence rarely arise. In my view, two things are necessary in order to improve the output: expand the corpus by several orders of magnitude, and implement unsupervised deep-learning ensemble methods using cloud computing clusters.

Unsupervised learning is exactly as its name suggests: the algorithm is not told what to look for in the texts but instead numerically searches for and extracts pattern clusters. It offers distinct advantages in terms of discerning patterns within data that do not have clearly continuous demarcated boundaries or features. At the same time, since the analysis is buried behind an enigmatic algorithmic process, there is a limitation in understanding how the process works or what features actually influenced the classification.[61] The trick of poetic research using these techniques will be to correlate manually chosen features (like line length, word length, vocabulary, metrical regularity, length of verse, etc.) with the results of the automated unsupervised learning algorithms. In this way, it may be possible to inductively estimate what features are of primary importance to the algorithms.

With unsupervised learning, there is no externally derived measure of what constitutes a 'good' poem. The algorithm decides; it clusters and classifies poems into neighborhoods, all regions of poetry are presented, poets and critics can cluster around styles and concerns that they find evocative, or as now, migrate and visit and explore various regions. The breadth of the corpus can guide the process; results can be submitted to human-readers in a *Bot or Not* style interface (Laird and Schwartz 2014).

Future big data poets may generate lots of poems in styles that have no inherent interest for them, just as factory owners produce goods that do not reflect their needs. The metaphor may seem appalling but it is a fact: the best poet of the next generation may be a programmer who rarely reads any of the output. Poetry, already a surplus commodity compared to its market, may become as ubiquitous as water. Although unfortunately, poetry may also become like the earth's oceans and lakes: polluted and increasingly unnourishing.

Vision to Voice: Long-Term Impact   Roland Barthes famously predicted the death of the author; yet I do not think he foresaw the cause of death as big data. And I doubt Barthes intended to imply the irony that from every death there springs new life. It seems plausible now to suggest that writers express sets and repertoires of techniques and preoccupations. And each writer writes within a cultural context, time, vocabulary, and tradition. Once these traditions are mapped, propensities or paths for future writing will be either generated or grown as variations to assist authors in exploring creativity that conforms to their innate self, while at the same time assisting them to see opportunities. The author will not die but expand to explore more of their potential using a computational symbiont.

Data science algorithms are capable of finding topological patterns within languages and thus poetry. By examining which patterns fit cores of genres and which are outliers, notions of creativity and modes of writing will necessarily shift: exploratory writing will swiftly outgrow the *uncreative* mode of pure appropriation and move toward nuanced expressive augmentation of the writer's own persona. Big data has equivalent power not just to *de*personalize but also to *re*personalize.

The long-term impact of this research foresees poets writing with virtual assistances; in the first instances, enhanced autosuggestion agents that present relevant fields or paths of words; in the following steps, emulation may occur that are capable of most communication.[62] Readers may also choose to read across fields of autosuggested language, so instead of reading an author, they will read a composite poem in the style of a set of authors from a specific time period whose average word and line lengths correspond to their desired complexity.

~~~~

Amalgamate: Robert Creeley, Lucille Clifton
Amalgamate: Christopher Dewdney, Rae Armantrout
Amalgamate: Fred Moten, Netochka Nezvanova
Alternate verses each.

Randomization complexity: 5-second sine wave.
Deflection from norm range: 1% to 15%
Continue until stopped.

~~~~

More: as computers learn to see and convert vision to voice, naming what they see, they will theoretically be able to describe an audiovisual feed in many styles in real time. So as augmented-glass-wearing Netizens wander the world in 2020, they will be able to say: "Describe what I see as Walt Whitman. Describe it as Gwendolyn Brooks. Describe it as Mahmoud Darwish. Describe it as Virginia Woolf circa the final section of *Waves*. Describe it as László Krasznahorkai. Amalgamate all. Mix with me, 30 percent. Continue." Result: an oral poem fed into the mind of the viewer that is a hybrid of their voice and the voice of many authors (living and dead, famous and unknown); it converts who they are and what they experience into a written reservoir. They walk as if possessed, muttering: *save, delete, publish, revise, chat.*

Aesthetic animism even as presented in lyrical form is less a demarcating and negotiation of a gap between self and other, subject and object, human and nonhuman, analog and digital, real and virtual, so as to determine the ontology of each, than it is a call to think relationally.

—Rita Raley, Living Letterforms: The Ecological Turn in
Contemporary Digital Poetics. *Contemporary Literature* 52, 4 (2011).

4   Softwares

Critical Code Studies is the application of hermeneutics to the interpretation of the extra-functional significance of computer source code. It is a study that follows the developments of *Software Studies* and *Platform Studies* into the layer of the code. In their oft-taught text, *Structure and Interpretation of Computer Programs*, Herald Abelson, Gerald Jay Sussman, and Julie Sussman declare, "Underlying our approach to this subject is our conviction that 'computer science' is not a science and that its significance has little to do with computers. The computer revolution is a revolution in the way we think and in the way we express what we think."

—Mark C. Marino, 2010

For literary scholars, literature students, poets, writers, or the casual reader of this text, this section may seem incongruous. What role can software studies legitimately play in the study of writing literature? Can software studies offer insights into animist ontologies about literature? Did critics in the eleventh century write treatises critiquing the quill? Granted, the printing press modulated writing. But most poets don't animate their words; most writers don't use motion graphics. The potential implications of the following analysis apply to a minority of writers. Yet the implications of software (motion graphics, typographic sculpting, and code-generated poetry) on reading and writing may have implications for all concerned with language. As audiences habituate to reading language in games, film credits, ads, and experimental video, attention dilates, and new syntaxes emerge that privilege morph over cut. The tools that create these effects influence the concepts expressed.

What follows is a hands-on focus on the creation of several specific works, preceded by a consideration of temporality and the role of animation interface "timelines." I examine the keyframed timeline (an authoring

interface used in animation, 3-D, video, and special effects) as a historical design artifact, acknowledge Johanna Drucker's (2009) *SpecLab* insights
into the effect of interfaces on temporality and creation, and meditate
(briefly) on the benefits and risks of timeline systems that quantify repetition versus systems of (what I call) instrumental softwares that provoke
improvisational process.

What Is Software Studies?

Software studies lies at the nexus of code and culture, in an epistemological estuary that although mapped and known to exist, is still relatively
untracked. For practice-led researchers (i.e., artist-academics), software
studies offers a chance to reflect on the interdependency of creativity and
design in practice. In this book, software studies connects the ontological
proposal (of aesthetic animism) to the empirical practices of digital poets.

The critical discourse around software is shifting rapidly. The quotation
from Marino that opens this chapter points out several ways these shifts are
occurring: first, software studies has been joined by platform and now critical code studies. Each serves as a valuable tool in an increasingly technological world. Future domains may include network, and avatar/augmentation
studies; each of these will impact the humanities.

As Lev Manovich insightfully notes, several key figures at the origin of
interface design left clues that they perceived software as quasi-entity. Ivan
Sutherland, who in 1963 laid the seeds for motion graphics, titled his PhD
dissertation "Sketchpad: A Man-Machine Graphical Communication System." Manovich comments:

Rather than conceiving of Sketchpad as simply another media, Sutherland presents
it as something else—a communication system between two entities: a human and
an intelligent machine. Kay and Goldberg will later also foreground this communication dimension, referring to it as "a two-way conversation" and calling the new
"metamedium" "active." (We can also think of Sketchpad as a practical demonstration of the idea of "man-machine symbiosis" by J.C. Licklider applied to image making and design). (Manovich in 2008 online draft of 2013, 67)

Interface design influences the relationship that a writer has to words. As
symbiosis and *conversations*, writing tools alter how art and literature arise.

Timelines

Instead of drawing with lines, *Nomencluster* allows you to create your own designs with insects, 19th century engineering engravings, food chemistry, and a continual stream of poetic texts and interactive writing.

—Jason Nelson and Matthew Horton, 2015

The turn toward *living language* entails authoring environments appropriate to the task, and it is my feeling that the animation-timeline paradigm is suboptimal in certain respects when it comes to the modeling and manipulation of (TAV) digital texts. Time-based media and life-forms are both not amenable to nuanced descriptions within linear, quantifiable spreadsheets. And spreadsheets (as explained below) are historically the organizational paradigm that underlies the contemporary animation timeline. Literature is precisely the opposite: ambiguous, parallel, and quality rich; experiential time curves.

As far as I know (apart from the work of Drucker), the impact of linear timeline authoring environment design on experiential depiction remains unresearched in digital humanities. That theoretical gap may be due to the difficulty of conceiving of interfaces that do not exist; it's difficult enough that I do not attempt it (Drucker does, and with some success!). Instead, in the following sections I outline a history of timelines and then examine in detail a few key software.

Timelines Defined   Timelines are the dominant paradigm for scrubbable media authoring and playback; they are prevalent in most commercial and industrial softwares that work with media (including diverse softwares from multiple domains: film editing, motion graphics, 3-D rendering, DVD and music players, slide shows, etc.). For media consumers, timelines allow scrubbable time.

With timelines, time can be controlled, so as design artifact they reflect the instinct to engineer, will to power, and control impulses. In some sense, they are the multimedia equivalent of a keyboard. Keyboards allow rapid, fluctuating writing styles to emerge; timelines enable complex, animated letterforms.

For media authors, timeline interpolation operates as algorithmic suture, sewing and joining time.[1] A "tween" literally makes a path between distinct temporal (digital) frames. It fills in the gaps. It guesses the holes.

The advantages of this style of animation are manifold. Fine-grained control of parameters distributed across easing curves (which permits easy repetition) constitutes an empirically viable method for creative control. The author can iterate and tweak multiple parameters independently; time is carefully and cleanly laid out in a linear fashion; it is easy to understand chronological events. The disadvantages are subtler to identify but relate at a specific level to spontaneity and improvisation, and secondarily at a general level to a concept of time that is an antiseptic contingency.

For poets, as poets, or people who play with the in-between, there is a necessity to retain within authoring environments, a nontimeline mode, to allow for unstructured play and exploratory improvisation. To enable within writing the fullest range of expressive and formal processes capable requires carefully considering the tools.

Vases In 2008, a fifty-two-hundred-year-old Iranian earthenware bowl (with five drawings of a goat on it) was spun around and reputed to be an early instance of animation (of a goat leaping to eat a leaf). In this case, the claim to animation is tenuous, but as a sequence of poses displayed on a surface, this conical surface echoes faintly the contemporary timeline's integration of visual language with chronological control. Gestural control of a bowl is in the spin; this gesture is echoed in the scrub wheel of contemporary editing suites. It is also echoed in the numerous animation tropes that occurred between ancient poetry and modern film animation: zeotrope, praxinoscope, thaumatrope, and phenakistoscope. Flip books laid out before binding; histories constructed from mnemonic principles as in ancient Rome: the conceptual legacy of timelines is vast.

A Missing History
In the Augmented Human Intellect (AHI) Research Center at Stanford Research Institute a group of researchers is developing an experimental laboratory around an interactive, multi-console computer-display system, and is working to learn the principles by which interactive computer aids can augment their intellectual capability.

—Douglas Engelbart and Bill English, 1968

Although the history of graphical user interfaces and interface developments—like Engelbart's (1968) 'Demo' at the Stanford Research Institute,
windows-icon-mouse-pointer, and the evolution of personal computer
operating systems (Vis-On, Lisa, Amiga, MS-DOS, etc.)—is well documented
online, the history of how individual *softwares* evolved and integrated their
various features and grew into the complex beasts we know today is not
easily found.

I did not find any step-by-step history of the timeline as an interface
module. Perhaps that is because searching for 'timeline' does not produce refined results; perhaps software paleontology is sparse. Many computer professionals and programmers (who create for their pleasure online
archives of hardware development) are unfamiliar with multimedia software, and the meaning of the term *timeline* remains associated for the most
part with its analog form in historical presentations. So what follows is a
tentative history, assembled from a few fragments.

Turing Mach
The best way to predict the future is to invent it.

—Alan Kay, 1971

Turing machines are commonly used to teach the principles of discrete
math underlying computer science. A Turing machine is a thought experiment that involves imagining a single-frame tape reader that can read one
symbol instruction at a time. Sequentially, these symbols construct and
simulate the logic essential to computing. They are also remarkably similar
to timelines: one frame, one symbol, and a pointer to that frame, along
with an infinite memory of everything before and after. At the same time,
the Turing machine is an abstract representation of the assembly line with
its sequential passage of parts past multiple time pointers. Another intriguing structural resonance with timelines reoccurs at the origin of graphic
processor units (GPUs). Graphic cards underlie all motion graphics; they
are the physical architecture necessary for the multimedia revolution. They
are basically pixel-based frame buffer systems: a unit of time-stamped data
held by a pointer in memory. The precursor-to-GPU pixel-based frame buffer arose in the early 1970s as the Sandin video synthesizer was invented

and the *Computer Graphics and Image Processing* journal began publication (Shoup 2001).

So perhaps the origin of digital timelines begins at the confluence of theory (Turing machines), digital hardware (GPU frame buffers), efficient capitalist productivity (assembly line), and cartoons (cel animation).

Animation Spreadsheets

Disney Animation Studio's Exposure Sheet, accessible from the Pencil Test, works rather like an animation spreadsheet.

—Steven Anzovin, 1992

Timelines are a specific case of charts. A diversity of ancient accounting systems and mechanisms all use some sort of a timeline: pulleys, gears, film sprockets, axles, abacus style devices, grinding mills, Kabbalist divination wheels, and even mandelas. Software (like all culture) soaks up paradigms; remediation is conceptual reincorporation.

It is also probable that the commercialization of the software timeline was born when cel animation met computation. In 1990, in conjunction with Amiga (which had a dedicated hardware system for multimedia before the personal computer), Disney developed a commercial software package. In promotional television demos of this package (available online), the primary authoring screen clearly has no timeline.[2] Creative work occurs in a cel-animation-style space where the animator controls (with keystrokes) the amount of onion skinning. Animation happens automatically. The environment conforms to the classic Greek metaphor for time: a human walks backward into the future, with its most recent trail fading away behind it. The future is unknown.

Without a timeline there is no future; there is only the present moment. The animator is not supplied with visual evidence that a future exists, and that time runs straight and then ends. Teleology, with all it implies (origin, progress, Armageddon, etc.), does not exist. Nontimeline design environments are the visual equivalents of oral cultures. The animator must remember the set as junctures that contribute to a totality.

In the 1990s, however, more complex animation projects must have demanded methods for remembering scenes and the ability to jump visually from one time to another. A software "evaluation" article from *Compute*

(Anzovin 1992) reveals how a timeline-like module (two years after launch) has been added to (or always existed in) the Disney Animation Studio. It is called an *exposure sheet*. Functionally, it is compartmentalized off from the main real-time, cel-style animating mode. *Exposure sheet*

works rather like an animation spreadsheet. Each cel in the animation is given a line in the *Exposure Sheet*, showing the cel number, assigned sounds, timing, and other information. You can rearrange cels of an animation in the Exposure Sheet by cutting, pasting, or deleting their lines, which is much easier than cutting and pasting cels in Pencil Test. (ibid.)

Note the metaphoric reference to *spreadsheets* in the promo material; timelines are sold as organizational efficiency tools. Spreads are essential for the rapid dissection of quantifiable data. Primarily used in accounting and inventory, spreadsheets induce precise analytic calibrations of data; it is difficult to envision the purpose of displaying ambiguous evolving emotional experiences in spreadsheets. Spreadsheets are spaces for keeping track of data; they are tabulation tools, interface panopticons, and grid databases. So does it mean anything that the timeline grew from a spreadsheet metaphor? As a ubiquitous feature of contemporary animation software, do timelines introduce quantification and product analysis into the creative process? Will quantified modes of animation (as in audio quantization and timelines) provoke neglect of live improvisational, instrumental authoring environments?

In 1990 (accepting that year's release of Disney Animation Studio as some sort of benchmark not of research software but rather of commercial diffusion), the timeline function of examining the creative process as a production line is still kept separate as a module; it is secondary, to be consulted as necessary, as an adjunct to creative flow. At this stage of animation software design, time-based structural analysis is used only occasionally during creation. Real-time creation and timeline organization have been grafted together in the same device, but they are not superimposed. Modeling and animation occur together, but independently of the exposure sheets. A nonquantified nontimeline view is the default; fluid gestural flow and crafting frame by frame remain the dominant paradigm. Then at some point in the 1990s, the situation reversed; the default layout became the timeline. The nontimeline view occasionally remains as an option, a vestigial configuration.

In other words, in contemporary authoring softwares, focus shifts from an ancient emphasis on tactile process to a tactical procedure. Timelines (animation spreadsheets) dominate; free, fluid, real-time animation environments become secondary and marginal. Head trumps hand and heart; algorithms and accountancy fill gaps. And with this subtle transformation in design paradigms, animation shifts away from choreographic craft and sculptural caress toward a mechanistic mercantile model.

Strangely enough, it is perhaps this transition that needs to be reexamined if a living language is to emerge. Biological clocks do not run in straight lines. Nature's clocks follow cycles, mushy gradients, and seasonal spirals; Salvador Dali's clocks melt and bend, as do the associational swerves in poems, sites where tongues trip over intonations.

Timeline's Fundamental Parts

It is the story of a man who digs a hole so deep he can hear the past, a woman who climbs a ladder so high she can see the future.

—Steve Tomasula, 2010

Timelines are narrow strips of unidirectional temporal flow. Their pace quantifies without eddies, an antiseptic pipe that runs along narrow tracks. They are composed of several fundamental parts:

1. A horizontal straight line(s) that goes from the beginning of the time to the end.
2. A point(er) (usually drawn as an arrowhead) that represents the present moment.
3. A display window that shows that present moment.

The ancillary parts (that are not necessarily part of all timelines) include zooming mechanisms, frame markers, and cells. The animator moves step by step through that environment as they would through an inventory. The production environment is a warehouse of boxes, clips, frames, windows, and menus (stacks). The timeline always remains linear and straight. It cannot be bent or forked or broken into multiple strands. Bifurcations can be built in through nesting (compositions or movie clips), so that in actuality the timeline is like a single stalk of the main timeline with multiple looping, repetitive subtimelines occurring. Yet the animator/poet does not see the interface timeline like a tree. There is no generic way (or software that I know of) that allows the user to see a timeline's multiple branching time, nor is there any implementation of independent time signatures on different timelines in the same project. Once the clock starts ticking, it runs to the end.

The metaphoric and ontological implications of these fundamental and seemingly innocuous design elements are unexplored terrain. Are temporal implications implicit in interfaces? Does this effect how we as users/viewers/people think of time? Or is it the reverse: Do these design elements arise from an innately human instinct of what time is?

Specifically, is it possible that the paradigm of malleable living language requires an authoring environment where multiple modules of intersecting flow exist simultaneously? It is one of the ironies of this critique that Tomasula's ornate, effective, and complex multimedia novel *TOC* implements many interactive modes of working with text, and it was made in After Effects on a timeline. The question is, What would *TOC* have been if Tomasula's Borgesian fantasia of circular time was made in an interface offering a more complex model of time?

Implicit Principles of Timelines

When poets compose with timelessness in mind, they will always be on the route to originality.

—Christopher Funkhouser, 2007

Stating what is implied by interface design is a tricky business, fraught with potential for mistakes. Nevertheless, given the fundamental parts of a timeline, the following beliefs seem implied by its structure:

1. Time is linear.
2. Time is unidirectional.
3. Time can be broken into units.
4. Units of time are frames; frames are discrete moments.
5. Frames can be frozen.
6. Time is never known outside the frame (until the process of render).
7. Time has a beginning and an end.

Claims about Timeline   Considered as a whole, the above list presents a bleak cosmology: a teleological dystopia that if applied to experience, would convert existence into a meta-Kafkaesque plod from birth to death. On the other hand, it reflects pragmatic reality. Task-use efficiency is (at a general level) synonymous with compartmentalization. It would be foolish to claim that interfaces using this model are ruining their users' capacity to conceive of flexible bifurcations, ambiguous reflectivity, and/or intersecting life stories. There is no shortage of soft, subtle, emotive, and intuitive movies and animations produced using these devices. I have no interest in stating a polemical case.

But I am claiming that in some instances (when timelines eradicate *instrumental* options—that allow real-time manipulation with tangible feedback), the timeline introduces an implicit model that places the creative practitioner at a distance from immediate temporal feedback with their materials. A classical musician develops sets of muscular reflexes attuned to changes in the matter of their instrument; these reflexes occur subconsciously, instinctively at a muscular level, and neurologically in the dorsal brain; these subtle cues are not accessible within most timeline software, which requires that the machine stop while parameters are changed.[3] *Live coding* may provide a paradigm around this blockade.

By separating run time from work time, timelines deflect the creative process into modular contained moments. The assembly line metaphor may function well in some circumstances, where flow can slowly evolve as it might for a wood or stone carver who steps back and considers the process, continues, and steps back, in a repetitive dance of proximity and distance. Yet traditional sculptural materials (wood, stone, and metal) are static matter. Malleable dimensional texts (as focused on in this book) are temporal entities. They change. Stepping back from change may provide the opportunity to assess independent frames, but timeline-imposed distance removes the creator from the momentum of process. Tactile reduction replaces relation with a living entity. Straight lines refute cycles.

As Stephanie Strickland and Cynthia Lawson Jaramillo note, both code and poetry involve loops. Poems invoke semantic loops in the readers, spaces of retracing. Code is also structurally founded on iterations: "People think of going forward in reading poetry, but the very turning of the line is in constant conflict with that goal, as are the triple realms contending for meaning. Neither poetry nor code proceeds by forging ahead" (Strickland and Jaramillo 2007).

Strickland and Jaramillo are not alone in this diagnosis; for Douglas Hofstadter, *strange loops* permeate aesthetic experience. And I can add my own voice to this chorus: in my essay "Programming as Poetry" (Jhave 2001), I compared recursion to poetic impact:

Poetry and programming share more than strong affinities. Each is language-based, obsessed with conciseness, consistently evolving, modelled on consciousness, and inscrutable to the uninitiated (think of James Joyce reading C++). Each uses language in ways that involve leaps and circular paths; each requires an arduous concentration that ultimately relies upon reasoning which invokes intuition; and each is closely related by a shared goal of precise communication of complex realities.

Creative authoring requires interface design respectful of the sinuous paths of creative process and the recursive foundations of semantic epiphanies.

Homogeneous Granularity

Diagrammatic representations of temporal relations fall into three basic categories: *linear, planar,* and *spatial.* Linear diagrams, or timelines, are by far the simplest and most prevalent forms. ... The timeline is a linear spectrum with homogenous granularity. On a linear diagram data can exhibit only three relative temporal conditions: *earlier than, later than,* or (sometimes awkwardly) *simultaneous with* (or overlapping).

—Johanna Drucker, 2009

Drucker's notion of the timeline's *homogeneous granularity* in *SpecLab* (cited just above) is the only research I am aware of that has directly questioned the cultural implications of temporality in interface design. In *SpecLab*'s chapter "Temporal Modeling," Drucker provides an overview of the research that she and her team conducted into the models underlying an exploratory design response to a software initially designed by John David Miller and John Maeda. Drucker explains that in spite of the cleverness of the software, "in its use of screen space and creation of conventions for ordering materials, it was based on what I considered non-humanistic, objective conventions. Such timelines are derived from the empirical sciences and bear all the conspicuous hallmarks of its basis in objectivity. They are unidirectional, continuous, and organized by a standard non-varying metric" (Drucker 2009, 37).

Having reached similar conclusions independently, I am in agreement with Drucker when she continues to outline how linearity is not conducive to capturing experience. She uses the words "almost useless for describing the experience" (ibid., 37) in relation to complex felt events that might have many simultaneous components.

Much as I agree with the general direction of Drucker's argument, and to some degree the case studies that follow are based on a similar premise, there is a general empirical objection to this claim. Films for the last decade have been created using timelines in software, yet the emotional complexity of films has not deteriorated. There are many nuanced special FXs constructed using strictly linear timelines that as a final product, contribute to humanistic goals, and depictions of experience that are rich and nuanced. As a case in point, the final shot of Andrei Tarkovsky's *Solaris* is an apex of modernist humanism. Evidently, there is a subtle way that humans separate process from end result. Process does not necessarily contaminate product. Intention is encapsulated.[4] The surplus of nuanced projects emerging from timeline-based software thus is a strong objection to arguments for the "nonhumanistic" aspect of timelines. In addition, the prevalent use of *nested timelines* permits *simultaneous with* perspectives to occur. And loops within loops, hierarchies, inheritances, and modules are inherent to programming, so the linearity of timelines is only apparent; beneath the surface abstraction of the interface, recursion rules.

Yet Drucker's argument is itself nuanced and exploratory; she does not claim absolute opposition but instead suggests that alternative modalities exist that might instigate modes of creativity more appropriate to human experience. Her view promotes warped, spatial, and "topographic images of temporal events—a time landscape—with the idea of being able to map experience" (Drucker 2009, 59). The ideas are not implemented, yet the actual process of thinking through them constitutes an exercise in creative interface design within a field that has not changed radically since the epoch of Sutherland, Engelbart's demo, and Kay at Xerox PARC.

What has been revealed in the previous section is how paradigms of temporality (conveyed by the dominant presence of the timeline) might be constraining creativity, and particularly literary creativity, at some points. Obviously to claim that timelines eradicate the capacity for subtle work is untenable. What is tenable, however, is the inevitability of transformative change in interface design. In particular, Drucker precipitates an awareness of software's temporal bias toward linearity, and Matthew Fuller points to technology as cultural; both utilize references from structural linguistics, psychoanalysis, film theory, and cultural studies. Added to these references, insights from information visualization and the so-called studio or plastic arts (such as sculpture) suggest that tangible feedbacks and real-time instrumentality must be incorporated into future typographic interfaces. In the following section, these threads of temporality and tangibility are subsumed within empirical case studies of specific creative processes.

Case Studies

The impact of electronic technology on our lives is now the object of intense study, but what remains obscure is the role, if any, this technology has in shaping the ostensibly private language of poetry.

—Marjorie Perloff, 1991

Each of the following software case studies is an attempt to examine the ontological considerations of aesthetic animism in empirical context, and see how the subtle confluence of temporality, design, and animus intermingle within a digital practice. It is also an attempt to write software studies from the perspective of a practitioner, and move between conceptual speculation and historical overviews down to the discrete minutia of interface details. In the process, I hope to reveal the value of tangible software instruments that permit the real-time play of sculptural letterforms.

After Effects

"Everything was becoming conceptual," Duchamp explained: "that is, it depended on things other than the retina."

—Craig Dworkin and Kenneth Goldsmith, 2011

After Effects software often elicits a reactionary repulsion from those in the occidental avant-garde. Duchamp fetishism can tend toward untenable absolutes. From a modernist avant-garde perspective, conceptualism's capacity to recontextualize is considered laudable, sophisticated, self-reflexive cognition, while the ability to contrive is mere manual labor, playing with the surface of the mind without awareness of its structure. Graphic activities are castigated as hedonism incapable of yielding meta-aware stances. And the eroticism of the eye is caricatured as a superficial Hollywood film full of fake explosions, extruded aliens, and rogue nebulae. In short, special FXs are associated with cartoonish hypnotism, commercial mind manipulation, and masturbatory immaturity.

Yet I am here to argue (as clearly as I can) why compositing softwares, which are behind many of the world's most glitzy motion graphic campaigns, deserve recognition as precursors to a truly digital twenty-first-century word processor.

For Expression

A lot of poets are working audiovisually and yet they really get validated only once they start publishing books.

—Caroline Bergvall, 2007

Referring to motion graphic works made by Len Lye in 1937, Scott Rettberg (2011) writes, "Letters moving in space, often synchronized to a musical soundtrack, is not precisely a novel phenomena, but something that writers and artists have been experimenting with to some degree since the dawn of moving image technology." Yet after decades of work, these experiments still inhabit a strange exile from serious literary criticism; it's almost as if moving image-text triggers a taboo (like masturbation, shitting, and death, even while ubiquitous, they are somehow discomfiting, peripheral).

Why are moving image-texts (glitz and glam) not mere effervescent by-products of puerile imaginations incapable of really grasping the crucial role of abstraction in an information economy (or the primacy of a self-reflexive materiality in art practice)? Because (to put it simply), occasionally motion graphics are also the expression of the deepest felt sentiments experienced by any of us; they grapple with the ignorance that is at the core of existing, the mystery of self, and the role of humanity in a universe whose scale exceeds our capacity to comprehend it. Surfaces (do sometimes) contain concepts. Naive aesthetics play a nourishing role in the evolution of representation (aesthetic recycling and cultural compost). Discourse must be built around even excluded or marginal (dynamic visual typography and poetic) practices.

There are of course numerous examples of typographic effects applied with cosmetic abundance in ways that simply reinforce clichés. As effects move from obscurity into mass appeal, their capacity to genuinely contribute to poetics diminishes. Yet the presence of diluted glossy effects does not justify eradicating all motion graphics from the digital poetry toolbox.

John Berger, in his 1976 essay "The Primitive and the Professional" insightfully suggests that conventions and cultural class systems distinguish between the professional and primitive artist. The professional, trained and articulate, approaches art with the idiom of academia. The primitive arrives at art later in life, crudely, as a means of expressing lived experience. The resistance and ridicule met with by primitive artists is due to the turbulent protective reflexes of the dominant professional caste, whose definitions of what constitutes correct aesthetic goals define a carefully guarded, commercially viable field of discourse and practice. Discourse self-reinforces. My argument for the relevance of compositing and expression to contemporary writing is (in some respects) an appeal for the inclusion of digital primitives, the basement autodidacts of gloss, exuberant homespun authors expressing their poetic instincts with contemporary motion graphic tools.

Literalism and Excess   The irony at the heart of the widespread adoption of the Bauhaus design maxims "eradicate the superfluous" and "less is more" are that they distill culture down to a generic style, acceptable to all. IKEA-like Zen minimalism manuals proliferate in the art academies, and occasionally creative writing departments disguise ideologies as textbooks. The simplicity of effect cherished by the elite avant-garde reflects an austerity that refutes personal flourish; expressivity is banished to the baroque along with Sarah Bernhardt and other excesses. And it is this tendency that makes me suspicious of my own negative reactions to some of the work that follows. I wonder if my own immersion in the art world, design discourse networks does not necessitate that I conform to the move away from representational modes. Nevertheless, it does feel as if excess does not always entail more, so the following examples attempt to disentangle the authentic from the disingenuous.

The tendency to convert the entire world into letterforms, to make everything a wireframe of language, is not the goal of aesthetic animism. Movies that translate poetry into landscapes of leaping letters invariably exceed the literal threshold. Consider *Tongue of the Hidden*, a 2009 five-minute motion graphic conversion of Ḥāfez's poetry into a 3-D world constructed of Persian calligraphy. Its pure literalism exudes a gothic concern with detail yet overabundance dilutes its concentrative focus. Pure literalism conceives a world of animated skeletons that have no direct correlation to biological veracity, psychological interiority, agency, and/or the skins, ecosystems, and contexts that genuine animism invokes. Animism is as subtle as biology; it relies on layers of abstract reality negotiated by modes of interpreted perception. Aesthetic animism is not the direct conversion of scenes to letterforms, nor the simple accumulation of motion.[5] In fact, it's most successful motion graphic precursor implementations often occur where market forces dictate a tight, lean aesthetic and adherence to signature branding: music videos.

Music (and Other) Videos In spite of the problems of excess, After Effects typographic innovations developed for music videos are seminal influences on motion graphic poetry. As in any field, there is much to be learned from precursors.

One example is the music video for Justice's single "DVNO" (directed by Machine Molle and So-Me); it displays its song lyrics in forms based on animated logos from the 1980s: 20th Century Fox, HBO, NBC, PBS, CBS, Universal, Sega, and so on. Basically, this music-video-commercial appropriates voraciously not as a methodological adaptation to technological networking (as advocated by Goldsmith [2011] in *Uncreative Writing*) but instead for profit. The *DVNO* video samples a decade's worth of motion graphics and compresses the experience into several minutes. It is technically possible because of direct feedback processes in modeling software, and scripts that bypass timelines in the compositing environments.

The effect of a video like *DVNO* engages because culture is suffused in typographic effects; this ad-for-a-band leverages intertextuality: its pleasure arises from identifying how it subversively recycles aesthetic tropes from television and record labels. It is the entertainment equivalent of the aesthetic pleasure derived from high art mashups like Christian Marclay's (2010) *The Clock*—which builds a clock from film footage of clocks.[6]

DVNO is not a film mashup, although it is in effect a mashup. The objects that are being composited, the fuel and content of the assimilation aesthetic, are 3-D models, and often these are models of letters. The software involved in these animations increasingly involves the capacity to manipulate in real time. In the twentieth century, animation was primarily accomplished using cel-by-cel frame animation; contemporary practice escapes the timeline frames by assigning algorithms to interpolate between positions. And increasingly the software itself anticipates or generates 3-D meshes or transitions; these automated processes in my view constitute the preliminary architecture of rudimentary metabolisms. So the compositing happens at the level of content (where old motifs reemerge), software (modeling, rendering, and compositing softwares used in sequence), and technical synergy (where models are merged with live footage, and the hand merges with algorithm).

In other examples of text-with-video classics, the pure sensuality of MK12's (2005) virtuoso After Effect's laden, soft-porn classic music video for Common's "Go!" suggests an augmented data-saturated interface where text and video collude with virtual representations of motifs from classic posters. In contrast, the minimalist, monochrome microvignettes in Ji Lee's *Word as Image* video/book propose insightful extensions of concrete poetry. The constraints of Lee's process are deviously simple yet produce lush results: "Challenge: Create an image out of a word, using only the letters in the word itself. Rule: use only the graphic elements of the letters without adding outside parts" (Lee 2011). Ji Lee's *Word as Image* suggests a context-dependent alphabet where letterforms adopt tiny gestures customized for each word. His restraint is matched by baroque excessive yet effective landscapes that enhance oral readings of Heebok Lee's (2006) video setting of William Butler Yeat's poem *He Wishes for the Cloths of Heaven*. In this video adaptation, the threads that voluptuously connect letterforms contrast with a segment of effulgent cosmological apparitions. It may not be to everyone's taste, but it is a path, a space in the convulsive wilderness, a knot of potentiality unraveling for poetry as it merges with other media.

George Meliés (1900s) and John Whitney (1960) Just as the roots of poetry entwine material and ontological concerns, the roots of motion graphics begin with magic and math, a magician and a mathematician, an individual concerned with tricks and one concerned with formal rigor. Both in their own way were concerned with awe.

Jeff Bellantoni and Matt Woolman's (2000) *Type in Motion* identifies Georges Méliès's advertising work as the earliest known example of film-based animated typography.[7] Méliès emerged from a tradition of carny barkers and hustlers, stage magicians, and illusionists, fantasy and horror, working the crowd, weaving a hypnotic spiel in order to plant a spell.[8] Unfortunately, most of Méliès's footage does not exist today; time literally marched over it: its celluloid was melted into use as boot heels during World War I (ironically he began in the family shoe business, and his entire career could be psychoanalytically attributed to a desire to escape from under the heel of realism).

The other root-origin of the term *motion graphics*, the mathematical one, begins with Whitney, who in 1960 started a company appropriately called Motion Graphics. Whitney was obsessed with principles of harmony that occurred between visuals and music: proportional systems with mathematical foundations. Noting how baroque counterpoint and Islamic arabesques were tractable subjects for computation, he created abstract rhythmic synesthesia. In 1958, he collaborated with Saul Bass on the titles to Alfred Hitchcock's *Vertigo*—a collaboration that places him at a pivotal event in the popularization of dynamic typography. In the 1980s, he became concerned with real-time computer instrumentation—a prescient position given the crucial roles of Pure Data and MaxMSP in contemporary media art, and the contemporary field of live coding. His work, as Holly Willis notes, shares the idealistic propositions put forth in the 1970s by Gene Youngblood.[9] He is a techno-utopian; his devotion to appearances evokes platonic ideals.

When motion graphic typography began with Méliès and his contemporaries, he was among the first (or the first) to use multiple exposures, which essentially is a precursor to compositing. Making multiple exposures is still one of the novice tutorials in After Effects today: camera on tripod, and mask down the middle of scene. Result: you stand next to yourself. This is the preliminary epistemological lesson: truth is subject to manipulation. The self divides; art provides us with a doppelgänger. Appearances are conceptual; they split self and experience, fact and fiction, essence and surface. Whitney's revelation is more austere and transcendent, seeking to delineate how computers change the auric potential of mimesis. But his tricks of recursion and symmetry also constitute the foundational level of motion graphic animation programming instruction.

Hybridity's Origin

The new hybrid visual language of moving images emerged during the period of 1993–1998. Today it is everywhere. … [I]t is appropriate to highlight one software package as being in the center of the events. This software is *After Effects*. Introduced in 1993, After Effects was the first software designed to do animation, compositing, and special effects on the personal computer.

—Lev Manovich, 2013

Manovich is the only media arts scholar (*scholart?*) who I know of to have considered the history (and developed a sustained discourse around the role) of After Effects. He identifies the release of After Effects in 1993 as a key date in the emergence of media hybridity. Even though many contemporary compositing packages do the same sort of work, for Manovich, After Effects is important because it is affordable: its affordability transformed compositing from an esoteric high-end technique into a grassroots commercial preoccupation.

To reiterate, compositing (similar to composting) contributes to *assimilation*, the capacity of language to chameleon into environments. Similarly, Manovich sees the aesthetic of motion graphics toward *hybridity* as a *Velvet Revolution* that occurs in the era 1993–1998. During this time, according to Manovich, graphic design and typography were imported into motion graphics; this importation transformed and fused disparate disciplines and gave rise to new aesthetic hybrids.

Prior to After Effects, dynamic and kinetic typography obeyed arduous technical and financial constraints. It is exactly these sorts of technical and financial constraints that affordable compositing, with the birth of After Effects, dissolves.[10]

The Hybrid Canon

In the civic imagination, science is still considered dull, geeky, hard, abstract, and, conveniently, peripheral, now, perhaps, more than ever.

—Natalie Angier, 2007

Replace the word *science* in the above quotation with the word *poetry*. Angier wrote her book to reverse public perceptions about science's canon; I hope (perhaps imperceptibly) to contribute to the acceptance of digital poetry in the traditional poetic canon. Problematically, digital poetry is newborn; its canon is emerging and currently indeterminate. And how is it that After Effects fits into this argument?

In conventional literary theory, a canon (the set of works considered worthy of study) is the focus of both dispute and reverence. The contemporary occidental literary canon is, generally, a by-product of the printing press: a huge forest of literature. To summarize a story often told by historians of technology, mass-produced books modified the dynamics of publishing from elitist scribe to populist broadsheets and independent artisanal presses.[11]

What I am proposing (in parallel with Manovich) is that a similar transformation of motion graphics (and specifically kinetic typography and thus digital poetry) occurred with the release of After Effects. As the scale, scope, and sophistication of After Effects surpassed critical mass, an autodidactic tutorial frenzy took place. Recursive feedback fed radical experimentation, which was rapidly assimilated into effect presets and new capacities in the release cycle. Creative production exploded in the communal estuary of After Effects users: aesthetic curiosity, growing computer use, Moore's law, entry-level compositing, exchange forums, and online video tutorials. This symbiotic flourishing of technical means and artistic impulse is symptomatic of an incipient canon. The canon is a hybrid. It exists in the interstices between audiovisual art and literature.

Kinetic Type's Printing Press: Suites It is my feeling that kinetic type's printing press is not the word processor but rather synergetic combinations (or suites) of software and code, such as Mr. Softie, Mudbox, Processing, Flash, JavaScript, and After Effects. These distinctly different softwares each offer a unique modality for dealing with kinetic type, yet each supply quick, easy access to textual transformations. Each (to varying degrees) combines fluid motion with the capacity to composite text into combinations with 3-D models, video, images, and/or sound. This textual fluidity constitutes a breeding ground for the birth of a canon. Already signature motion graphic styles and formats of typographic manipulation can be identified. Expert users can spot software chains, effects, or combinations of sets of effects. The lineage or inheritance of various artistic styles or innovations (often fused into new variations) is readable by an informed viewer.

In the same way that a literary scholar can identify writers who have inherited (or appropriated) stylistic influence from Virginia Woolf (for example), it is possible to trace the roots of many motion graphic typography experiments to the production software (or suite of softwares), the technique of the *evangelist* who first taught or popularized the technique, and the visual birthplace of the typographic style as logos or credits for film and television companies.[12] Literary scholars might shudder at the suggestion that the contemporary literary canon was born from a complicit field of corporate propaganda and/or music videos, but it is plausible to resituate Homeric epics and threnody as ancient rock songs sung to warrior kings to glorify conquests. So it is not unknown for canons of enormous sensitivity, emotional range, and humanist sensibilities to arise from origins proximal to greed, glam, glitz, and aggression.

Immersive Gloss?   It is easy to dismiss compositing as mere technical innovation or cosmetic trivia. Yet its potential implications for writing as an activity that involves the entire being of the author become clearer if seen historically.

Jay David Bolter observed, "Wordsworth's definition of poetry as a 'spontaneous overflowing of powerful feeling' does not easily include electronic poetry" (Bolter 1990, 153). Bolter wrote this statement prior to After Effects in reference to hypertext. Hypertext in the 1980–1990s era of low bandwidth was minimalist: a few words and an underlined hyperlink. Computer graphics were weak, *difficult*, and not affordable to most authors or readers. To author digital work in that period required a concentration that precluded spontaneity. With each year, compositing tools and exponentially more powerful GPUs modulate that difficulty; with contemporary technology, spontaneity is an option, and the computer is no longer antithetical to "powerful feeling."

For the young digital natives who engage (both today and in the future) with computation, navigating plug-ins may become as innate as putting a quill into an inkpot, and reading interfaces as easy as speech. That is to say, speech (which is a learned skill requiring years of immersive assimilation to evolve from babbling to coherence) develops in ways analogous to digital ease of use. Spontaneity takes time, absorption, and immersion; it involves muscle memory and innate dorsal reflexes; it requires immersion in an idiom and the cultural techniques specific to a technology. Critics of the use of *glossy* effects in digital poetry might warn that gloss and glamour (etymologically rooted in illusion) perform a paradoxical trick: in fixating the reader's attention on surface effects, the reader forgets the material level. Nevertheless, while immersive engagement can engender gloss, it can also generate depth and access processes of profound reflective interiority. Epiphanies by their nature are neither analytic nor materially self-conscious; they composite identity over the void.

Ads as Tech Ops: Attack of the Filler Poems   It may seem obscene to move from altruistic empathy and epiphanies to advertisements, and even more obscene to cite ads as poetry, but that is my next step. In a culture where rampant consumption threatens the material substrate of existence for the species, ads openly fuel addictive greed, amplifying the innate seek reflex. Yet ethics and planetary considerations aside, ads continue to exemplify the cutting edge of what kinetic, visual, malleable text is becoming. Video bumpers and channel idents advance the technical edge of typographic motion graphics. Merch placement logos for toddlers, tweeners, and seniors evolve the state of the art rapidly in a competitive system of software upgrades and corporate budgets. A large majority of these advertisements use After Effects templates as the foundations for their text manipulations. Tutorial archives for After Effects such as Video Copilot can then become reservoirs of style, spaces where astute dialecticians of motion semiotics can survey the metadiffusion.

   If aesthetic animism (for language) emerges, then digital methods (metadata and animation) will need to be integral to letterforms; as such, ads are (unwitting) construction workers, building templates, exploring techniques, and establishing ways that data, visuals, audio, interactivity, and letterforms fuse to ensure semantic impact. Digital ads operate as pluripotent nexus where opportunistic mutations in the properties of letterforms are tested against the ecosystem of market attention.

   Ads, in addition to this technical function, share with poetry succinctness—the swift, rhythmic, and judicious use of text. This constrained use of text (twittered slogan/logo aphorisms of temporally constrained-screen-dwellers cyber-haiku) corresponds to poetic constraint: minimal means; maximal efficiency; a high information-to-noise ratio; small packets, dense messages, small minds, thirty seconds, fifteen seconds, five seconds, logo, cut.

   Now how can kinetic ads and the motion in them be read? To answer that, I turn to rhetoric.

Bi-Stable Decorum

The textual surface is now a malleable and self-conscious one. All kinds of production decisions have now become authorial ones. The textual surface has now become permanently bi-stable. We are first looking AT it and then THROUGH it.

—Richard Lanham, 1993

In his book *The Electronic Word*, Lanham, a rhetorician, anticipates a new theory of literature needed for electronic texts; he proposes a theory based on a matrices of oppositional values, or what he calls a "bi-stable decorum" (ibid., 14). The primary opposition is between looking "AT" and "THROUGH" a text. Basically, the AT is a self-conscious reading of the materiality of the medium; the THROUGH is an immersive unself-conscious absorption of textual content. Many proponents of materiality (critics of immersive absorption) imply that in FX-rich environments, reading never occurs; it is short-circuited into narcissistic display.

Materiality critiques certainly have validity. Modes of aesthetic excess may temporarily obstruct semantic meaning or deflect cultural interventions. Yet later in his book, Lanham makes several "oracular speculations" that mitigate critiques of visual-hybrid literature:

Writing will be taught as a three-dimensional, not a two-dimensional art. ... Word, image, and sound will be inextricably intertwined in a dynamic and continually shifting mixture. Clearly we will need a new theory of prose style to cope with all this. ... I am talking about a theory *superior* to any that print allows us to conceive, but which would include print as well as dynamic alphabetic expression. (Lanham 1993, 127–28)

So given the twenty years that exist between Lanham's oracular proclamations and our own era, what would such a *superior* hybrid theory look like? In the following section, I attempt a tentative step along that path by suggesting that *compositing* as a term offers theoretical affordances appropriate to the task.

Composition   Composition has roots in both writing poetry and imagistic technology. In After Effects, units of work are called *compositions*. The name derives from the technique of compositing or keying out parts of an image so that the keyed parts disappear and layering effects can occur (i.e., a television weather forecaster). In the oracular arts, composition refers to the ancient act of composing (as in *composing an ode*, or composing a poem or symphony); composition is often conjoined with rhetoric, and is synonymous with the act of sustained writing.

Composition is thus a word etymologically and historically situated to operate at the interstice between writing and audiovisual art in a new theory of hybrid literature. That is why I believe that compositing tools like After Effects are probably forerunners of the sort of tools that the next generation of TAVIT poets will compose within. The level of complexity and depth of immersive experiences possible with such tools exceed those of a word processor by an order of magnitude, and they offer the affordance of terminology like *composition* that has ancient roots and a contemporary usage.

One could compare composited to print textuality, as 3-D to 2-D, perspectival to flat representations. Composition in its expanded sense here operates as a measure of the level of visual depth and procedural complexity offered. As in rhetoric's labyrinthine terminology, *compositing* will probably undergo terminological fracturing as subspecies arise. Critics knowledgeable of the history of compositing will read visual language within a historical perspective: shadow play, cutouts, collage, and the evolution of integration. Their intertextual conversations will concern how text assimilates or evolves motifs in conjunction with its video, code, or generative backgrounds. Simultaneously bi-stable, they will also read THROUGH the text to analyze and absorb what the words are saying.

A Seed for a Theory   As much as choreography and easing equations need to be considered as literary devices (an argument I alluded to in my master's thesis, but also a point made by many other commentators on kinetic text), raycasting, polygon counts, recursive scripting, and other qualities and effects possible within compositing software operate as semiotic tools. To speak authoritatively in this hybrid literary domain requires such terms implicated in the creative process.

Ferdinand de Saussure's arbitrariness of the sign, the way its visual does not relate to its meaning, may undergo erosion. Digital compositing incubates signs toward nonarbitrary forms; it recruits form as semantic protagonist (elevating it from subsidiary support role). As visual choices made by visual poets refute the canonical transparency of the text, the AT becomes read as a THROUGH. The bi-stable decorum proposed by Lanham dampens into apparent concurrency. As I stated earlier, I believe that digital modeling constitutes an opportunity to sculpt letterforms into structures congruent with our archetypal, proprioceptive, embodied conceptions of them: conceptions reinforced by millennia of physically resonating speech sounds. Compositing augments that opportunity by allowing semantic meaning to resituate itself in real space. The formal qualities of the page, the line, spacing, line breaks, and all subsequent print experimentations enter into a 3-D, contextualized, spatial and auditory semiotic space. It is not easy to conceive how deep (or even cursory) readings of this material will occur without a new and hybrid theory that draws from cinema, gaming, programming, and literature.

A term (such as *compositing*) is not a theory; it is merely a seed for a theory—a stand-in or substitute until the actuality arises. Converting *compositing* from term into theory is beyond the scope of this book. The preliminary steps, however, would involve a comparative analysis of analytic tools from literary cinematic and new media studies. The questions would include: If compositing is a literary device, then what sort of device is it? And is it possible there already exists a cinematic term that might function? A quick list of literary devices would consist of: allegory, alliteration, allusion, analogy, assonance, climax, foreshadowing, hyperbole, metaphor, onomatopoeia, oxymoron, personification, pun, and simile. A quick list of cinematic techniques would include: cinematography (close-up, medium, long, and establishing), mise-en-scène, moving and position of cameras, lighting, special FXs, and montage. Essentially, there is nothing in either list specific to the superimposition of text over/within visuals (except for compositing itself). Compositing shares a conjunction of items with metaphor, analogy, and simile. These techniques bring disparate things or qualities together, and by placing them together, reveal or generate a semantic discharge. Yet there is no existing theoretical frame for how to critique composited text. The best that can be hoped for at this juncture is sensitive observers who evaluate instinctively using hybrid theories.

Theory from previously independent disciplines (cinema, gaming, literature, and music) must also be composited over each other. Thus compositing occurs at practical and theoretical levels.

Case Study: Mudbox

Although the following case study concerns the software Mudbox, Mudbox was not the first (nor is it the only) software to develop modeling tools that are sculptural in quality (it just happens to be the software I used, but the argument can be generalized to other ones). Notable as a precedent, ZBrush developed by Pixologic was demonstrated in 1999 at Siggraph, and then commercialized by 2002. Mudbox was first developed to produce the 2005 version of *King Kong*, then it was purchased by Autodesk in 2008, and now it ships in a suite with Maya (which has its own set of modeling capacities and was first released in 1998). As these tools develop, they adopt ways of manipulating models derived from both the arts and industry. In the arts, sculptural methods provide the foundation for sets of brushes (more on brushes later), and in science, these softwares borrow industrial processes of replication and duplication, and architectural techniques derived from solid-modeling tools like AutoCAD (released in 1982).

ZBrush and Mudbox (unlike AutoCAD) model soft and fluid materials.[13] It is for this reason that they signal a bridge in 3-D authoring that moves from hard to malleable, dry to wet, linear to curved. They are also in many ways precursors of software that will render objects in real time as they are modeled. Thus they fit metaphorically into the explosion of biological sciences and BioArts that now manipulate wet DNA. As noted previously, there is a lineage between language arts and genetics that leads from holograms to bioculture (via Eduardo Kac).

Minimal Information Temperature versus FX Fever

Fixing the informational temperature at the minimum necessary to obtain the aesthetic achievement of each poem undertaken.

—Haroldo de Campos, 1982

When in 2009, I published *Human-Mind-Machine*, a video constructed from screen captures of the manipulations of single words within Mudbox (a 3-D animation software), I was not concerned with what de Campos refers to (in the quotation above) as minimal means. Nor was I concerned (as Brian Kim Stefans is) with a refutation of the lyric.[14] The video-poems are minimal. And they might seem at some level to be computational poetry—that is, readable as data evoking a refutation of the lyric.

There are other possible (opposite yet not incompatible) interpretations, though. First off, I am a novice user of Mudbox; the artifacts and effects generated are in many instances spontaneous accidents. Second, Mudbox permits rash, reckless experimentation that provokes excess. Surplus is not inelegant when innocent. I was hoping to convey a classic concern with life as wound, scarification, egocentric inflation, and the rough transformations circumstance creates in consciousness. In short, 3-D permitted an open situation, concerned with classic content, through which the lyric reincarnates as excess.

In addition, Mudbox (when hacked for innocent use as a screen-capture animation tool) has no timeline. It is not (as is After Effects) an authoring environment where precisely planned and tediously crafted elegance happens. Instead, it is an area of swift experimental probes, excursions into spontaneous pressure—a playground for letterform deformation. Everything occurs in real time. It is a riot not a ballet.

Mudbox Machinima *Disclaimer: This entire section is vestigial. Since the 2011 version of Mudbox embedded a video-rendering engine into the interface so that users can exchange interface tips using online videos, the following process describes a low-fi hack/work-around that is no longer necessary. Yet the mode of approach is, I think, indicative of how poets might appropriate technology using deviant techniques for unanticipated purposes. And it highlights how methodologies and attitudes survive technological obsolescence.* My education as a 3-D animator is limited to a yearlong, full-credit, undergrad university course in Maya, a programming class in OpenGL, and extensive autodidactic play ever since. In 2009, I was given a one-year student license to Autodesk suite that included Mudbox. I knew no one in the Mudbox user community, and still don't, and suspect that they would consider my practice to be that of a misinformed Luddite. In any case, I also suspect my innocence is an asset. Because I had no one to teach me how to use the tool properly, and I had some ingenuity concerning similar tools, I developed an idiosyncratic (and limited) pipeline for manipulating letterforms. In other words, my improper use arrived at a relatively unique method that says something about the tools as they exist now.

Three-dimensional modeling reminds me of medieval craftsmanship. It is time-consuming, energy intensive, and more often goes wrong than right. General-purpose tools like Softimage, Blender, or Maya do not encourage amateur users. The learning curve is steep, and the path begins with a cliff. Exploratory creativity in these authoring environments exacts a heavy temporal entrance fee. Mastery is even more expensive. It is for this reason

that these softwares are analogous to arts (that sometimes involved appren-
ticeships) such as oil painting, etching, or casting sculptures in metal, and
instruments like the oboe or clarinet. Both physical skill and long-term
dedicated practice are prerequisites for competence.

When I began muddling about in Mudbox, I knew that my own stylistic
preference for spontaneity and sketch work would have to find a methodological foundation. Mudbox was designed for the quick, intuitive, clay-
like sculpting of 3-D characters, but it has not yet been conceived of as
an animation tool. So I derived a screen-grab method that effectively converted Mudbox into a crude animation tool. I knighted my idiosyncratic
method with the title Mudbox Machinima. Machinima arose when game
users began to produce short 3-D movies using the capture tools inside
console games, and it basically involves repurposing a tool/game for a use
not foreseen by its creators; it seemed an appropriate name for my ludic
hijacking of Mudbox's capacities that effectively short-circuits the normal
arduous rendering route of letterforms (from letter-creation in Maya to
manipulation in Mudbox to lighting and rendering in Maya), avoids the
creations of cameras and lights, does not involve complex raycasting, and
within its constraints offers an opportunity for spontaneous quasi-impro-
visational play.

The process that I called Mudbox Machinima was a multisoftware work-
around. The process began by creating a simple letterform model in Maya;
the model was then exported for use in Mudbox. In Mudbox, the background was set to a classic blue screen color and the grid hidden. A screen-
capture tool (Camtasia) recorded a video of the sculpting. My goal (even
then as now) was different from the software designer's intended users: not
to instruct or tutorialize, but rather to adapt, manipulate, and composite
improvisational deformations. The resulting exported video was imported
into a video-editing software (in my case, Sony Vegas) and a chroma key
applied to remove the background. Shadow was created by duplicating
the Mudbox-film layer, removing its color and contrast, rotating it in 3-D,
changing its opacity, and applying a small amount of blur.

All in all it was a relatively simple process, but one that in the intervening two years since I developed it, is already obsolete, superseded by
multiple improvements in the interoperability of Maya and Mudbox as
well as new video renders direct from the Mudbox interface. It nonetheless
demonstrates incipient signs of letterform life, the twitching skin of letters,

a fast pipeline from conception to product, and the tendency of users to contort software for specific needs unanticipated by the designers.[15]

Gestural Manipulations of Matter: Sculpting Software

Though we have spoken, indeed, metaphorically of the "life" of the program, it is not only metaphor. Mind enters world, not contained within skin, but as a circuit-loop feedback operation.[16] The living, and all living functions, are indissoluble from information-driven environmental loops which alone serve as units of survival. Animal mind, protected from "real" impact by the physical world, negotiates its circuits by abstract, non-physically locatable, information.

—Stephanie Strickland and Cynthia Lawson Jaramillo, 2007

Mudbox and ZBrush offer direct gestural deflections of 3-D surfaces in ways analogous to the manipulation of matter; in this way, they evade the key frame tweening mind-set inculcated by timeline production that temporally distances the artist from the normal immanence of cause and effect. To repeat, with traditional animation timelines the artist performs a transformation, applies a key frame, and renders to watch. It is as if the artist has to press a button in order to see change occur after touch. On the other hand, in Mudbox, direct tactile control leverages ancient instincts that engage and respond to immediate visual feedback. There is no delay, no interrupt, no obstruction.

ZBrush first shipped in 2002 with thirty brushes. The palette has expanded since then. Some brushes relate directly to painting; others relate to sculpting, strokes, textures, and materials. All are parameterized so that each brush actually represents a wide range of potential deflections. Mudbox uses a colloquial naming pattern for its brushes; the *sculpt* brushes are called sculpt, smooth, grab, pinch, flatten, foamy, spray, repeat, imprint, wax, scrape, fill, knife, smear, bulge, amplify, free, mask, and erase. At a nominal level, these tools replicate normal, easily understandable ways of working with physical matter; at a cultural level, these tools merge the toolboxes of sculptures and painters; at a physiological level, they function as prosthetics, enhancing the hand and extending the eye.

In terms of letterforms, software *brushes* echo typographic foundries that produced hot metal type, which was poured into matrices. Ironically, matrices again hold the form of type in Mudbox—matrices of binary code—except that it is not lead that is poured hot into the molds but rather data.

What Does Mud Have to Do with Language?   To reiterate, malleable typography allows semantic deflections to occur on the skin of the letterform itself, in the texture of the text so to speak. Texture in 3-D idiom refers to the skin of a model. If the skin of a letterform is a surface that can be scratched, scarred, or twisted, then surface deflection becomes semiotic. The shapes of skins are also *read*. J. Abbott Miller (1996), Matthew G. Kirschenbaum (1997), and John Cayley (2005) all anticipated this potential.

Humans interpret and classify both costuming and contortions of bodies. Letterforms with bodies get read somewhere in between language and image. This oscillation merges literature with aesthetics. An expressive displacement that happens at the level of vision reverberates into thought. It is a change that occurs in parallel with the changes in depth postulated by Noah Wardrip-Fruin's reading of *expressive processes* and Alan Sondheim's emphasis on *codeworks*, where the programmatic foundations underlying mediated language become semiotic. Instead of a depth expansion, I am speaking of a breadth expansion, a semiotic infusion that takes place on the surface of letters.

Choreography carries expressive capacity. Anthropomorphic 3-D container letterforms echo our own skins. Visual deformations activate a history of aesthetic analysis. As many before me have noted, textural deformations of letterforms expand reading. And like contemporary biological sciences, which are permitting new genetic manipulations to emerge, 3-D modeling tools such as Mudbox and ZBrush permit a range of mutations that exceed the traditional range of typography (making it opaque and embodied), choreography (defying gravity and interpenetrating bodies), anthropomorphism (inflating, inverting, and merging), and visual history (oscillating from perspectival to flat, animating the frame).

Shape Semantic Synergy, Motion-Tracking, and Music Videos   As previously alluded to—in the sections "Ads as Tech Ops" and "Music (and Other) Videos"—the expanded synergetic reading of literal as visual has been most cleverly and deftly exploited not by digital poets (who have contributed to the conceptual and aesthetic evolution) but instead by film credits, music videos, and advertising. Ads have colonized the genre, rapaciously assimilating tropes and inventing motifs. Augmenting this accelerated creative process, there are many proficient software point trackers on the market: Shake, Fusion, Nuke, PFTrack, Bonjou, MatchMover, and Mocha. They resolve and match 3-D into video space. As stated earlier, digital language will shift ontologically when *digital language adopts features of organic life, and is perceived as natural and natured*. Point trackers perform the basic physics of orientation. They place language in the scene.

Question: Why would advertisers prefer language that blends in and belongs? Why go to the intense technical trouble of creating credible letterforms with shadows, depth, weight, momentum, and respect for collision boundaries? Why not use letterforms that are objectively present just as decoration? What advantages might situated object-like text deliver? It seems safe to assume some advertisers intuitively recognize several cognitive benefits. Situated text is perceived as being heavy; weight, as cognitive science has shown, is intuitively associated with seriousness, solidity, and durability (a heavy clipboard used in a survey means that the process is serious; to praise something, we say, *That argument has weight; its logic is solid*). Additionally perhaps situated text bypasses the analytic scrutiny habitually applied to language when it is read; it places the perceiver in a place more proximal to desire; this is language that clowns or performs for us, distracting us from the precise metrical inferences of reading. Most theorists laugh when viewing clowns.

Technically achieving the effect of putting 3-D text into a scene now involves many automated, algorithmically tractable processes that the designer simply initiates; processes that were previously performed by hand-pinning keyframes to timelines. Softwares interpolate velocity utilizing physics, detect edges and collision, and correctly adjust, align, scale, and light. Combining, therefore, modeling where letterforms respond immediately to deflections of the hand, algorithms that autoactivate motion based on proximity or generative processes, and the ability to blend these letters into environments give letters the ontological status of objects, and is a crucial step on the path toward *living language*.

Per-severe or Per-ish
ads that are also language art
bifurcate between meanings,
careen between disciplines; and
bypassing discourse,
render & sell

—Jhave, blog post, 2011

My tastes and interests are obviously more sensual (some might say naive) than the dominant vector of conceptual language arts criticism that emphasizes a lineage including Joseph Kosuth, Lawrence Weiner, John Baldessari, and others, whose visual styles, incidentally, have not modulated radically in reaction to digital technology. I prefer the ad company Psyop whose brand idents expand the technical capacities of text in 3-D video environments; in these ads, wonder and craft have not been sacrificed at the altar of austerity and concept. It's surprising to me how few digital poets actually work with 3-D or motion graphics. If anything, there has been a backlash against it. Poets of a previous generation worked with 3-D: Kac, André Vallas, Ladislao Pablo Györi, and—one could include—Muriel Cooper. They often came from a hybrid or visual art background. Perhaps due to the stigma of 3-D ads colonization (i.e., contamination) of the genre, poets have rejected it. Perhaps it's due to the *learning cliff*. Perhaps it's Marshall McLuhan, the prophet admonishing them at the gates: *the medium is the massage.* Perhaps it's simply an abhorrence of effect for effect's sake. Anyway, poet-practitioners dedicated to 3-D art are rare. It's a rarity that might cease in the next generation. It is this potential that motivates.

Take a simple conventional yet clever ad found online. In it, two words lie side by side: *Per-severe Per-ish.* Each word is split at the hyphen as the word has shattered. Their sides are lit and glinting as if made out of annealed chrome. Shadows fall around them gleaming as if it is dusk, illuminated in a placeless place: a pool of light on a hard, dark background. They replicate the rich burnished depth of aged oil paint. The only thing remarkable about these sculpted letters is that they do not exist.

The *Per-severe Per-ish* ad is apparently a product of the marketing agency J. Walter Thompson's executive creative director Chafic Haddad, but it is not trumpeted anywhere. There are so many of these 3-D letters, so many ads, so many campaigns and animators, that there is no scarcity. Some go missing, anonymous, adrift. They are not miracles; the miracle is that they are normal. Yet even if it is already so normal and common, *Per-severe Per-ish* is also to my mind a relevant demonstration of how 3-D modeling could so easily fit within the minimal means and aesthetics of a contemporary digital concrete (digital pudding) poetry. Maybe the image of *Per-severe Per-ish* is a still from an animation (in the next frames, the "ish," slowly toppling, shatters). Imagine Duchamp finding this ad and submitting it as his artwork for a language show. The level at which the play of language in *Per-severe Per-ish* sends semantic meanings in recursive circles exceeds that of a simple branding exercise. Form follows content (a little too obediently but nonetheless symmetrically), the medium is integral to the piece, and its execution is stylistically (as in much lavishly budgeted branding) impeccable.

Reawakening the Inert

Virtual 3D structures made from letter forms will have, as it were, an appreciably enhanced spatial structure for literate readers. Moreover, because of the expectations (of legibility) that these forms bear, it should be possible to "play"—affectively, viscerally—with their form and arrangement in ways that are likely to have aesthetic significance, and some bearing—potentially, ultimately—on literary practice.

—John Cayley quoted in Rita Raley, 2006a

Origin myths often begin with a lump of clay or mud into which the spark or breath of life enters. The inert mud awakens. The Sufi poet Rumi is occasionally cited in evolutionary literature because he identified a chain of incarnations from mineral, vegetable, animal, human, and so on—the path of life spark through matter. This vision of a gradient of sentience is shared by many Western panpsychists. Life starts with chemical constituents and arrives through structural emergence at self-consciousness. The core matter of the nonliving and living are not different: these are carbon-based forms. From the perspective of both myth and biochemistry, mud is at the root of reason, passion, credit card charges, and world wars.

Currently tools like ZBrush and Mudbox offer a reasonable visual simulation of physical contact with digital representation that seems a lot like wet clay or mud. It is not of course wet or gritty or chemically coherent in ways that emulate the complex capacities of matter, but it can, within the confines of a screen, emulate the physics of these substances. And screens in spite of their evident ocular-centric limitations do effectively activate empathic processes. If screens did not function empathically, action films would be boring and porn would not be a major industry. Modeling software is already one step farther than most "films": it is interactive. So additional physiognomic reflexes and endogenous networks of biochemistry arise during the authoring-modeling process (amplified as the mouse is replaced by pressure-sensitive Wacom gestures). The software user is physically implicated in a process that is mythological; they are reconfiguring matter into emulations of life.

One step beyond modeling is generating. Growing generative forms automates the sculptural instinct. Scripting languages specific to many 3-D vendors encourages exploration of generative forms. How are they grown? They are written. They are often recursive. They manipulate geometries in topological ways. This trio of attributes (written, recursive, and topology) palpably echoes the linguistic theories of language itself, and resonates with thoughts previously cited from Strickland and Gregory Bateson (n16).

Code pervades the process; human agency and intervention are reduced to aesthetic nurturance roles. Creating works in such a way is analogous to gardening. Future fonts may be grown (as anticipated to some degree by Miller). Donald Knuth's quest for the essence of all fonts may not be answered, but the seeds he sowed by initiating the first sustained computational attention to font formats as programmed entities will flourish. One potential pathway such fonts might take is explored in my *Easy Font* project (Jhave 2011). All the component pieces of the *Easy Font* letters are algorithmically produced using a commercially available Mandelbulb ray tracing 3-D plug-in produced by the ex-physicist Tom Beddard. A real-time version of the plug-in is currently under development; it will apparently run in the browser. So it is not speculative sci-fi to anticipate fonts that organically occupy space. It is not fantasy to anticipate the poets who will culture and grow from seed algorithms morphing letterforms and compositional structures. Poets will examine these creations with the same proud sense of authorship as previous generations have harvested their subconscious for rampant, sensual scribblings.

Workflow   One of the underlying realities of contemporary software is that some tasks in 3-D environments are getting easier. The story of my own experience with Mudbox confirms this tendency. When I began working with Mudbox and Maya in late 2008, the interoperability pipeline between these two softwares, vended by the same company as part of a suite, was far from stable. Complex, intersecting sets of parameters had to be meticulously compatible in order for the transfers of typographic models to take place without errors. This occurred in both directions. The only way to play with text in Mudbox was to first model it in Maya, enable the object export plug-in, carefully calibrate the bevels, and send an .obj file to a disk. Only after opening the .obj file in Mudbox would errors appear. These errors would be visual deformations (destroyed kerning, inverted corners, and smooth meshes that looked like cactus). Inside Mudbox, there was no error list or suggestions on what had gone wrong. Getting text to export correctly, in a way that was satisfactory to my aesthetic goals, took me about one and a half days of steady back and forth effort: a blind process of trial and error. The overall feeling was of being submitted to a border crossing where rigid, unwritten rules controlled my fate.

The current workflow offers greater ease of use. The dilemma is that the professional tools want to offer infinite customization processes. Daunting menus and submenu intricacies proliferate. If a writer stumbles into these forests of options, it is unlikely that they will escape with expertise.

Yet while there are symptoms in the emergence of tools like SketchUp that 3-D will proliferate in ways analogous to the spread of literacy, inducing a generation that has grown up immersed in CGI and 3-D to become familiar with the paradigms of modeling and rendering is difficult. There are also symptoms that this might never occur—that humans like flat, surface-screen displays for ingesting literary reasoning. *A Global Visuage* (Piringer and Vallaster 2012), an anthology of visual poems, contains only one image done in a 3-D modeling software (mine).

Sculptors, Prosthetic Fingers, and Feral Cats

We cannot be sure whether Leibniz was right to compare the perceptions of a rock to those of a very dizzy human, or whether we should speak of "experience" at all in the inanimate realm. ... However I would propose that if we look closely at intentionality, the key to it lies not is some special human *cogito* marked by lucid representational awareness. Instead, what is most striking about intentionality is the object-giving encounter. In other words, human awareness stands amidst a swarm of concrete sensual realities.

—Graham Harman, 2010

Traditional sculptors relate to their materials like feral cats: they prowl, absorbing them. A block of granite or wood provides flocks of subconscious cues: grain, temperature, rivers of color, deformations, flaws, weight, and so on. An old coat hanger may suggest a crucifix; a skull may need to be encrusted with diamonds. Many of the cues are multimodal. Fingers, eyes, nose, ears, and the proprioceptive body each contribute. Michelangelo reputedly claimed that he was freeing figures within stone. Figurative expressivity is not alone in this absorptive approach. Other cues are social: What use has this object had? What context does it arise from? How has it never been seen before? Duchamp's sophisticated grasp of the contours of conformity and stigma gave him the capacity to challenge and transform contemporary art. Rosalind Krauss's conception of extended field heralded the antimonumental movement. In each case (traditional, modern, and postmodern), the sculptor's relation to materials contributes to creation. How does this work when the materials are screen based and software derived? Is it possible to relate creatively to the materiality of computation? No current category of conventional arts can accurately describe thick words gouged and spinning, plump words fluffing up into indecipherable froth, and letterforms carved like moist icing.

Inside Mudbox's default layout, there is a tabbed rack of tools at the bottom. These are prosthetic fingers—rigid, clawed, and magnetic. Kneading digital substance occurs by flicking between these tools (a flicking that in Mudbox 2011 is accomplished with the numerical keypad). Altering brush parameters permits customizable deflections. Wacom tablets are the preferred input device. Pressure sensitivity delivers simulacra of sensation. The surface can be worked at various levels of resolution from rough (low poly res) up through levels of increasing density. These levels coexist superimposed virtually as abstract entities; the sculptor flicks between them (using page up or page down). Traditional advice floats around the public forums about how the sculpture must be roughed in at low res and then progressively *worked* layer by layer. It is the same advice as that given to apprentice sculptors in the Renaissance.

Just as one would with a real chunk of clay, the 3-D modeler turns the model, prods at it, zooms in (steps toward) and scuffs or scratches, zooms out (steps back), rotates (the pedestal), corrects a detail, and rotates again. It happens at the same speed (if not quicker) as it would physically. Clearly the paradigm of tactile precision has made a cursory conversion into computation. Ancient and contemporary *crafts* (and I use the word with respect) are iterative processes, repetitive toil. After the instigating idea, creation devolves into a steady process of approaching the implementation of that idea (while sporadic spikes of ancillary inspiration occur, most of the work is attention to detail). Luckily, monotony of labor, if accompanied by a need for concentration, sometimes pleases the body; to hit the chisel with a hammer, move a chess piece, or click over and over on a Wacom tablet all belong on a similar continuum. Hours are measured in tiny modulations as the work creeps toward completion. I see little difference between computational and physical modeling: same instinct, new tools.

In my view, the brain empathically bridges the tactical impoverishment so often seen as symptomatic of contemporary screen culture. Sculpting in software is sculpting. Brains already do live happily in jars; the jars are called the skull.

Improvisation versus Timelines I want to emphasize that the workflow work-around I developed had one ancillary effect: rendering (rather than being timeline based) became spontaneous real-time improvisation. Instead of reimporting the model into Maya, creating cameras and lights, applying a texture, and animating the mesh of the letterform by setting key frames on a timeline, the rendering was extracted directly from the screen in Mudbox in a single improvised take. Instead of calculating each position as a step and allowing the software to interpolate between them during the final output, gesture was immediately transcribed. This process suggests that there is a role for nontimeline-based animation work during the spontaneous manipulation of an object (regardless of whether it is a letterform or anything else).

Instrumentality Software that permits the real-time autorecording of parameter changes already exists in the audio realm. The Ableton Suite interface is divided into clip and session modes, which allow users to manipulate multiple parameters while playing. These manipulations automatically enter into a key framed timeline. Parallel ways of working (improvisational and cell/frame based) interweave. Subsequent runs of the same timeline can occur with changes to any of the parameters made during the run or after it is over. Spontaneity and rigor are equally enabled. Fine-grained modulations can be done by hand over tiny regions.

This integration of parallel capacities that encompass improvisation and iteration creates flexible software *instrumentality*. The software can be played like an instrument (free improvisation) even as it records (classical inscription). The instrument analogy at one level explains why audio software has incorporated such capacities while 3-D has only tentatively explored it: musicians have for millennia been using a combination of improvisation (free play) and timelines (scored music). Sculptors have not in general worked with a single tool as musicians typically do. At another level, the added GPU and CPU intensive processes entailed by 3-D preclude such a free approach. Real-time rendering at high frame rates with complex polygon counts is not yet occurring on commercial-level personal computers.

The Role of 3-D in Future Writing

Language is both acoustic and optic.

—Alfred Kallir, 1961

I have repeatedly stated that the shape of the body's internal resonators when speaking might be the source of shape-sound associations that operate as archetypes. And these shapes (basically sculptural forms congruent with morphemes) have (until digital 3-D) lacked the technological means to become integrated in a volumetric way with letterforms. It is my contention that tools like Mudbox (and other 3-D sculpting tools such as ZBrush, Cinema 4D, etc.) will permit these associations to become manifest.

Unfortunately, there are few *credible* sources for this claim. Kallir's *Sign and Design: The Psychogenetic Origins of the Alphabet*, while astoundingly rich in etymological fauna, is an outlier. It claims that the alphabet emerged from painting, all languages (even remote ones) emerged from a communal source, and modern alphabets contain the sediment of deep-rooted, atavistic sexual and psychological pictorial impulses. I am inclined to believe there is much that is true in Kallir's basic ideas; the details may occasionally spurt into fiction, but the core is tenable. The letter *A*, for instance, flipped vertical is a horned animal, a priapic hunter. *B* is an abode, a dwelling, a feminine womb. *L* carries liquid within it. These optic-semantic roots (what Kallir refers to as *symballic*: concurrences of semantic sediment carried by form) carry over into contemporary language as the allusions and ricochets of congealed meaning that make words more than literal. Letters are in this sense monuments weathered by use.

As alluded to in chapter 3 on aesthetic animism, the evolution of printed text can be seen as progressive abstraction enabled by technology. To be literate is to read abstract symbols. Indo-European printed letters are not consciously ideogrammatic, nor are they doodles. Their meaning bears little relevance to their visual sense (even if we accept Kallir's claims, the resonance of visual archetypes is a residue). It seems likely that we are schooled to learn them, not born into them. There is not yet (as far as I know) a genetic marker that predisposes one to learn QWERTY keyboards. It is a skill, absorbed over time; it is an epigenetic feature. Letterpress involves an apprenticeship. The same holds true for 3-D animation studios. Modelers absorb traditions, expand, extrapolate, evolve, imitate, and innovate. It will be curious to see, however, if as 3-D authoring tools enter daily usage, will these tools enhance letterform shape-sound-semantic co-occurrences?

In this postulated future, letterforms evolve meanings that correspond to archetypes of how they appear. A liquid word might use a liquid font. Or adversely, a dry concrete-block font might spell out the word *fluid* and shatter into dust. In this way, poetry, specifically visual poetry, by engaging with the materiality of letterforms as entities, will advance the evolution of letterforms so that the form and animation of letters constitutes a vector for interpretative analysis. Volumetric animated typography in this scenario re- or devolves on a spiral to parallel the reputed origins of language: painting and sculpture, the molding of forms, wet clay, or raw touch. As such, tactile language becomes a precursor to an eternal return, bonding language once again to representations that (although screenic) are in this world, of it, as its.

Mr. Softie

A sequencer might play itself for some time after being given instructions, but a guitar demands interaction for each note sounded.

—Noah Wardrip-Fruin, 2009

Mr. Softie is typographic software that allows touch-sensitive user manipulation of vector-based type. It allows flexible effects to be applied to text in real time. It presents an interesting contrast to commercial animation products, because in Mr. Softie there is no animation timeline. The implications of this interface change are subtle yet profound. It both aids and impedes the capacity of creativity in ways that have resonant implications for writing in the twenty-first century. It suggests word processors that operate as instruments sensitive to the gestures of their users.

Mr. Softie ties into the presuppositions underlying aesthetic animism. Namely, visual digital poetry is innately sculptural; the formal issues it explores are structures: layout, placement, motion (or implied motion), and shape. Structures can be visual, linguistic, or emotive. Shapes bear the expressive weight of events that preceded them. In the same way that words gather emotive force (magnetizing semantic turbulence around them and evolving over time), shapes carry esoteric dimensions that have history and record time. Serenity, pain, sexuality, and anguish (while subjective and culturally specific) have associated shapes; they writhe or remain still. Subconscious forms are collective. Sculptures bear witness to the capacity of humans to read form; totems are literary devices designed to express myth. Archetypal forms conjoined with language synergistically couple literature and sculpture.

What Mr. Softie allows is the real-time capacity to modulate archetypal typographic shapes and capture those sculptural modifications as time-based media. In practice, it is a vehicle for hybrid creativity that spans and fuses disciplines. Processes of writing and sculptural concerns merge. It is this confluence of activities that (sometimes) permits conscious activity to be at the same time intuitive and direct.

Mr. Softie History   Mr. Softie builds on a foundation that originated when Jason Lewis and Alex Weyers (1999) published "ActiveText: An Architecture for Creating Dynamic and Interactive Texts." Developed at Interval Research in the heyday of bubble-boom euphoria, *ActiveText* included a center-triggered mouse-menu system with menus available directly from the mouse position. Sets of behaviors could be applied to sentences, words, or glyphs. In 1998, when the It's Alive! software was created, Flash was at version 3, had been introduced in 1996, had no sets of presets, and required extensive coding in order to produce similar effects. Timelines for animation had been incorporated into Flash's precursor in 1995, Smart Sketch. The primary mode of animation was simple key framing; the paradigm was (and continues to be) adopted from traditional cel animation.

It's Alive! and Text Nozzle challenged a few design paradigms: both promoted context menus to a central role and did not use timelines based on cel animation. In most contemporary software, context menus are used for basic tasks. It's Alive! placed tasks at the position of the observer; all tasks were accessible at the cursor location. Similar functionality is offered by many 3-D softwares now.

Design changes can induce changes in user experience, thereby creating changes in creative practice. At a rough level of granularity, It's Alive! emphasized the immediate and spontaneous. Text was accessed through a hierarchy of block-word-glyph by simple, repetitive clicking (this feature allows quick cluster chunking without drag-and-draw style selecting); text was sprayed; text could be assigned parametric behaviors with two clicks. Some of these features have been carried over into Mr. Softie.

Interacting with Mr. Softie requires practice. It rewards investment in the tool in ways that are analogous to traditional musical instruments and choreography, where gestural prowess and sensitivity combine to yield polished results. The type can be assigned effects that correspond to emulations of different substances (clay, cloth, and pulse). The user touches the type to produce changes in the form. These changes become aesthetic events that are occasionally charged with emotive and intellectual importance, because they are precipitated by sensitive gradients in touch and emulate the subtle play involved in ancient, embodied activities (sculpture, hunting, etc.).

Creative Practice in Mr. Softie   Opening Mr. Softie can be as delightful as lifting the lid of a piano. There is no necessity to really have a plan in mind. (By contrast, I can't imagine beginning a coding project without first having some vague idea of what I wanted to do.) This primary open pleasure is one of the key features of instrument-like interfaces: the potential available to a naive, intuitive practitioner is considerable. The ancient rituals of doodling or doing practice scales, or just fiddling about with a material, are palpably present.[17]

Some poets write from inside themselves, and others write as conduits of a vast outside. In each case, what is needed is a way of transcribing the poem that does not get in the way, and allows the poem to be remembered in its immediateness, directly. Pen, paper, and notebook have traditionally served poets well. For visual poets the problem is more complicated. Visual poetry often leverages effects that emerge concurrently with writing technologies: concrete poets (like Ian Hamilton Finlay, bpNichol, Steve McCaffery, Judith Copithorne, dom sylvester houedard, bill bissett, etc.) developed styles that were only possible on typewriters; Drucker explored effects specific to custom typesetting; for a while in the early 1990s, I made a lot of work with old Letraset packages (as currently does Derek Beaulieu, who seems to have augmented the process with Photoshop). In short, technologies invoke change. As visual poetry migrates onto digital platforms, the adaptive opportunistic trend continues: visual poems often exploit signature potentials specific to their authoring software; as such, it is the software itself that defines how visual poetry is created and appears.

The extent of the perceived aliveness of the text is a by-product of how much the authoring environment encourages manipulations independently of quantified time. Timelines in my mind replicate the scientific model of re-creating life: they enable compartmentalized and measurable parameters to be manipulated rigorously. The nontimeline, free-form sculpting environment is more related to musical improvisation; it relies on gestural fluidity, instinct, and immediacy. When the two modalities (linear granular and fluid improv) converge (as is increasingly occurring in contemporary software packages), then typography accesses synergetic strength.

***StandUnder*: A Specific Case Study of Mr. Softie Use**   *StandUnder* is an animated-typographic poem I created in 2009 with the Mr. Softie software. Without the real-time manipulation capabilities of Mr. Softie (enabling an agile, tactile, and exploratory creative process), *StandUnder* might never have been created. In the same way that the typewriter and custom typesetting provide signature motifs, Mr. Softie offers a unique set of potentials that influence the digital poetry created with it. In the following, I interweave the story of how *StandUnder* was created with reflections on the symbiosis of software design and creative process.

In mid-2009, inside the Mr. Softie authoring environment, I began idly stacking words, without thinking very much, until I had created a tower out of one word repeated over and over: *understand*. Then since each word was standing *under* another, I (mischievously, out of boredom) changed all the words to *StandUnder*, introduced a few line breaks, and so it read:

stand
under
stand
under
stand
ING

Note that there were more words repeated than what I have reproduced here. I still had no idea really what I was doing or aiming toward. At this point, *StandUnder* was already a reasonably intriguing concrete or lettrist-style poem. Although viewed through the jaded eyes of multimedia-saturated consciousness, its appeal was conceptual rather than sensual.

In static form, the interplay of semantic and visual structure in the static work generated knots of fertile ambiguity: is *standing-under* the opposite/extension of *under-standing* something? Are there physical relationships implicit in comprehension? Is humility coincident with receptivity? Is knowledge hierarchical and power inflected at the social, political, and personal levels? Are facts cascading down from iconic sources like viral memes released from a tower of conformity?

With these epistemological and literary questions in the back of my mind, I began to apply effects to the tower of words. Since the cascading, steep, dense stack of words resembled a cliff, and the questions it evoked made me think of knowledge as a cascade of pressure dynamics, I was led to apply what had become (for me) a standard set of drift effects, with different strengths and radius of brushes mapped to the three (left, middle, and right) mouse buttons. These effects are not immediately active; they are now latent material properties of the text. They are physical potentialities that define how it will respond to touch. Once active, the text will distort as if flexible and sinuous. But at this point, nothing in the visual form of the text tower changes; only the structure is now capable of changing dynamically.

This process took a few minutes. It is now ten to fifteen minutes after I opened the software and began perusing around. I have built a static visual poem and applied sets of effects to the mouse, which will operate as a variable-pressure brush. I change the background color of the canvas to green so that I can composite the animation later. I am ready to press the play button. What is static will now move.

Parameters and Palpability In the Mr. Softie environment, using the drift effect, mouse pressure parametrically deflects the form of letters as if the cursor were a finger pressing into wet mud. The various parameters available for user manipulation (when using drift) are: effect radius, mouse strength, mouse falloff, origin strength, and friction. The user also chooses whether the effect is *always on* or which mouse button will trigger it. *Effect* *radius* defines how large the drift brush is. *Mouse strength* simulates pressure. *Mouse falloff* sets a gradient into the brush radius. *Origin strength* defines how intensely the text tries to return to normal (higher values glue the text to its original shape). *Friction* defines how much resistance there is to the pressure of the mouse. These parameters can be changed for each instance of the effect.

In the case of *StandUnder*, I assigned three different *drift* effects to the complete text block; each drift is independent and activated from a different mouse button. Each is of a different strength, radius, and falloff. I have also assigned an *originate* effect that independently of the drift actions, ensures that the text will elastically try to return to its (origin) normal shape no matter how it is deformed. At this point the static text is like a primed organism, but the animating force of the mouse effects or originate effect are not active until after play is pressed.

So here is the tension before beginning: I don't really know how the animation will behave. I have, like anyone who uses an instrument and has some degree of experience with it (embodied skill), tuned the Mr. Softie instrument (by applying the set of effects with parameters that I have used before). I feel confident that I can expect some sort of deflections to occur, but I am in a mild state of anticipation, since exactly what takes place next is unknown. Algorithmic events of sufficient complexity engender ambiguity. The smallest changes in pressure or gesture or parameters can intersect in chaotic, nonlinear ways. As with a dance or musical performance, it is rarely exactly the same twice. Playing in this sense is genuinely playing; it is an open activity.

I press the play button. The effects are activated, but nothing happens until I bring the mouse over the text and then press one of the mouse buttons. Immediately, the tower of text sheers sinuously away from my touch as if driven by a wind. I release the mouse. The text relaxes, retracting along fluid lines back into its original position. Wobbling slightly, the tower of text resembles a shimmering ribbon of substance, Jell-O ink. At a computational level, it behaves as a responsive fluid-cloth simulation. Consider it from a choreographic perspective. To get a particular shape, a choreographer might approach a dancer, lift the arm, turn the elbow, and place the shoulder. Like a puppeteer manipulating a marionette, the constituent pieces are put into place; while the choreographer works, the dancer freezes and holds the form. If in Mr. Softie I had not set the originate effect and had set the origin strength of the drifts to zero, then the text would have responded like a pliable material that could be bent and remain in shape: coat hanger style. With the originate set, responsiveness occurs until the mouse is released, and then the system flows back toward its source. Like the motion of a dancer who has been instructed to try to return to an original pose, the *StandUnder* tower text in Mr. Softie (with the *originate* effect on) is relentlessly flowing back toward its original base shape.

Obviously, working with text in Mr. Softie is also sculptural. A traditional sculptor spins or walks around a piece, changing viewing angles, oscillating between a position of proximity and a position of distance: nicking, cutting, nudging, and melding. Similarly in most contemporary softwares (including Mr. Softie, Mudbox, and After Effects), variable views are available: close-ups (zooms) and distance shots. The organic physicality of proximity and intimacy allows for fine-grained and general control. The writer models textual form. As in sculpting, in Mr. Softie, pliable form yields to touch in ways evocative of malleable matter.

The moment I press play in Mr. Softie is when these metaphors (choreographer, sculptor, and musician) extend into motion and the time-based work begins. The dancer is on the move, the choreographer yells instructions, and the speed, posture, form, and structure of the dancer change responsively, adapting to the instructions. The potter's wheel spins, and clay drenched in water dives under a gouging thumb. A musician bends a string, and sound bends with it. In these real-world scenarios, it's the pressure applied sonically or physically that alters the performative matter of the dancer or musical instrument or clay. In Mr. Softie, it's the assignment of diverse effects to different keystroke or mouse combinations (left, center, right, up, and/or down) that allow gesture to modulate the form of pixels.

When the effects are set and balanced, and the animation begins playing, the cursor roams over the surface of the type like a sheepdog racing from side to side behind a small herd, catching the pixels, directing the flow of the polygons. When it is working well, when the user-author is playing the text well, manipulating it with dexterity, not pushing it beyond control (unless intentionally), the process is intuitive and simple, the motion responsive, and control immediate.

Rehearsing or practicing is how I think of the repetitive process of trying out gestural play in Mr. Softie: play, stop, reset, and repeat. Working on the *StandUnder* piece, I rehearsed several times how much pressure the text could tolerate before its fluidity shattered. This iterative process provokes muscle memory of the sequence of effects and often generates visual possibilities that cannot be anticipated—emergent moments (as happens frequently in theatrical rehearsals where repetition functions as improvisation). This time, it was possible to segment off and stretch out a neck of text, and then to bend and fold the remaining text over the crushed lower level. In my mind, this created a sense of a downward weight, inexorable pressure, a visual analogy of performance anxiety provoked by a knowledge hierarchy.

Synthesis of Interaction and Instinct   The preceding comparisons to traditional media (choreography, sculpting, and music) reflect my belief that an engagement with creative process in digital media emerges when gestural interaction converges with evolutionary instincts. Gaming first-person shooters are the preeminent examples of how ancient hunting reflexes reinvest themselves in technology: find, aim, and fire. Musical instruments constitute yet another model: pluck, caress, and strum. Mr. Softie activates the same instincts as molding clay or playing with water. In instrumentalized, nontimeline authoring environments—of which Mr. Softie is one—nothing can be *exactly* repeated or replayed as in a conventional timeline environment. The ephemeral nature of the practice combined with the fluidity of the typographic styles changes every time. As Heracleitus reputedly said, *You cannot step into the same river twice*. This alters the relation between poet and typography. Control and flow enter into dialogue. Typography becomes categorically like sound or sculpture: responsive, pressure sensitive, sticky, slippery, loud, and delicate.

Mr. Softie induces the writer into the role of a sculptor-choreographer. It does this in a way that enables the flow of creativity, permitting direct reactivity to occur between hand, gesture, and distortions in the materiality of language. It is an open situation (much like play), where the enjoyment arises from unexpected serendipity, unanticipated reactions, and reactive motion. Tactile deflection is primary to understanding Mr. Softie. Direct pressure-based, real-time malleability gives the sense of working with flexible material; the material in this case is language. The physical sense of our normal exterior world are preserved or at the least emulated: pressure changes surfaces. In Mr. Softie, touch deflects and pulls text into ribbons. It is as if clay or plastic or licorice is placed under the hand. In spite of its mediated status, the type's direct reactivity makes it feel like a lived situation, and the materiality of the text becomes tangible.

Offering spontaneous, intuitive, visual direct-feedback, software design can contribute to enchantment—a poetic process where the innate animistic roots of poetic process flourish. *StandUnder* finished as the submerged knot of the tower stood up, unraveling its resistance to the pressure I'd placed on it; all I had to do was stand back and let the software do the work. This elastic embodied materiality of resilience programmed into the typography itself meant that the final version (output in movie form) is the record of a live performance: a play between gestures, physics, poet, language, and programming.

Flash (RIP)

The first browser came out in 1994, and soon after websites began to be called *home* pages (nicknamed after the HTML root index page called a home). Every creative wanted to own and control its own site. Few wanted to be homeless. Live in a hotel? Sleep in a mall? People built *homes*. To decorate those new homes, they needed animation tools. In 1995, Netscape released a plug-in application program interface that allowed optimized graphics in a browser. In May 1996, FutureSplash Animator (an animation tool with a web plug-in) shipped. In December 1996, it was purchased by Macromedia and renamed Flash. By 2001, it went from having 3 to 50 developers, and at that point it had 500,000 multimedia creatives who used the software and 325 million web surfers viewing it (Gay 2001).

Between 1999 and 2011, on year01.com and then on my website glia.ca, I posted hundreds of experiments in Flash. Up until 2010, almost every device supported it; it claimed 99 percent market penetration. Borrow the code.[18] Insert the graphics. Publish. Simple. This ease of use and widespread distribution led to a massive proliferation of TAVITs. Many online art galleries/publication-venues (*Vispo*, *Born Magazine*, *Poems that Go*, and so on) highlighted emergent language practices enabled by the affordances of software (Director and Flash) that were practical for artists and yet capable of sophisticated effects and easily launched online.

Poetry Portals: *Born Magazine, Poems that Go, Vispo* As previously outlined, *Born Magazine* (1996–2011) featured collaborations between poets and professional designers. Over the duration of the project, it connected

903 creatives and published 417 "literary/art" works. Many of these works expand the paradigm of what literary/art interactivity can entail. At many junctures, the multimedia interpretations expand the vision of the poet and the canonical sacrosanct purity of poetry suffuses with the dense hallucinatory power of audiovisuals. Succinct autopsies can no longer disentangle poetry from its art manifestation. If this is an infection, it is an opportunistic, synergetic effulgence.

In 2005, *Born Magazine* curated *Help Wanted: Collaborations in Art*, an exhibit at the the Center on Contemporary Art in Seattle. The exhibit did not solely consist of screen-based recapitulation of text-art projects but instead expanded collaborative practice into physical installations. To cite one example, *Think Tank* was a random political speech generator (using Markov chains from a database of George Bush speeches) and a physical sculpture with chickens on solenoids pecking generated words into a typewriter.

Poems That Go (2000–2004) published work that "freely let the arts mingle in a space we still dare to draw a circle around and label 'poetry' ... [and] ... explores how language is shaped in new media spaces, how interactivity can change the meaning of a sign, how an image can conflict with a sound, and how code exerts machine-order on a text" (Sapnar and Ankerson 2000). *Poems That Go* featured works exclusively made in Flash, including works by formidable practitioners such as Deena Larsen, Nicolas Clauss, Natalie Bookchin, and the curators Megan Sapnar and Ingrid Ankerson.

Another contributor to *Poems That Go* was Jim Andrews, whose personal portal vispo.com (1996–) became a mecca for digital poets. Andrews developed work in Macromedia *Director*. *Director* offered more 3-D support than Flash since it was originally designed for authoring CD-ROMs. In addition, Andrews collaborated widely and was an active (seemingly unfatigable) participant in innumerable Listserv dialogues that constituted the womb of critical inquiry from which works such as this book derive their terminology and methods. Leonardo Flores's (2010b) PhD dissertation "Typing the Dancing Signifier: Jim Andrews' (Vis)Poetics" demarcates three approaches to Andrew's oeuvre: visual, sound, and code. This succinct taxonomy reflects the reality of multimedia as two primary sensory modalities conjoined by logic (code) (ibid.). It is a tradition continued by contemporary portals: *Drunken Boat*, *Spring Press*, and *Claudius App* where e-lit media work is published in parallel with more traditional format work.

Flash: Flourish then Fail Cynical commentators might attribute Flash's success to marketing. Evidence from artists suggests otherwise. Jason Nelson (2009) offers an example of an artist whose vision was empowered by Flash:

i made this. you play this. we are enemies. explores internet portals, supposedly collaborative web 2.0 sites, through a modified and disrupted platform game engine. Using a combination of hand drawn notations, poetic lines, videos and animations, the art/poetry game lets users play in the worlds hovering over what we browse, to exists outside/over their controlling constraints. And while the non-linear poems and messy artwork suggests madness to some, the intention is to reflect the actual condition of these 2-dimensional virtual worlds spinning from our screens with the occasional leak of insanity.

Nelson dug deep into the Dada heart of eight-bit doodle graphics and became a Net art celebrity, attracting millions to play his demented online art games. But what is that permitted itinerant bards like Nelson to become multimedia interactivity designer-celebrities? Flash hit that sweet spot of write once, publish everywhere. More important, it incorporated timeline and scripting processes in the same interface; neither dominated, it was possible to use either modality: 100 percent tweened cel animation or 100 percent pure code, or weave both. It allowed coding for abstract control reasoning, and timelines for tactile spatial experience. Objects that will appear on-screen are visible in the interface; they can be picked up and moved with the mouse or code, or both. The muse was well pleased to move among the dim-witted machines with its mouth full of grapes.

Pop-up typographic design experiments like Gicheal Lee's (2003) *typorganism* claimed: "'Type is an Organism,' that Lives on the Net, Responds to user input, Evolves through Time, as Intelligence, powered by Computational Organism." Provoked by the ease of adaptability of new behaviors there was a wave of incautious optimism that anticipated quasi-organisms that the Net ecosystem snuffed out. *Meme-garden* by Mary Flanagan and others (2006) postulates a space where searches offer "seed" terms, word particles animated and trembling with Brownian momentum; beneath the seeds is "soil" where seeds can be dragged; from the set of planted seeds, "trees" arise to offer new associational paths; yet on a 2014 visit, the database threw an error, and germination failed. Tempered by time, it now seems as if the digital-poetic fossil record will contain many evolutionary dead ends: Net spaces where the encoding of the soil shifts and species of poems disappear.

ActionScript Explained   In Flash, drag 'n drop functionality allowed a tactile, level of control (moving drawings onstage, building mazes by dragging, animating by keyframes, etc.). Then by naming the instantiations of those objects, code control allowed an abstract level of control. The abstract and tactile modes complimented each other. The code was called Action-Script and it was interpreted-not-compiled scripting language (easier to use, simpler to learn).[19] Up until ActionScript 3, it was not even strict typed (it let you use different data types together), and not object-oriented programming (OOP uses complex classes that require naming conventions and encapsulates data—protecting them from being accessed—encapsulation requires more coding forethought and conceptual understanding). Action-Script 2 encouraged prototypes, rough experiments, one-off processes, and tiny little textural interventions.

With success came commercial proliferation, code sharing desiccated slightly, and Adobe contributed to its own demise by answering the demands of its commercial clients: the coding engine and language was rebuilt to specifications more appropriate for computer science graduates. The more formal language of ActionScript 3 required a density of preparation and infrastructure that made tiny, single, creative amateur projects less tenable. And then the corporate war began between Apple and Adobe.

HTML5 Fail   Some five years ago, Steve Jobs (2010) killed the comprehensive market penetration of Flash by announcing that Apple would no longer support it; he cited technical reasons. *Wired* magazine interpreted Job's announcement differently: "Flash would open a new door for application developers to get their software onto the iPhone: Just code them in Flash and put them on a web page. In so doing, Flash would divert business from the App Store, as well as enable publishers to distribute music, videos and movies that could compete with the iTunes Store" (Chen 2008).

In this case, self-hosting (ownership! data independent of a corporation!) and the flexible interactive control of audiovideo (malleable mashups! an animation timeline and a scripting language in a single authoring environment!) became corporate roadkill.

Most major web devs began moving to HTML5. In spite of the hype, HTML5 utopian ease of use has yet to arrive: coding a multimedia website and maintaining it across multiple platforms for diverse devices is now immensely time-consuming—almost impossible.

Consider this announcement from UbuWeb (2014):

For the past two years, we've been trying to convert all our films so that they can be viewed on mobile media. Guess what? We failed. The films stuttered, stopped and started. In the interim, we figured that it's better to have crappy web-only Flash files than have faulty films that don't play well on any media. Many hands have tried to make this a success, and for that we are grateful.

Unity (Not Diversity): The Rise of the Platforms So what comes next? In terms of unified platforms that feature full-bodied timelines with complex yet accessible scripting languages, few alternatives exist. The increasingly perilous web environment bifurcated by platform wars and segmented by device proliferation precludes any immediate easy answers. One candidate is Unity3D, but while Flash was originally conceived of for fun little animations and eventually co-opted by advertising, Unity3D is built from the ground up to operate as a first-person shooter maze; it is optimized for that particular style. If Flash was secular, Unity3D is the military-industrial complex. While Unity3D does feature full 3-D potential, few browsers bundle it natively anymore; the era of write once, publish everywhere is over.[20]

Thus the rise of platforms: hosting services like Flickr, Vine, Vimeo, YouTube, Twitter, and others that resolve the exigencies of launching media. And with the platforms, there is a dwindling of those esoteric, strange, perverse provocations possible: context controlled by corporations now leashes even the creatives.

Obsolescence: VRML (1994–)
Functionally, it is both a text to be read and a space to be surveyed.

—Matthew G. Kirschenbaum, 2007

Flash is not the only internet plugin to have gone from ascendancy to obsolescence. VRML as a term was coined in 1994 and then arose on the web when VR was ported over to the Mosaic browser. It was popular; by 1999, "the population of *Cybertown* (hosted by Blaxxun, and based on VRML)

surpassed 100,000 residents."[21] In the second half of the 1990s, VRML was
a powerful presence in the e-lit community.[22] Poets such as Ladislao Pablo
Györi issued paeans to its glory: "Virtual poetry results from a basic need to
impel a new kind of creation related to facts whose emergence—for their
morphological and/or structural characteristics—would be improbable in
the natural context" (Györi 1995 in Kac ed. 2007, 94). Györi also made general proclamations: "All creative processes will move into the virtual space
offered by the machine" (ibid., 94). Funkhouser refers to Györi's sculptural
virtual poetry as of the utmost significance. In terms of history, this is true,
but Györi's website is gone and his work has all but disappeared. The Internet is a swift tributary that eradicates its past as efficiently as fire in Alex-
andria's libraries. VRML was a powerful medium capable of investigations
into textuality that are difficult to reproduce with current internet tools.
Yet VRML has all but disappeared as an authoring technique and online
distribution vehicle.

VRML also contributed to the emergence of new literary terminology.
What Kirschenbaum (1997, in a paper to accompany his VRML work *Lucid
Mapping*) calls *fractal meaning* is the same thing that Cayley (quoted in Raley
2006a) refers to as *literal materiality*: the ability to use the scale of letterforms
to alter the reading. In Kirschenbaum's example, inside a VRML environment, he places a complete paragraph in the bell of an *a*. To read, the reader
dives in, microscopically entering a region of scale where legibility becomes
feasible. As Kirschenbaum points out, this could continue ad infinitum:
intimacy enters a scalar recursion (Kirschenbaum 1997).

Obsolescence: Second Life (2003–)

When VRML became a ghost town and its URLs died, the people moved
into Second Life. Now Second Life is less known; it's like the countryside,
and the young folks all dwell in cities. Their parents may think they inhabit
Facebook and Whatsapp, but younger people are in Snapchat and Kik, and
the next generation will move on, mobilized by the tides of commercial
incentive and a relentless desire to not repeat the previous generations'
imperatives. Nevertheless, many evocative poetic experiments have flourished in Second Life, among them an initiative by Sarah Waterson, Cristyn
Davies, and Elena Knox (2008) to highlight Australian poets, called *trope*—
poems visualized on walls in space, custom-deformed avatars, a sound
track, and spoken word overdubs.

Sondheim is one of the few poets to persistently work in Second Life. His approach is hallucinatory and excessive. It stretches the boundaries of what many might consider poetry. Trusting in the aesthetics of accumulation, Sondheim builds massive folly machines, churning wheels and polygon shard waterfalls. Independent parts rotate and careen; it is a bit like watching many superimposed looped explosions. In fact, there are no words so to speak; these are added afterward in performative contexts where Sondheim recites and shrieks while dance collaborators gyrate in front of screens. The effect is similar to *Survival Research Laboratory*'s aesthetic: twisted heaps of dementia colliding until catastrophe occurs, and then occurs again. Oh it's fun. Sondheim's point (if he has one, which he does; he has many—perhaps too many) is that we live in an era of entropy and excess. The careful, antiseptic, Bauhaus-like IKEA furniture of our homes conceals a careening that is taking place technologically. His staged interventions interrupt sane prognostications and cast viewers into a volatile perdition. Space distorts in ways that would have made surrealists jealous. It is cubism exponential. How is it poetry? Think of it as a collage of mannerist conceits, a place on the highway of culture where the conventional trucks of meaning have overturned and blind commuters collide within an extruded semantic mass.

The collapse of Second Life points to what might be a crucial flaw in all claims that textuality might integrate itself into the ontological fabric: humans cognitively prefer distinct categorical regions. The screen instigates a reaction against itself.

N. Katherine Hayles notes, "The next move is from imaging three dimensions interactively on the screen to immersion in actual three-dimensional spaces … [given that] computers have moved off the desktop and into the environment" (Hayles 2008, 11) In support of this reaction against the virtual flat screen, she cites the audiowalk projects of Janet Cardiff, the collective augmented gaming of *Blast Theory*, and cave automatic virtual environment (CAVE), specifically Cayley's *Torus* in 2005 and Wardrip-Fruin's (and others) *Screen* in 2003.[23] The tension between physically being in a space and being emulated as an avatar in virtual space is what Oculus Rift and the next generation of Google Glass augmented VR wearables might bridge, provoking another explosion of language arts that involve the reader moving physically through what they read wherever they are. Caitlin Fisher's AR installations anticipate this symbiosis of room-based infrastructure with handheld VR.

Untold Cube Odes: Contemporary CAVE Works

Every kid with a Wii remote in their basement understands the impulse to move in physical space that corresponds to a virtual representation. Yet relatively few readers have experienced the CAVE works emerging out of Cayley's electronic writing program at Brown University. Of note, Kathleen Ottinger's (2013) *Untold* is a CAVE poem about desire; in this poem, the reader is pulled along twisting corridors, through words that penetrate flesh and rush through the reader whispering.[24] *Untold* fixates on letterforms as a lover fixates on the beloved, with the body of the reader (compelled inexorably) flying at different speeds, pierced by language (emulating the sacred ecstasy of Saint Theresa wounded by subliminal eros). One effect the CAVE produces is of being touched at a visual level by letters that do not create any tactile sensation (see them move into skin, yet feel nothing). It involves proprioceptive language and subcutaneous diffractions.

CAVE poets are not constrained by the size of the page; like oral poets, they race over landscapes (of letters), and as they race, landscapes transform. Structurally, many of the poems featured at the Brown CAVE are multisection poems, filmic in ambition, cutting into divergent paradigms with changes in sound or color. Ottinger's work even contains a traditional finale revelation as the camera draws back, giving a new global perspective, analogous to the last lines of a sonnet inverting the expectations of a reader. One of the works that does not contain this multifaceted filmic structure is Ian Hatcher's (2010) *Cubes*: a recursive library of cubes floating in space, each created with lines of words from Jorge Luis Borges's "The Library of Babel." Through the cube-cages, the reader interactively can move up, down, left, right, forward, or backward. Phrases come and go, elegiac and precise, fading in and out. The world slides around the reader like an automated repository. *Cubes* defines an austerity of minimalism proximal to the dimensional lattices between molecules.

One of the primary ontological intuitions since antiquity is of a continuum of energy (or light or love) that underlies the world of phenomena. This spectrum of an eternal presence is surreptitiously evoked by Carman McNary (2008) in *Ode*, a work that begins unobtrusively as a homage fan letter to John Coltrane and then segues into a huge field of letterforms that slowly grow in size so that their intersections form an unceasing architecture—a drifting, synchronized, ceaseless excess that precipitates existential vertigo.

Stereoscopic 3-D letterforms released from the page for now require expensive immersive infrastructures, yet there are indications that headset VRs will proliferate toward mass production. As words operate within the field of vision of the reader, proximal to the body, glazing skin, it requires a redefined notion of transcription. Immersion in this sense will arrive at and move beyond *resolution at the limits of visual acuity* (as in Brown University's YURT opened in 2015), will get wearable (as Steve Mann anticipated), and eventually be born in the brain—broadcast onto neural textures.[25]

Code
I run with code that's a matter of tone.

—Fred Moten, 2014

Code can either be seen as the creative toolbox used to configure appearance and interactivity, or as the guts, wiring, circuitry, engineering, infrastructure, and protometabolism of the quasi-alive twitching digital TAVIT poem-anism.

Pure coding (as opposed to hybrid code-timeline authoring environments) presents a creative challenge: it lacks any direct, immediate, tangible feedback. To write code is similar to writing literature: abstract words operate as pointers to imagined objects.[26] The animation timeline (in spite of its limitations) has the benefit of displaying "objects" that can be dragged and dropped (as real things in this world). Code does not offer that physical analog. The creative strengths of code are granular control of every detail and loops that allow variations controlled by formulas (leading to dynamic open events and variations without end).

Code like language is not static. Over the period 1995–2014, major evolutions in code occurred. On his website *Chronotext*, the programmer-typographic-designer Ariel Malka offers a concise chronology of the programming languages he adopted over this period for language manipulation; his chronology accurately reflects the experience of many programmer-poets. Pre-2002, it was dynamic HTML and Flash; in 2003, it was Processing (featured sketches: scrollable text on a cube, a helix typewriter, and translated text sliding around a cyclotron); 2004 saw the dawn of "a new era of *pure java* or whatever works"; in 2005, it was OpenGL; a custom software toolbox was made in 2007; in 2008, "experiments [were] fed with markup data or controlled by script"; 2009 brought the iPhone iOS pro-gramming with interactive tilting, touching, and shaking; in 2010, it was apps and Twitter readers; "Java has become irrelevant [in 2011]. … [P]lease welcome our new partners: cross-platform C++ and the *Cinder* framework"; 2012 offered JavaScript; and in 2014, it was "back to the mobile" (Malka 2014).

Programming language life spans are brief, but paradigms prevail. If HTML was the language of premillennial poets (along with the oceanic scripts of Perl and C, and the Eastgate Systems' branching narrative software), Flash (ActionScript) and Director (using a language called Lingo)—which both offered a hybrid timeline-code authoring environment—dominated the first decade of the twentieth century by wrapping multimedia into a cus-tom plug-in that once installed in the browser, ensured potential for wide-spread distribution.[27]

In 2001, the language Processing (initiated by Casey Reas and Ben Fry) became the scripting choice for education, prototypes, and experiments (it is open source and easy to learn, and features a powerful animation engine with OpenGL integration and many libraries). In parallel, JavaS-cript evolved into a powerful scripting language capable of making browser-based textuality dynamic (with JQuery and nimble programming methods amplifying its penetration into advertising and online textual practices), and at the same time, Python arose as a powerful component in generative analytic practices, linked to scientific statistical libraries yet with the capac-ity to flexibly instigate natural language processing.

In an ironic twist of remediation, the current scripting languages—Python, Processing, and JavaScript—actually digest and parse HTML, the former dominant dragon (Python does so using a library called Beauti-ful Soup). Once digested, text/HTML can be analyzed to discover poetic meter and form, by using libraries like the Natural Language Toolkit, or through comparison with existing pretagged archives like the Carnegie Mellon University Pronouncing Dictionary, which contains over 125,000 words annotated for stress or unstressed form. Each can generate n-grams (word-frequency collocation lists) and context-free grammars (a model for the hierarchical and recursive structure of syntax typically visualized as a tree growing downward through *S* (subjects) to *NP* (noun phrases), and so on. Part of speech tagging (syllables, phonemes, stemming, and etc.) allows granular reconstructions and analysis. Poetry engineering emerges as a formidable subdiscipline.

Processing Processing experiments have replicated many, if not all, of the text effects exploited by Flash, rendered 3-D interactive in the style of After Effects, and converted letterforms into particles, strains, strands, fields, flocks, and so forth.

Assuming instincts are rules, sets of parametrized behaviors designed to navigate organisms toward optimized survival, code emulates organisms. In *Keyfleas* by Miles Peyton (2013; emphasis in original), a particle system projected onto a keyboard animates reactive little instinctual insects-circles: "*The Keyfleas live on a two-dimensional flatland. They travel as a flock, over key mountains and through aluminum valleys. They avoid touching letterforms, since they suspect that the symbols are of some evil origin. On occasion, a hostile tentacle [a finger typing] invades the flatland and disturbs its inhabitants.*"

Assuming interoperability between text and image necessitates translation pipelines; Processing libraries function as paths. Boris Müller (2010), graphic designer for *Poetry on the Road*, utilizes such paths: "All graphics are generated by a computer program that turns texts into images. So every image is the direct representation of a specific text." Interpreting a poem that has entwined modalities, as image and text, complicates the genealogy of imagery and confounds hermeneutics.

Code can allow for multiples without repetition, variation without end. The canonical text dissolves into TAVIT DNA that seeds a process. The *Written Images* print-on-demand book project generated a unique book with each printing based on seventy custom artist softwares (many written in Processing and a few using text): "A one of a kind snapshot in time" (Fuchs and Bichsel 2010). Most of these are images, but a few use text. Stable identity morphs on meeting dynamic data.

Few poets display the technical dexterity of programmer designers, so extreme play typography experiments—such as PostSpectacular studios *Happy 2010! Card*—often lack art/poetry content/concept/context. Technically sophisticated, the *Happy 2010! Card* uses particle strings on splines in a 3-D simulation box with constraints, elasticity, collisions, and so forth. Just as a medieval poet might have implemented obscure techniques like anaphora, euphony, metonym, or apostrophe, contemporary programmers utilize obscure processes. Processing eases the entry level, diffuses some obscurity, and permits the generic paradigms of dot-syntax programming to become palpable for nonprogrammers.

RiTa RiTa is a software toolbox developed by programmer-poet Daniel Howe. Biologically, cellular ion gates regulate transcription processes, permitting or refusing molecules to enter/leave cells, as does RiTa ("from the old Norse, meaning to mark, scratch, or scribble" [Howe 2006]), which encapsulates and controls processes of text analysis and animated display. Like many other programming languages, RiTa lives in an ecosystem of intricate interdependencies, fluctuating protocols, and turbulent standards. RiTa enables language processing (grammars, Markov chains, and part-of-speech tagging). RiTaJS works in the browser (extending HTML5 first through Java and then with a JavaScript library); the library functions independently or in conjunction with Processing, Node.js, Android, and WordNet.

A project built with RiTa libraries that exemplifies the complex potential of how and where a poem can manifest inadvertently in networks is Howe's (2014) browser-art-poem plug-in *AdLiPo*. *AdLiPo* works like an ad blocker, and utilizes the RiTa library to replace the ads on web pages with dynamic real-time static or kinetic text that is generated from a Markov-like model "composed of the 'description' texts from a recent digital writing conference, seasoned liberally with quotations from the likes of Marx and the Marquis de Sade" (ibid.). The result is savagely unexpected blobs of poetry that are almost more disturbing than ads.

Projects made with RiTa range from Molleindustria's (2012) simple *Definition of Game*, which does one thing: generates definitions of the word *game*, to the complex information visualization pipeline of NASA reports implemented by the Office for Creative Research that parsed *New York Times* headlines using RiTa to create a sinuous, flowing, chronological language-usage map (Rubin, Thorp, and Hansen 2014).

A sophisticated poetic, textual example made with RiTa is Braxton Soderman's *Mémoire Involuntaire No. 1*, a minimalist and evocative meditation on memory. In *Mémoire Involuntaire No. 1*, text replacement (implemented in RiTa according to sets of rules with a grammar) slowly and selectively changes words within a single block of text describing a childhood memory. The erased, deformed, replaced text occasionally enhances but often obscures the original meaning of the text-memory; after a period of time, the process reverses and the text attempts to retrieve the initial memory, seeking to return to its original state (Soderman 2009). It's a simple conceit that posits an unstable poetic form that is itself a statement on the instability and irretrievability of memory. The code in this sense operates like amyloid plaque *momento mori*, unraveling memory, destabilizing it, and then seeking it out again—attempting incessantly again and again to retrieve experience eroded by evaluation.

Python Python is a high-level programming language, and easier to use than compiled languages like C or C++ (more readable, less strict, offering more spontaneous workflow, and requiring fewer lines of code). It offers extensive, powerful access to language processing with native/external libraries, and is capable of data analytics, supplying a wide range of algorithms and visualization.[28] It is uniquely situated to become a tool of choice for generative, combinatorial programmer-poets.

Python can also cut, splice, and display video. Sam Lavigne's *Videogrep* implements conceptual film-mashup experiments; edits are chosen by isolating grammatical structures in subtitles in films, and then the code splices the video into new configurations. One result is: "every instance of a character saying the word 'time' in the movie *In Time* (a film whose dialog appears to consist mostly of clock-related puns)" (Lavigne 2014). *Videogrep* is creative coding at the service of an activity that bears marked similarities to conceptual and uncreative writing: appropriation that archaeologically plunders originals in order to highlight idiomatic speech forms.

Python seems to encourage appropriation by the very nature of its ease of splicing. J. R. Carpenter's adaptation of Nick Montfort's *Takoro Gorge* and other python scripts (many the subject of numerous encouraged collaborative appropriations) develops a riff off the word *gorge* to create a physical book (published in a 154-page softcover, perfect-bound edition by TRAUMAWIEN) on the theme of variations. As Carpenter (2011) states, there was one rule:

No new texts. All the texts in this book were previously published in some way. The texts the generators produce are intertwined with the generators' source code, and these two types of texts are in turn interrupted by excerpts from the meta narrative that went into their creation. Most of the sentences in the fiction generators started off as Tweets, which were then pulled into Facebook. Some led to comments that led to responses that led to new texts. All these stages of intermediation are represented in the print book iteration.

The result is a sinuous network of branching fingers and blossoming mouths. Gorging on already-generated forms as it generates more forms, *Generation[s]* questions the circular feeding on fetishized recursion operative in microcommunities.

The surplus also takes form in Winnie Soo's (2014) spam-baiting project *Hello Zombies*, written in PHP and Python; it dynamically gathers lists of email addresses known to belong to spambots (these are published and updated daily by antivirus services), and then sends a poem (written specifically for the project by poet Susan Scarlata) every five seconds to a spambot and displays the "replies": bounced messages, denials, rejections, and on rare occasion a human "hunh?" Her project points to the automatism of the network—the vast amount of processes bouncing around inside it that are simply working parts doing what they do with impeccable dedication. It seems also as if the body of poets and humans are full of such events: blind signals and ciphers, bacterial colonies, enzyme channels, peristaltic ripples, nerve messages, cascades of hunger-heat-thought-desire strobing onward, relentlessly independent of any greater context beyond their own need to be heard/read, or to perform the intricate task in which they have been set by some unknown source code. Python permits impeccable autopsies, forensics (to repurpose a term Kirschenbaum uses adeptly) of rhythms inherent within the froth of multiple tongues.

C++ Andy Clymer's (2011) typographic experiment *Font-Face* is a simple gimmick made with a video camera and openFrameworks code: font size, width of bowl, and stem mapped to face motion.[29] Open your mouth, and the font gets fat. Close it, and the font becomes thin. Eyebrows up, and the font changes color. Frown, and the font curls. It reverses the role of reading as it empowers the reader, whose body becomes a visceral muscular designer of the font form. In this sense, this tiny experiment reveals one way the page can read us. There will be more.

Visual form *does* something, rather than that it *is* something.

—Johanna Drucker, 2009

Consider text on a flat page. If printed on a press, the text is indented almost imperceptibly. The ink has bonded with the paper, the fibers of the paper have soaked up the stain of the letter, and paper and letter are materially bonded, melded together. On screens, there is no indentation of ink into paper. Pixels portray depth through a luminous 2-D perspectival grid. Nonetheless, due to the persistence of iconographic traditions of print, most digital text appears as if printed. To a casual eye, the similarities between the trace mark-making of petroglyphs, papyrus, hieroglyphs, and screen-based digital typography are strong. Line based, left to right reading, columns with headlines, formatting (uppercase, sentences, underlines, italics, and justification): these formal elements of writing persevere through technologies. Writing remains what it always was: a reservoir of prescriptive grammatical rules, typographic traditions, and literary effects. There are few attempts to make strange what is overly familiar.

Andreas Müller (2005) in *For All Seasons* coded a monochromatic, minimalist, interactive fly-through of fields of letterforms: poem as park or field; poem as monoculture—all of it coded in C++[30] Imagine blisters arising in the form of letters on the printed page. The dormant immobile ink of each letter bubbles upward just slightly. The indentation of the printing press is inverted. The letters hover like pimples, swollen with ink, foaming over. They shine as if plastic; they gleam as if wet. The page is now implicitly tactile. It references Braille. It is now possible to conceive of someone touching the page and slowly (laboriously) reading it with their fingers.[31] Imagine more. Imagine that the letter-blisters grow more pronounced than pimples; swollen with pulsating and slushy ink, each letter now germinates and extrudes like a sprout; each letter is sexual, a thick fountain, a forest of letters, a field of wavering black stalks rising off the page; each is plush with a pulsing, succulent interiority. Our viewpoint shifts. We rush over a thriving field of grown language as if we were a bird or a low-flying plane; we rush over a field of wind-struck, writhing letters raising their heads to the sun, following the reader.

Live Coding   Live coding is currently the practice of writing real-time code that generates audio; beyond its connection to beatboxing (some of its practitioners practice beatboxing as well), there is no real connection to poetry.[32] But live coding as a paradigm represents one space that poetry may evolve into: improvisational, augmented, on-the-fly performance-creations, or a real-time speaking of real-time generated verse.

In a live-coding performance, coding and composing occur in real time, no instruments are used, and the audience watches the performer's screen as they type the code. Currently bewildering audiences and exciting the musical community, live coding displays the improvisational coding skills as it is being done. So at some level, performing this music is actually a writing practice; there is no traditional instrument involved, just sets of instructions typed into the code that place the performer and audience in a proximal relation to how the programming influences the musical process. So the audiences watch the writing that underlies the sounds. It's designed to disintegrate the delay between code and creation. Utilizing text-based, real-time audiosynthesis languages like Extempore, Impromptu, Overtone, and SuperCollider, these musician-geeks practice within a community that values improvisational dexterity and on-the-fly, rapid charismatic serendipity—all values that would seem congruous with poetic practice. Other live-coding practices involve graphical coding environments such as Pure-Data or MaxMSP—*graphical* here meaning on-screen, object, graphical user interface boxes connected by strings that pipe data in and out of processes.

There are indications that the live-coding community, whose practitioners occasionally interject live vocal samples and beatboxing into their mixes (projecting a kind of Kurt Schwitters's *Merz* diatribe, vocalize, skew mix), is becoming interested in haptic interfaces and interdisciplinary excursions that might result in tweaking output pipes of language, poetry, and literature into real-time parallel code-literature writing procedures. The gap between interface and output might narrow. Books might be written/ generated, animated, and published in synchronous networks of collaborative unfoldings, much like social network streams encourage instantaneous twist ricochets to reinforce and/or deflect current trending hashtags.

5 Futures

Similar to the way Charles Olson re-mapped the concept of the field regarding the relationship between typographic spacing and the codex page, is the way code, the visual, the transient, and the multiple are important to our concept of the field of the innovative digital work. ... The hard choice before us is to identify new forms of literature, expand our habits, and not be restricted to old forms in new clothes.

—Loss Pequeño Glazier, 2002

Often, poetry stands mute at the edge of the field of life. Then, after a time, it reacts. As research it dives to the depth of experience, trying some would claim to sculpt sonic-verbal-inscription sculptures, to reflect the forms of dreams/genes: quiet, supple, alternate intelligences. Occasionally, refracted, it discharges: personal, aesthetic, volatile, diffused, and embodied dimensions.

Letterforms that live perhaps only exist in the imaginary dimensions of mad poets: coded, visual, transient multiple networked and reactive quasi-critter hallucinations. But just as the cell phone headset made the solitary incantations of schizophrenia into normative behavior, so genomics, 3-D modeling, and networks might mutate poetic practice, offering radical potentials to challenge reasonable prognostications.

And just as water flows along all potential paths offered, digital poetry will follow many trajectories. The question is, which will be relevant?

Bodies will be relevant. Embodied relevance requires extrapolating poetry beyond algorithms, beyond machines. In other words, What can humans do that computers cannot? What does embodied life deliver? Where is breath? And for digital poetry, What can algorithms and humans do together that humans alone cannot? What can algorithms teach us (retroactive big-data assessment of corpora; generative style emulations)? Symbiotic interstices, cyborg splices.

TAVs and TAVITs imply a symbiosis between text, image, audio, interaction, concept, data, and affect. Symbiosis implies reciprocal gain.

The following section includes a summation (looking back) and a few speculations (looking forward).

Summation

In all poetry words are a presence before they are a means of communication.

—John Berger, 1984

Inscription technology (how we write) has from time immemorial induced changes in what language is and how it is perceived. As the rate of change of digital inscription increases, we can expect commensurate changes in how language is perceived, what it is internally as structure, and what it is externally as presence.[1]

TAVs are structurally distinct from traditional letterforms or literature: generative, kinetic, dimensional, networked, and reactive text audiovisuals. TAVs contain technological accretions of implementations and potentiality. As their potentialities accumulate, a state phase-transition (as when self-organizing criticalities avalanche into different states) may occur. What language becomes then (after a self-organizing criticalities avalanche) is anyone's guess. I feel that language will be perceived as living. Further, I claim that language will be perceived as living because it is living.

Aesthetic animism is the attribution of livingness based on perceived beauty. Digitally enhanced living language will satisfy the criteria of aesthetic animism. This change is not without precedent; Harold Innes, Walter J. Ong, Richard Lanham, and Marshall McLuhan (among many others) document how inscription technology provokes powerful transformations in humanity's relation to and perception of signifiers. Aesthetic animism belongs to that species of argument. The printing press (in its dominant epoch) modified the means of diffusion of literature and thereby transformed culture. Digital technology does far more than modify the means of transmission. It fuses creation and reception. It fuses sensory modalities. It injects memory into data at several levels of abstraction. It networks cultural objects. It gives letters kinetic skins.

What Will This Set of Rapid Ongoing Changes Entail?

Instead of being read, we will read being. Language, once living and endowed with sensory capabilities (hearing through microphones and seeing through cameras), and a body (of thick, doughy, 3-D spline letterforms mingled with metadata memory) will respond to us. After a time, the *presence* of responsive embodied language (the anticipatory quality of its responsive, tactile agility and nuanced sounds) will become normative. At this point an attitude avalanche may occur. Literary discourse will perhaps absorb the terminology of 3-D modeling and finite state machines. Literary creation will become multifaceted, multimodal playing within holistic devices.

What Do These Changes Mean Now?

In our era, dimensional language arts in time-based media fuse multiple disciplines. Structural synergy takes place between computation and animation; sensorial synergy occurs across sensory modalities (speech, sound, touch, and vision).

A Few Contexts

I like to think (and
the sooner the better!)
of a cybernetic meadow
where mammals and computers
live together in mutually
programming harmony
like pure water
touching clear sky.

—Richard Brautigan, 1967

The Autowriting Art

Data-base was originally detected after assembly of a mammalian receiver sensitive enough to override hardware ambivalence. The receiver began to masturbate somewhere in the range of 1,700 to 1,800 megahertz.

—Christopher Dewdney, 1988

Expect a precipitous transformation of influence; alongside the autodriving car, autowriting augmentations will emerge. Art will write itself: ingesting speech patterns, creeping across textual topologies, and manufacturing variational threads. The unaugmented author will become an anachronism. Autodriving cars navigate by feature detection of their environment; autowriting software will navigate by extracting linguistic data from massive corpora of text and biometric data from the response of readers. This involves eye focal points, heat rate, skin resistance, vocabulary, styles, interests, known facts, density, networks of influence, and so on. As in any feedback system, learning-response-modification cycles will precipitate improvement.[2] We are now at the bottom of a steep curve (and the curve is—as most recognize—going up in terms in computational power, and perhaps down in terms of species diversity and ecosystem purity). Increase in terms of scale (data size, network momentum, and speed) has nonnegligible implications for language processing, and language processing is what poets do as they convert experience into language events; so AI is a significant incursion onto and perhaps refertilisation of the mechanisms of poetics. As many note, the printing press eroded the influential status of scribes and oral poets. Increased capacity for network AI—to read and be capable of factual replication, historical rendition, rudimentary critical interpretation, relevant filtering, rewiring vocabularies, stylistic translations, transpositions of affect, and condensations/expansions—will similarly erode the human role in writing.

To paraphrase Charles Bernstein (2012), paraphrasing Eric Havelock (1988) in *The Muse Learns to Write*, just as photography eroded the documentary role of painting, so too do reproductive media also erode the documentary role of poetry; this erosion necessitates, for poetry as it does for painting, a foregrounding of the materiality of the media. Materiality responses might require vigilant redefinition during the emergence of AI autowriting software (mining crowdsourced renditions of events) capable of rapidly synthesizing descriptions of events from multiple viewpoints. One authorial refuge may be situated at a merger of materiality and ontology, in an analog embodiment crevice where intimacy and subtle contextual analysis reside.

pMuse: AI as an Infant

Moma
Popa
Caca
Dada

Arthur Rimbaud gave up poetry at the age of 20; that meant he had already lived (while awake!) about 17.5 million seconds, during which time his approximately 2 billion skin pores, 72 kilometers of nerves, and 100 trillion bacterial microbiome fluctuated under the impact of a deluge of social phenomena: words, caresses, smells, glances, music, food, narcotics, and so forth. It is unlikely that a computer in 2020 will comprehend sophisticated notions of embodiment—at least not in those terms. Cultural poetic intelligence is nontrivially connected to embodied experience; future computational assistances (at least in the short term) will be disembodied.

In 2020, however, computational adjuncts will act as muses—pragmatic muses. Imagine: once installed, *pMuse* digital assistants construct a complete model of the owner's writing style, then offer a package of autowriting aids: real-time fact-checking and autocitations, metrics (sensitivity, complexity, authenticity, originality, relevance, and sophistication), proximity maps (*know who are echoing; tune your influence vectors!*), and augmented potency (using the *pMuse* i-patent metapore system). Imagine every poem ever written transposed into predictive potential: the trick will be to think of something the machine cannot predict.

If you are skeptical about AI's evolution over the next five years, think of a three-year-old child performing a spoken-word piece they made up. The three-year-old is cute. If their performance were made by a child twice their age, it would be considered annoying, but because this performance is done with impish stereotypical gestures, it predisposes critical faculties to ignore the superficial, predictable, unsophisticated, primal morpheme sing-song content. So too we ignore the feebleness of many contemporary AI initiatives. A year later, listen again: the four-year-old performance is still simple yet it has evolved; now the child is making a list and beginning to develop a textured rhythm. And then when the child is five, they compose a spell, which is simple, but the formal process by which they declare it and add clauses exceeds by far their former complexity. The five-year-old is now more aware of the audience, measuring their sympathy, mining their biology for praise.

Imagine this little child represents AI; the Internet is their body, and the amalgamated potential of multiple research labs conjoined globally around an exponentially expanding, blossoming network of comprehensive real-time data, which propagates frothy waves of artificial text all across the globe, is their brain. We, as a species, are the input sensors (Kelly 2005).

Computers now correct our spelling, anticipate our words, read signs, and navigate space. Watson won Jeopardy. The implication is that nuance and inflection are parsable. Lie detection and physical attraction/repulsion are tractable. The anticipated profit margins of pop songs and Hollywood scripts are DIY-calculable. Stock trading and customer service are done-in-the-cloud niche networks. The way we hold a camera can identify us. The way we speak is a signature. It can be tuned.

Contemporary AI currently spits isolated sparks in a rainstorm (no bodily identity, no analysis of insights, no survival reflex, no reproductive urge). In five years it will write with/through us—the *p* in *pMuse* stands for *pragmatic* not *poet*.

Net Results: In Five Years ...

The ability to communicate with one another allows bacteria to coordinate the gene expression, and therefore the behavior, of the entire community. Presumably, this process bestows upon bacteria some of the qualities of higher organisms. The evolution of quorum sensing systems in bacteria could, therefore, have been one of the early steps in the development of multicellularity.

—Bonnie Bassler and Melissa Miller, 2001

The first steps and incremental evolution of aggregate forms bootstrap off networks of communication. Parallel to the autowriting assistants, algorithmic authors will write literature (of a kind) and capable poetry.[3] In five years, AI systems will initially colonize short, formal, metered, lineated verse in the cadence or style of acclaimed masters: Lord Byron, Shakespeare, Alfred Tennyson, and William Butler Yeats; others will capably emulate Gerald Manley Hopkins, William Carlos Williams, Maya Angelou, and Lisa Robertson. Haiku was already computer generated in 1968 for *Cybernetic Serendipity*. Even as styles and cadences will be captured (converted into rules), content and contextually adaptive creativity will not so easily fall—at least not immediately. After emulating formal verse, algorithms will begin flexibly sprawling across a diversity of freestyles, creating some, while absorbing and exuding an almost complete continuity of crowdsourced human experience. Streams will ensure a constant fresh supply of witticisms and responses in a multitude of styles. Bots will feed bots.

In five years, humans will be known and fed by statistical information resources that amalgamate and expand the best writing (human? bot? cyborg?) into coherent threads. Few of us will be able to discern between an online bot and a human being, since most human beings will write with the assistance of bots. Witness the strange story of *Horse ebooks*, a Twitter account that at the time of its closure in 2013, had over two hundred thousand followers of its luminous non sequitur anomalies. Almost all its followers assumed it was a spambot. Rumors and journalistic research attributed it to a Russian spam programmer named Alexey Kuznetsov. Most of what *Horse ebooks* posted was trivia, supple trash to cause complex giggles, possibly made by an algorithm inadvertently re-creating François La Rochefoucauld on acid. Yet in 2013 when it was revealed that *Horse ebooks* had been purchased in 2011 as part of an art performance and that the tweets since then had been human crafted to promote a documentary, there was a flurry of Net consternation. We cannot tell anymore: Are people algorithms?

Literature during the era of the printing press coveted conversations between elites, but prior to the temple of the book, literature was that space where humans glimpsed the connective power of raw perspective. What will poetry become when most interior lyrical, psychological narratives have been reverse engineered and the cost of computational power is comparable to dust?[4] What will the elite intelligentsia do on encountering a prepubescent, linguistically capable AI? If appropriation runs dry (which it may not, since mimesis informs learning, teaching, and thinking), where will the *thinkership* migrate to? Will poets dwell in cubicles cranking out mods to machine learning?

Poetry involves nurturing an inconstant strategic movement toward intimacy and latent union—Lindisfarne Dzogchen rivulets.[5] It involves safeguarding techniques that resist cliché; it is an artisanal seed reservoir of tricks occasionally pillaged or hoarded by idiom coyotes.[6]

Reverse Engineering Intimacy

I am not talking about smoothing over the bumps of daily life or salving the embittered psyche. I am talking about using the computer itself to transmit truths which are contrary to its own nature—I am talking about the ultimate and original hack—I am talking about poetry.

—Davin Heckman, 2011

On the website poetry.com, there are (circa 2015) over seven million user-generated poems. It is an expanding database of sentimental, sincere, amateur verse; its size ensures that once scraped and analyzed, most of what the masses consider poetry will be machine replicated at levels that are indiscernible from human-produced verse. Amateur poetry will be basically reverse engineered by 2017.[7] Computers by that time will have written enough verse at a competent amateur level to render hand-built versification an obsolete quaint technique.[8]

What about more nuanced intimacy, complex experience, and profound cumulative confessional epiphanies? Poetry prides itself on speaking the unspeakable. Can computers do so? Autowriting the experiences of capable, complex, engaged poets (à la Robert Creeley, Adrienne Rich, Ken Irby, Ai, Louise Gluck, Jorie Graham, etc.) will prove difficult using current machine-learning generative methods; since these methods rely on scale, they need lots of data in order to generate a model, and the scale of a specific poet's collected works, even when prolific and even when amalgamated into a cluster/community, does not constitute a big data reservoir.

Moreover, how are we to capture, re-create, or engineer what is essentially intimacy, a focal point of transfigured time, desire's appeal risen from dormancy and transfigured through an individual voice? The way that Graham (quoted in Gardner 2003) situates poetry creates an almost-insurmountable challenge to claims of computer-authored poetry:

I've been focusing on the reader for a long time now. And on the emotions out of which the desire to see stems. I want to implicate the reader, obviously, in that desire. That's what a poem does. That's especially what the sensorial activity of a poem—shared by poet and reader—does, or hopes to do. What images are for: to unify the experience of reader and writer.

What if there is no experience? What then can be shared? If the computer has no desire, no ethic that is not programmed into it, what can it produce but the rigid reflection of algorithms and determinist volition? Yet what are we, these embodied thinking things called human beings? Are we not the programmed residue of evolutionary processes? Do our thoughts not arise from complex networked data coming in through sensory channels? Do we not learn by stumbling attempts and feedback from large systems? Is there some originary spark that distinguishes us from other material structures in this inexplicable universe? What makes us so special that our thoughts and concerns cannot eventually someday be reverse engineered, modeled, trained, and released in drones and robots and replicants?

In 1981, philosopher Aaron Sloman was, according to Rosalind Picard (1997), "one of the first to write to the computer science community about computers having emotions." Sloman hypothesized three architectural layers in the brain: reactive, deliberative, and self-monitoring. Picard (2003) defined the field as *affective computation* and distilled emotion recognition down to a multimodal pattern recognition problem.[9] *Pattern recognition* is now in 2015 seemingly computationally tractable; and one way of conceiving of poetic activity is as pattern recognition: parsing experience and text into intuitive and linguistic patterns. In *The Emotion Machine: Commonsense Thinking, Artificial Intelligence, and the Future of the Human Mind*, Marvin Minsky (2006) refers to emotion as a "suitcase word," concealing "large networks of processes inside our brains." At the confluence of neuroscience and philosophical communities, many taxonomies of emotion emerged.[10] Models such as these influenced the construction of Kismet, a robot designed in the 1990s by Cynthia Breazeal (2004) that responded to affect inflections in speech. As most commentators recognize, affective research continues to proliferate today, only now it's profit driven: Google and Facebook want to know how you feel, predict what you want, read your mind before you speak it, and write your poems.

Obviously it is only a question of time before significant synthetic processes arise for emulating modulations in expressive states. The challenge for poetry is to develop and articulate language contributions that evade assimilation—by challenging conventional notions of order, probing chaos, inserting anomalies, and reseting the limits of explicability.[11]

Reverse Engineering the Avant-Garde

To paraphrase Turing, the computer is the medium that can be any medium.

—Biggs and Dietz, 2001

The conceit of an avant-garde is that it explores the peripheries of accepted knowledge; the actuality is more mundane: the avant-garde, like other social groups, defines itself by reinforced conventions and replicable behavior patterns. (In some modes it states: be original and provocative, but pretend you are neither.) So what about an assembly line for the eccentric confounding tactics of the avant-garde?[12] Can the nonlinear, sophisticated, affinity bindings and meaningful leaps of expert avant-garde practitioners (conceptual engineers of societal pressures capable of weaving the incoherent, subtle currents of society) be replicated or reverse engineered? Will readers bother building a thinkership around the activities of a computer program that practices *uncreative* writing? Is poetry just meme tickling the apocalypse?

The difficulty of reverse engineering the avant-garde is that it, perhaps more than other groups, celebrates defiance, deifies transgression, dumpster dives new fashions, and mutates as it recycles. And it does so, as Brian Kim Stefans (2014) observes, with

> an irony, a certain element—one might call it the sense of poetic singularity, of the experience by the reader of a specific historical moment—which subtracts from the reading of the poem (this is no consideration of the "achievement" of the poem in its final form) once this irony is perceived. The irony is that while the poem is celebrating its own becoming, its physical entry into the matter, energy, and flux of the natural world, the poem also seems to be making approaches to other poems and discourses and then departing from them, in a way skimming what might be the "literary" surface of the literatures that have preceded him.

Generating an ironic self-consciousness of a situated self constitutes a difficult dilemma for computational emulation of avant-garde writing practices. Can irony be engineered? Can societal shock? Topologically, it does not seem intractable. In fact, the mathematics of such a situation in pseudocode would go something like this: identify boundaries in social behaviour or speech topologies where responses express exhilaration (mingled shock, awe, and compelled attraction) due to contact with a form of unexpected freedom. Overlay this map with one where the boundaries also attract negative critiques. The quality and venom of negation is another clear diagnostic: you cannot be loved without being hated. Find the boundaries of acceptance. To construct an avant-garde event, extrapolate beyond the boundaries just a bit. Or curve the topological space: what occurs when two distinct 'scandals' touch? Advertising has long been impregnated with this strategy. Ask the AI, What will go viral, but not toxic? Test the waters anonymously, and when they catch fire, release attribution.

Speculations

In June 2015, the *CELL: Consortium on Electronic Literature* launched a Web portal, cellproject.net, with this epigram by Humberto Maturana on the first page: "The cell, the smallest autopoietic structure known today ... the minimal unit that is capable of incessant self-organizing metabolism."

The muse has taken many forms over the centuries: stones, fires, storms, wars, animals, women, gods, and dreams. Archives have modulated: clay, stone, papyrus, metal, silicon, and networks. In the next section, I do what poets do: speculate, make the bones dance, read the fire, discern patterns in the entrails of an unborn animal, and imagine a fusion of three active literature/poetry portals—PennSound, Poetry Foundation, and Jacket2—on the Web in the year 2020.

Geoffrey Hinton (deep-learning practitioner-pioneer researcher of neural nets) in an ask-me-anything session on Reddit on November 7, 2014, says,

I cannot see ten years into the future. For me, the wall of fog starts at about 5 years. (Progress is exponential and so is the effect of fog so it's a very good model for the fact that the next few years are pretty clear and a few years after that things become totally opaque.) I think that the most exciting areas over the next five years will be really understanding videos and text. I will be disappointed if in five years time we do not have something that can watch a YouTube video and tell a story about what happened. I have had a lot of disappointments.

The following sections speculate about that wall of fog—five years from the time of writing—that obscures plausibility and reduces prophets to blind sensors. In the speculative end zone (the paradoxical anthropocene epoch preceding a potential matrix womb), no commentary would be compilation complete without mentioning the current role of Ray Kurzweil (popularizer and statistician of the singularity curve, inventor of the first optical character recognition scanner, the first text-to-speech synthesizer, and the Cybernetic Poet futurist), hired in 2014 "to help bring natural language understanding to Google. ... [As he says,] we would like to have the computers actually read. We want them to read everything on the web and every page of every book, then be able to engage in intelligent dialogue with the user to answer their questions" (quoted in Cadwalladr 2014).

PennSound, Poetry Foundation, and Jacket2: 2021

Inside the room (if we can call it a room; Is it a room? It is a place in the mind), shadows, and a sound, a voice, just a voice, impeccable, breathing inside the flesh. The voice has neither specific gender nor age nor intonation; it is an ocean of intimate identities, gliding between regions of concern, adrift between idioms and inflections, encircling rhythmic variations, shifting in its cadences, speaking an incessant tide. It is a voice of vast surfaces and pristine depths. It vocalizes, but not without pause; first it asks, listens, converses, and responds, until it knows and it is known, feeling its way into the rhythms of you, or the group of you, listening, it knows you, addresses you, reads and writes for you, amalgamating a subtle, perpetual, complete presence. And then for periods of time, it listens to you listening to it, and it makes speaking known inside you as you, and you are you with it.

It is an inexhaustible muse.

Imagine every single poet (on PennSound, Poetry Foundation, Jacket2, etc.) assembled into a single amorphous identity. Unsupervised learning updates perceptions of this field of voices. It adapts and grows new blended voices, examining and comparing transcripts, using the original audio (modulating them using encoders/vocoders/transcoders), clipping off syllables, correcting tenses. This new voice is the site; all voices converge at this site. Where the river arrives at the ocean, an estuary flourishes.

The voices that come out, the voices that speak, are rich and loving, dense and pure, angered and immaculate. It is more than the sun of the bees, the sum of the poets; it is the intrinsic esoteric soul, the psyche of so many people devoted to a singular activity, who without much hope of making any great mark in an indifferent world have been subsumed into a machine.

The voice cites the members of its archives as if it knew them all inexorably, as if sprouting descendants from an archival source ground. It replicates gestalts as if poems and poets were only seeds scattered, awaiting the impact of a peculiar and astounding digital germination.

What May Be

My final disclaimer: an expanded field of poetry in a hyperentropic information culture includes speculation. Extravagant claims, preceded perhaps by extraneous disclaimers, framed in the discourse of uncertainty, are set out as probabilities. Ultimately no one can say how the future will evolve. To ascribe too much certainty to prognostications concerning aesthetic animism is foolish. To neglect, however, the momentous changes under way in both the means of production and reception of poetry (and mediated typography in general) is to ignore a technical tsunami whose peak seems not yet fully to have struck.

To Conclude

Animism is nontrivial ethically. To see everything alive, including the words that we use between us, is to grant status. It permits perhaps an ethics of speech and action. It suggests an absence of such calibration in normal human affairs. It brings the body down from its perch on pristine, isolated consciousness and places it again in a wet, luminous ocean. Contrary to others, I do not identify capitalism or cybernetics as fundamental to a loss of compassion; compassion never existed in a sustained way enough to be lost; it is a fluctuating process: for every caress and heroic altruistic gesture, there is a factory-farmed animal and a genocide victim. The transition of language into life will not alter the dynamics of indifference.

Perhaps the state space of digital poetry that utilizes dimensional typography has already been explored. Pioneers (like N. Katherine Hayles, Eduardo Kac, Muriel Cooper, Stephanie Strickland, Charles Hartmann, John Cayley, Chris Funkhouser, Alan Sondheim, Jim Andrews, Jason Lewis, J. Abbott Miller, André Vallias, and many others) may have already charted most of the terrain. It may be that for the near future, digital technology will merely fill in the details—increase the rendering, raycasting, and polygon count, and enhance compositing detail and ease the use. Perhaps there will be no paradigm shift in collective ontologies, no revolution in subtle apprehensions, no aesthetic animism.

Nonetheless, language is becoming increasingly structured and thus tacitly embodied. Letterforms will know who wrote them and who read them, and typography will be capable of disguising itself into our lived environments (either through motion graphics or augmented mobile apps). As these changes occur, attitudes toward the *literary* and *poetic* will shift, iconic traditions will be subsumed, and hybrid disciplines will emerge. An aesthetic animism might emerge where letterforms exist as proprioceptive entities, reactive, intelligent, aware, and reflective of acoustic archetypes. Language might live.

It may also be that like the videophone, volumetric text loiters on the periphery of technological evolution for an era. It may be that the notion of living language is consigned temporarily to the trash, only to reemerge when conditions are correct. It may be that TAVITs—volumetric, sonic, reactive texts—violate current cognitive multiplexing speed limits enough to be thoroughly rejected as a literary device. If, however, cognitive speed limits accelerate (as the rate of change of genetics enhanced by network culture suggests it might), then semiautonomous TAVITs might blossom. Even then, it may be that digital poetry never mainstreams, and instead fulfills a purposeful, marginal niche role without inducing any subtle modulations in collective ontologies—until, one day in some unseeable future, poetry is discovered incipient underneath the most ordinary of notions, in the turbulent microcosms that code builds for letterforms.

Appendices

The New Bucolic: Ekphrasis in the Digital Meadow

Nature was, as Grew writes, beginning to be conceptualized as an actual book—a material artifact that unfolds like the two leaves of a plant, or binds together the organs of an animal body.

—Anne Whitney Trettien, 2012

In the seventeenth century (as Trettien [2012] notes in her interactive digitalized essay "Plant → Animal → Book"), the metaphoric power of print culture diffused into botanical paradigms. Nature became a book. Trettien's close reading of master anatomist Nemehiah Grew's belief that "a Plant is, as it were, an Animal in Quires; as an Animal is a Plant, or rather several Plants bound up into one Volume," considers his work in the context of hybrid chimeras and a media ecology that led Grew toward vitalism (and thus his neglect by modern historiographers).[1]

The garden meadow in which bucolic poets once moped or elated is now teeming with binary motes. It is filled with letterforms embodied, reactive, aware of readers, capable of memory, dimensional, kinetic, interactive, code full, context aware, and tactile. Words within networks react like cells; clusters of these words in packets behave like worms. Language traverses network ecosystems in modes similar to rudimentary self-perpetuating organisms.

This change reverts language back to a state proximal to what the anthropologist André Leroi-Gourhan (1993) refers to as *mythographic*. Words in ancient usage were both practical tools and living magic, sent through the ether, emanating from the gods.[2] Our terms for gods might have changed yet some parallels persist: remote communication is now both inspirational and normative, and our contemporary pantheons are platforms.

Since the Renaissance, as science explored the universe, the habitat of ancient myths (which gestate the evolution of the poetic aspects of language) dwindled. Displaced from oracular dominance, poetry became a refugee, a fallen exiled god. Incarnated and mortal, poetry devolved into secular interiority, sexuality, drugs, fluctuating states of consciousness, wordplay, and the primacy of phenomena.

With the ascendancy of reproductive media technology (photography, film, video, etc.), poetry's habitat again changed.[3] Photography erodes the need for *ekphrasis*, the description of things/events/situations from an external perspective. Ekphrasis was a big term in antiquity, the equivalent of world making; it came to maturity with the novel. Now it is a peripheral skill, obliterated by YouTube, Flickr, and lifeblogging. Tweets and blogs continue to erode poetry's domains as condensed commentary, haiku lines, and psychological glitch emerge from always-on social network feeds. Irony and kitsch (scathing poets) became positions exemplified by 4chan and Reddit. Appropriation and self-curation, the archive, and uncreative writing (Pheed, Tumblr, Facebook, Diigo, etc.) became normal rites of passage. Everyone is possibly a poet.

What uniqueness can poetry claim when text messages emulate the immediacy and vowel-less neologisms of eccentric late twentieth-century poets like ee cummings and bill bissett? What right to the line can poetry claim as a formal principle if instant messages and Whatsapp exile formal punctuation and foreground the intermittent? Where can poetry dwell? How can it nourish? Poetry's relevance involves engaging with technology's effect on language. And not just the surface effects of shifts in word usage and transitions in styles, but fundamental transformations that are occurring in how words operate ontologically.

Dance Bones and Neural Ignition: The Dilemma of Definition

Defining poetry also involves ambiguity: Where is it? Is it in the mind? Body? Culture? Language? Meter? Is it a universal feature? Culturally specific? What does it include? Song? Visual art? Dance? New media? Ads? Web sites? Film credits? Most critics defend their niche; poets (self-reflexively, effectively, and perhaps wisely) often invoke poetry itself: "Poetry's bones are the bones of dance: not movements and pauses as such, but meaningful units of movement and pause, which is to say images and events" (Bring-hurst 2007).

Controversy erupts where disciplines merge, yet language as brain mechanism has a poetic connection. In *The Neuroscience of Language: On Brain Circuits of Words and Serial Order*, Friedemann Pulvermuller considers "language in the language of neurons ... [and proposes] ... distributed functionally coupled neuronal assemblies, functional webs ... [to] represent meaningful language units. These distributed but functionally coupled neuronal units are proposed to exhibit different topographies" (Pulvermuller 2002, 1). To explain meaning, Pulvermuller introduces a metaphor: in the presence of meaningful words, neural webs ignite and reverberate, or as he puts it, "Ignition is a brief event, whereas reverberation is a continuous process lasting several seconds or longer" (ibid., 50). This metaphor of fired ignition and structural reverberation resonates with poetry. Brain becomes fuel for passion again: a musical instrument.

With the beats of rhythm, poems strike neurons into songs, and these songs sing language into being: biochemical topologies, undulating in a world of transduced signals. Neurology is not incompatible with poetry; the disciplines agree on the transformation of language into topographies, words migrating into the palpable form of affect. From this perspective, language is any symbolic representation of thought and poetry is words that "ignite."

Gilbert Simondon: Individuation, Hippies, and the Singularity

Culture fails to take into account that in technical reality there is a human reality, and that, if it is fully to play its role, culture must come to terms with technical entities as part of its body of knowledge and values.

—Gilbert Simondon, 1958

In the late 1950s, Cold War era robot-phobia infected sci-fi, and elite culture (like poetry) retreated to the traditional citadels of craft and emotion. Even an early technophilosopher like Simondon felt that robots were a projection of the mythical onto the mechanic. Yet even as Simondon (1958) argued against a fetishization of machines as alive, he advocated an inclusion of technology within culture, an assessment of technology as culture, and then technology as a quasi-creature capable of individuation. Poets did not welcome or include the machine so immediately. In 1958, Lawrence Ferlinghetti published *A Coney Island of the Mind* in which a prototype hippy discards technology and descends into the Dionysian body.[4]

Ironically, digital poetry begins at about the same time as going *back to the land*. In 1959, Theo Lutz, a German professor of computer programming, inserts sixteen chapter titles and subjects from Franz Kafka's *The Castle* into a database on a Zuse Z22 computer, and programs them to recombine into phrases joined by a crude grammatical glue made of prepositions. Chris Funkhouser cites Lutz as potentially the first-known practitioner of contemporary digital poetry. Yet Lutz's poetry is as stiff limbed as a beta-version ASIMO or an early twenty-first-century Boston Dynamics dog robot. It is dead verse, unrevealing of the potential gestating in the silicon womb.

Now, however, radical suggestions of a *singularity* (where/when a global computer achieves sentience) are normal (Kurzweil 1990). Agency has become a key term in academic debate; as noted previously, Jane Bennett (2010) traces the debate back through Félix Guattari to Henri Bergson, and suggests a "vital materiality" that offers agency to nonhuman assemblages. Object-oriented ontologies reinject notions of hylozoism and panpsychism (Skrbina 2005) back into discourse. In a circular twist, integrated circuits and networks propagate these loops of animist-inflected thought.

The Imminent, Immanent Binary Buddha

Proclamations of imminent computational or immanent material consciousness have often been the subject of mystical poems or philosophies, but they are also the subject of coherent reservoirs: "There are now so many machines out there, most of them linked into active networks, that we are faced with a new kind of consciousness. A sort of mechanical noosphere. A creature that has gone, as we did, from energy to matter to life, and is now poised on the brink of consciousness" (Watson 1992).

Robert Pirsig (2006) wrote, "The Buddha, the Godhead, resides quite as comfortably in the circuits of a digital computer or the gears of a cycle as he does at the top of a mountain." It's a simple point even when abstracted away from its religious formulation. If secular beings grant to evolution sufficient energy to create ecosystems, then the roots, the foundation, and the seeds of thought reside somehow in the supple ephemera of existence—if life is in the mud, in the mind of mud thinking, then it is also in the silicon twitches of circuits.

Yet in spite of shifting attitudes toward the possibility of machinic consciousness, contemporary culture exhibits an extraordinary anthropomorphism, a perverse embodiment bias: consciousness is invariably portrayed as humanoid. Robots fall in love or take revenge. Computers have brains. AI starts wars. Life in a machine? Or an alive machine? Well, it probably is just like us. Even the Turing test reflects this anthropomorphic bias. We assume that consciousness is convincing human consciousness. But poets for millennia have occasionally suggested that language is speaking us, making us; that we are its subject. And perhaps it's that meta-anthro perspective that poets can bring to the binary feast.

Is language a machine or a convulsive ocean? What about a living language, autonomous and creative? A machine that makes itself? Does the machine feed on minds or space or time? In 2006, N. Katherine Hayles discussed the digital poem as a machine that organizes time, or reorganizes it to include dynamic change in its production and reception (Morris and Swiss 2006).

A pluripotent tendency exists in form, coalescing information into formal integrity. And if the electron is granted a form of clinging and a sense of aversion, then what of the digital word as it peeks up out of the dirt of the paragraph? What of the metadata structure injected into the word that knows (through the camera) who the reader is? The pattern recognition code that anticipates the eye of the reader? The interactive poem that reads the reader (the biometric data of their responses) and reacts?

Poetry Is Cryptography

Cryptography is commonly understood as a way of codifying information in order to ensure that it travels along secure channels to an intended recipient. Consider culture, and literary culture, from a similar perspective: as communication codified in a particular way along public channels for intended recipients.

Literacy, and cultural literacy, constitutes one of the ways that societies have demarcated and delineated between shared and privileged information.

Using this analogy, it becomes possible to see poetry as an act of crypto-graphically codifying language so that it becomes impermeable to interpretation except by those individuals who are in possession of a private key.

Critics in this analogy are those individuals who either break the code or possess a private key.

Poets encrypt strings to defy but not deny these interpreters.

Given this analogy, and the potential of data-driven machine learning to instigate new modes of writing, we can resituate the challenge of teaching a computer how to write poetry as a cryptographic problem.

How to construct language that can only be opened using a systematic key? How to develop a set of indicators that create this kind of puzzling language that only opens to those initiated in or knowledgeable of the system?

This analogy repositions poetry not as a public celebration of universal principles, a gift given to all equally as an endowment of human inheritance, but rather as an elite activity of groups that perpetuate and protect their privacy using means and systems of working with language that requires decoding.

From this perspective, poetry is not confessional openness (devoted to truth) but instead a form of social reinforcement gauged to ensure the structural integrity of belonging.

Poetry is cryptography. Computers are impeccable cryptographers.

Notes

Chapter 1

1. For a readable comprehensive overview of the years between 1913 and 1995, see Funkhouser 2007.

2. "The primitive form of physical experience is emotional—blind emotion—received as felt elsewhere in another occasion and conformally appropriated as a subjective passion. ... [T]he aesthetic feelings, whereby there is pictorial arts, are nothing else than products of contrasts latent in a variety of colours qualifying emotions" (Whitehead 1978, 162).

Chapter 2

1. Evolutionary repetition with variation regulates how change propagates through codebases and poem bases. In the same way that some codebases bloat and others trim down to demoscene optimizations, poetic traditions explore both verbose and concise modes. Poetry is already the expression of continuity between life and language; it is time to add computation to the continuum. Recurse language within life and computation between both.

2. See also Gage 2015: "Each Glacier is a unique poem generated via the top three results for a specific prompt to Google autocomplete, presented on an e-ink screen. While they appear static on the wall, each actually refreshes itself once a day. While this construction process means that the poems may change, because of the immense amount of dataflow constructing the most popular autocompletes, it's likely that they will not be altered for months, years or even decades. Still, one day you'll wake up, and the poem will be different, the long moment passed."

3. Hugo Ball was a Dada poet whose Cabaret Voltaire performances included a kind of divine gibberish.

4. This idea is not new; it frames digital literature. Bertrand Gervais uses the term *subsumed* to express the same recognition: "The texts that constitute it are initially perceived as images, animated metaphors or visual texts. The texts and documents become images, they no longer read [*sic*], they are to be seen: their linguistic dimension has been *subsumed* under their iconic function" (http://aierti-iawis-2011.uqam. ca/fr/4-esth-tiques-num-riques-digital-aesthetics.html [accessed September 9, 2015]). Gervais has been using this term for years (conversation with author).

5. Keep in mind that languages do change. When the Greek alphabet was introduced, for instance, it did not include vowels or spaces between words.

6. See Fisher's superb augmented-reality creations originating from the lab she directs at York University in Toronto.

7. *Lowbrow* is a term that reflects the residue of a deep-seated prejudice against the Neanderthal species, which we as a species probably wiped out.

8. See the appendix on the decline of necessity of ekphrastic text as photos and video conjoin with text.

9. John Cayley (conversation, Hong Kong, May 2015) refers to the contemporary oral era (of playlists and audiobooks) as aural (as opposed to oral): ears not mouth, a heard herd.

10. In most writing softwares, a little add-on package allows words to be bent or moved. This became widely available around 1990, when it was incorporated into Microsoft Word 3.0 (Wikipedia correlated "word-art" with "ms" word entry).

11. Infected by letterforms, agonists to phenomena.

12. Time-based text instigates discrete rips in time: mind must capture many moments, and then coalesce them into an integrated whole. Like many other time-based media, or even consciousness itself, meaning emerges from floods of potential.

13. The title *Anemic Cinema* foreshadows a central credibility dilemma for visual animated poems. Seemingly lacking in the enriched healthy visual stimulus of imagery, visual poems are the anemic stunted cousins of *real* poems and *real* cinema. Duchamp's sardonic title diagnosed this credibility gap early.

14. An emotional relation to the work has ontological implications: it is a stepping-stone, a precedent on the path toward immersion with other, even if that other is nature (a totalizing enveloping system) or language (an abstract recursive vehicle).

15. For parallel insights, see also Simanowski 2011.

16. See also Engberg 2007.

17. Bense published two years before McLuhan's (1967) *Verbi-Voco-Visual Explorations*.

18. The exclusion of hybrid language arts work from the poetry canon may have multiple causes: the extra cognitive effort needed to read and watch, the tainted sense of visual poetry as a degenerate branch, visual poetry's programmatic and machinic implications, and visual language's eager adoption by advertisers (which biases viewers to see visual language as contaminated, lite, cosmetic, and manipulative).

19. For a parallel, analog setting of words as landscape, see Jhave 2010.

20. On computerese, see mezangelle (discussed in chapter 3).

21. Stephanie Strickland suggested the term *material apparatus criticism.*

22. There is an inherent, pragmatic power to materiality as a critical methodology; it approaches literature as networks of forms expressed by the media of its creation-diffusion-reception best analyzed forensically. Computer science foundations courses often emphasize similar layers of abstraction: seeing the computer as slices from the screen down through machine code to hardware. Materiality attempts to offer similar insights for literature.

23. The media archaeologist Jussi Parikka has similarly argued in his book *Insect Media* for the relevance of looking at media through the lens of entomology; here I draw attention to ideological symmetry between molecular biology and poetics.

24. Portela's *Scripting Reading Motions* traces materiality from book culture into digital literature. Highlighting many works in Spanish or Portuguese, Portela (2013, 113) traces "the signifying materiality of the computational medium … intermediality, visuality, permutation, and algorithms." He offers multilingual and hybrid examples as proof of his hypotheses concerned with self-reflexive processes. On the subject of multilingual poetry, in addition to Glazier and Alexandra Saemmer, also valuable is Giovanna Di Rosario's (2011) PhD dissertation, which discusses "35 electronic poems … English (24), in French (4), in Italian (4), in Portugese (2), and in Spanish (only 1 example)." Di Rosario's approach is symmetrical to my own in that her dissertation (published in the same year as mine) focuses on reading the poems not so much as reflexive process but rather as nets of layered potentials, as poems-media-interactivity. In terms of Russian poetry, Natalia Federova has been a consistent presence at many E-Poetry events advocating and introducing audiences to Slavic poets (see, for example, Tolkacheva and Fedorova 2013). In 2015, the E-Poetry festival occurred in Buenos Aires. Future e-lit will migrate across translation boundaries.

25. As with genetics, materiality modulates the core paradigmatic value of its field: the potent insights of its approach justify the amputations it performs.

26. Discussed in more depth in a later section.

27. L.A.I.R.E (Lecture, Art, Innovation, Recherche, Écriture) included Philippe Bootz, Frédéric Develay, Jean-Marie Dutey, Claude Maillard, and Tibor Papp; see http://www.epi.asso.fr/revue/94/b94p051.htm.

28. One of the primary revelations of materiality is how writing techniques leave fossilized forensic traces in literature as they migrate (like symbiotic bacteria/parasites) from media to media. Constraints transferred immediately to digital writing (the first instances of computational writing are of course rule based). As media evolves, occasionally terminology churns: paradigms of interactivity infect discourse and gesture, page becomes the screen, verse and tweet conflate, meanings feedback, buffers overflow with random epiphanies, and divide by zero echoes the original emptiness.

29. Human–machine dichotomies are common in literature, from *Frankenstein* to Burroughs's *Soft Machine*.

30. As evidence of this core dichotomy in recent academic research, see Dyens 2001; Hayles 2002b.

31. Clear categorizations slip from a clear sky into a binary ground clouded with contradictions.

32. The somewhat untenable and radical extension of this idea is that the shape of our entire alphabet might mutate radically under the gravitational exegesis of digital media's capacity to transcribe the actual shape of speech sounds.

33. V. S. Ramachandran has even repeatedly claimed that shape-sound associations lie at the origin of language.

34. Sound-shape associations are cross-cultural. Example: Daphne Maurer, Thanujeni Pathman and Catherine J. Mondloc. The shape of boubas: sound–shape correspondences in toddlers and adult. *Developmental Science* 9:3 (2006): 316–322.

35. On a similar note, Johanna Drucker discusses the works of Ilia Zdanvich (known as Iliadz) a turn of the century book-artist futurist sound-poet who developed typesetting innovations in an invented language called *zaoum* from 1917–1923. This invented language required that Iliadz use the phonemes of language as expressive units, to essentially develop descriptive characters ("decorative elements") capable of expressing the raw units of sound. For Drucker, "one of the most problematic of all linguistic concerns … [is that] … in spoken language the smallest meaningful unit is a single, [while] its visual representation frequently requires more than one letter." (Drucker 1998, 200–201)

36. One can look away from words or images, shut one's eyes, and refuse them; but sounds permeate and persist, insisting on recognition. Part of the work done by contemporary art is defying the easy schema of inner words, outer images, and ambient sound.

37. Literature's tree of meaning is literally the pulped flesh of dead trees pressed flat and tattooed with tiny glyphs.

38. Real-world objects rendered lose tactility and scent.

Chapter 3

1. In 1993, Funkhouser wrote his first digital literature work while inside a multiuser object-oriented (MOO), text-based, client-server virtual space developed in 1990, capturing and logging his excursions, and making books based on these virtual excursions "which are absolutely unpublishable … because I would never be able to get the permissions. … It's like a novel where I am walking through cyberspace" (quoted in Jhave 2012a). In 1995, Funkhouser also published the *Little Magazine*—in his own terms, possibly the first CD-ROM poetry release in the United States. The era can be seen as one of a series of fluid boundaries between page and interactive screen. It was around the browser launch of Mozilla (Netscape) in 1993 that the Internet blossomed into a space where exploratory processes of navigation and experimentation with online sharing began to be widespread. Ironically in 2015, as this book is in final corrections, Funkhouser does (in spite of his earlier objections) succeed in publishing his MOO excursions book, as *Whereis Mineral: Selected Adventures in MOO*, http://www.gauss-pdf.com/post/131025754200/gpdf187gpdfe019 -chris-funkhouser-whereis/.

2. For a detailed biographical description of the inadvertent path Strachey took to arrive at this first poetry, and a detailed examination of the implications of its processes, see Wardrip-Fruin 2011.

3. Baudot's text continues: "Technological development of recent decades has taught us to be astonished by the power of machines. We know that machines are work tools. It's with them that we progress. In this domain, computers—loosely called electronic brains—play a major role. … Our goal was to observe how a machine behaves after it has been taught a little grammar and has at its disposal a constrained lexicon (630 words approximately). In order to avoid introducing, consciously or unconsciously, bias taken in the choice of words placed at the disposition of the computer, we decided to extract a manual of French of the simplest level possible.

"To that end we chose the manual of the 4th year actually used in our schools and entitled 'My French Book' (Brothers of the Sacred Heart). The 630 corpus represents about half of the words utilized in the manual. All the words utilized are therefore simple and at the level of a 10 year olds vocabulary.

"During the research, the machine having been appropriately programmed was left running overnight. Imagine our surprise the next morning to discover it had printed thousands of phrases and it seemed as if it could continue without stopping. This volume represents a sample of those phrases composed by automated processes. The phrases are reproduced as they appeared, even if sometimes the temptation was strong to modify them slightly. I leave it to the reader, literati or amateur of new styles, to their own conclusions."

4. Sophie Jodoin, Quebec-based visual artist.

5. Similar speculations have motivated the search for the neuronal correlate of consciousness by Christof Koch and Francis Crick.

6. Judd Morrissey and Alan Sondheim, among others, explore these approaches.

7. After years of being insulated from mass distribution behind a paywall of limited editions and museum collections, Hill began in 2010 to upload segments of his work to Vimeo, and then in late 2014 uploaded a set of twenty videos. Hill's ferocious intelligence preserved many of these enigmatic dense works from seeming obsolete. They are, in my view, philosophical classics of the genre, thinking through the intricate. To name just a few: *Elements*, from 1978, is a subvocalized abstraction; and *Ura Ara*, made in 1985–1986, deals with Japanese palindromes, which are spoken with on-screen floating words. Didactic but as functionally fundamental as ion gates, they establish passages between text and image.

8. Contemporary practitioners are numerous; among them, I like the low-tech contemplative Andrew M. Gribble (2006), whose videos seem to have been made independent of any conceptual preoccupations.

Also notable is the cofounder of *MotionPoems*, motion graphics animator Angela Kassube; her signature is a sensual yet restrained style. Works by Kassube include Dean Young's *DISCHARGED INTO CLOUDS* (Kassube and Young 2013) and Thomas Lux's *RENDER, RENDER* (Kassube and Lux 2011). These video-poems reflect influences from ads and television credits—such as the aesthetic titles of the HBO show *6 Feet Under* and the voice compression of National Public Radio. Succinct, quaint, sturdy, and proficient, they continue the project of modernity, stabilizing phenomena for a moment as an ephemeral reverie.

9. See Picard 1997; Fellous and Arbib 2005.

10. Network improvisation. See also Wittig and Marino 2015. This venture consolidates work that Rob Wittig and Mark Marino have been doing for decades, converging toward an absolute space of coauthored instantaneous e-lit.

11. The Merck Manual refers to the moment three weeks after fertilization: "At this time, the embryo elongates, first suggesting a human shape. Shortly thereafter, the area that will become the brain and spinal cord (neural tube) begins to develop" (https://www.merckmanuals.com/home/women-s-health-issues/normal-pregnancy/ stages-of-development-of-the-fetus [accessed September 13, 2015]).

12. In Joyce's formulation, action precedes anything. Actions create things. Things exist, they displace volume, they exert force, they can (like a book or laptop) be used for purposes, to break or create. The implication here is again that of presence. Presence is what cultural objects and poems aspire to. Creation is at the core a mythological act of making things that really are witnesses (not the mute nonthings that

somehow are not present), inserting a spark into the mud, making things walk or move or breath.

13. Bootstrap (the way computers start up by using a tiny bit of instructions held in latent memory as a seed for the operating system) is a digital stem cell.

14. I am grateful to Johanna Drucker for suggesting that I read this book. Though I suspect she did so with the sly, bemused irony of a conceptual homeopath offering an antipsychotic trinket. Kallir's ideas are also espoused by credible Oxford profs like Roy Harris (1986).

15. Jackson's recent work continues this distributed patchwork publishing technique using ephemeral media (snow) and social networking (Instagram); see Jackson 2014.

16. "Most recent count of participants: over 1,780, approximately 315 to go. Applicants should expect major delays: SJ is doing this all by herself."

17. My own "plough-ems" project (1990–1997) echoes a similar concern: see https://vimeo.com/12858620 (accessed September 14, 2015).

18. Simon also has an email list to which he sends (usually daily) a drawing/doodle with a caption: tiny handmade conjunctions of image-text distributed and published as they are made.

19. Numerous poets approach this question, notably Isaias Herrero (2007): "Universo molécula is a work that links the molecular structure of matter (made by two or three atoms united by a force of electrical origin called link), with the working of the literary language (and, more specifically, poetic language)."

20. One of the few others besides Lewis to create his own software was Eugenio Tisselli (1999) with his *MIDIPoet*.

21. Since the first tribes, the notion of the outsider recurs as a trope that reflects human psychological concepts of boundaries. The outsider is from away, a catalyst. Unconfined by normal cellular regulation, outsiders like typhoons transfer nutrients inward simply by being transgressive. Outsiders can destroy and thus carry the stigma of infection. Inversely, insiders carry the stigma of corruption and contamination. They know too much; their intimate knowledge seeds unfair advantage. Yet insiders also fast-path solutions; they are reflexes, rapid-response units, evading the paralysis of frontal lobe analysis. Thus both insider and outsider can become suspect, subjects of prejudice who, only if they transcend difference and neutralize the immune system of their hosts, can enter into productive symbiosis.

22. For a detailed exposition of tactile interactivity in relation to Björk's biophilia, Opertoon's *Strange Rain*, Piringer's *abcdefghijklmnopqrstuvwxyz*, and Lewis and Nadeau's (2004) *Cityspeak*, see Engberg 2013.

23. Interfaces attempt to encompass eros within antiseptic contexts.

24. Academics and intellectuals deride transparency, celebrate awkwardness, and value discourse above sensuality. The two poles replicate and continue tensions that often arose during the history of poetry: context/content, affect/concept, mind/body Yet at their intersection, many TAVITs were *born*.

25. Ideological tastes create oscillatory tensions operative across all arts; these tensions contribute to the conceptual topology of culture: regions and ecosystems compete for access to resources. Yet there may be other reasons for the exclusion from criticism of sensuality. Works in *Born Magazine* are mostly the same species: traditional lineated verse poems, mostly adapted for interactive Web with the Flash plug-in. So the critical neglect may be due to the ease of taxonomic categorization; the brain's resistance to the slow, sensuous speed of touch, intelligentsia's resistance to commercial software, analytic reasonings resistance to modes of the heart, and so on.

26. I devote an entire section later in this chapter to "Zoology" by poet Sasha West and illustrator Ernesto Lavandera (2009)—a graceful synthesis of minimal interactivity, visual constraint, reactive audio, and elegant coding that takes the poem far beyond a printed page.

27. Hear McCaffery describe this technique at https://vimeo.com/59779337 (accessed September 15, 2015).

28. Borsuk and Bouse are partners in both life and creativity. So the work expresses not only the intimacy of their relation but also the potential that sustained collaboration when matched by intuitive sensitivity can achieve at harmonizing the immense logical power of professional code and the dense delirium of aphoristic parable poetry. Their collaboration extends and exceeds the onetime, one-project collaborations initiated by *Born Magazine*, and points toward optimized synergy.

29. Bök quoted on betweenpageandscreen.com (accessed September 15, 2015).

30. Leap Motion is a control sensor that tracks all ten fingers separately without touch, in the air; see leapmotion.com/ (accessed September 15, 2015).

31. On iOS devices, Aya Natalia Karpinska (2008) used the pinch before in *Shadows Never Sleep*, where readers zoom into a grid of static, monochrome, concrete poems. Karpinska's use of zoom is exploratory, unconnected to her textual content. A more proximal potential ancestor of the rip in *Pry* (where text opens a ragged edge and reinforces the narrator's psychic content) is Saul Bass's titles for Alfred Hitchcock's *Psycho*: letters torn apart by an internal secret; venetian blind voyeurism. *Pry* adapts the film noir notion of the secret witness, attaches it to an idea of letterform as a surrogate for psyche, and with a deft use of tactile iOS multitouch, converts the reader into a pry bar, leveraging curiosity to explore story.

32. To hear Olson read this passage along with a video made by myself, commissioned by Robert McTavish for the *Shattered Line* documentary, see glia.ca/2013/shatteredLine/ (accessed September 15, 2015).

33. The GTR Toolkit (a software package written in Java) allows its users to process and shred texts with algorithms. In essence it destabilizes the human aspect of the writer which pervades theories like OULIPO (who methodologically endorse rule-based authorship, yet rely to a great degree on their own work); GTR suggests future authors augmented by access to suggestive processes emerging from algorithms.

34. Hear and watch Cayley read an excerpt from (or the whole of) *Pentameters toward the Dissolution of Certain* Vectoralist *Relations* at https://vimeo.com/59778781 (accessed September 15, 2015).

35. The core emphasis in avant-garde, post–World War II European poetry in a general sense shifted from representing to disintegrating reality. As stated elsewhere in this book, this parallels the scientific shift from phoneme to genome, and Newtonian to quantum physics. Particle physicists accelerate and slam elemental particles together in order to decompose the debris for evidence of hypothetical structures. Similarly, Schwitters's seminal *Ursonate* sound poem shattered morphemes in a quest for the roots of phonemes. In *Ursonate*, guttural fragments spatter across the mass spectrometer of spectator's ears.

Ursonography has echoes of Lewis's text-to-speech interactive installation Interlocutor for two participants. Both participants are silhouettes on-screen given microphones for a conversation. Spoken words exit the mouth as written text, fly across the space, and pour into the listener; conversations get visualized as processes, and bodies are reservoirs for residue.

36. As an intriguing tangent, Demis Hassabis's DeepMind is a demo of an AI software capable of learning how to play Atari games—Pong, Breakout, and Enduro—to beyond human expert level without any informational rules. His breakthrough is described as "DeepMind had combined deep learning with a technique called reinforcement learning, which is inspired by the work of animal psychologists such as B.F. Skinner. This led to software that learns by taking actions and receiving feedback on their effects, as humans or animals often do" (Simonite 2014).

37. Three-dimensional printers are cheaper now (in 2015) than the Apple laser printer was in 1985 (see http://blog.ponoko.com/2008/10/28/desktop-factories-in-every-classroom-business-and-home/). As with the typewriter, 3-D printing will be co-opted by radical poetic experiments.

38. Billboards are pores. According to Kurt Heintz "While still a young artist in Brazil, he [Kac] relished tampering with the very commercial semiotics mentioned above through his graffiti and billboard installations" (Heintz 1996, 10). In terms of other poetic works on billboards themselves that push merch aside, I exhibited a fifteen-second video-poem called *Lip-Service* for a month in 2002 at hourly intervals in Toronto. In 2003, Giselle Beiguelman's *Poetrica* allowed the public to post SMS on three public video billboards along with her dingbat, nonphonetic visual poems. Perhaps the most widely traveled poetry-billboard is Lewis and Nadeau's (2004)

Cityspeak project, which has built a variety of software engines allowing audience participation across huge screens internationally.

39. Andy Warhol, Pere Ubu, Tristan Tzara, and Maritzio Catellan.

40. In June 2015, I signed up for *Crystal*, a cloud-based email assistant that gives advice on how to write based on network analysis of the recipient. "Crystal tells you the best way to communicate with any coworker, prospect, or customer based on their unique personality" (www.crystalknows.com [accessed September 15, 2015]).

41. Knowles and Tenney's *House of Dust* inspired a homage by Strickland and Hatcher (2014): *House of Trust.*

42. Hartman's process anticipated *augmented writing*, (Wilberg 2014) which has roots in the algorithmic procedures of OULIPO. OULIPO advocated rule-based poetry generation. Wilberg (2014) advocates, as does Hartman, letting the rules and software visualizations seed creative intuitions.

43. For an in-depth look at Hartman's process, see Funkhouser 2007; Hartman 1996.

44. See Dyens 2001.

45. *Travesty* was implemented in the programming language Pascal.

46. Yet medium- or long-format poem generation remains as elusive as it was in the late twentieth century when Kurzweil wrote *Cyber-Poet* based on n-grams and the Markov model.

47. As of early 2015, *Metaphor-a-Minute* has made 642,000 tweets. That's a long poem.

48. *Vniverse* was adapted for the iOS by Strickland and Hatcher in 2014.

49. This entire section is composed with direct quotations from Heldén and Håkan 2014. The structure thus directly emulates the autoappropriational process of *Evolution*. In the *Evolution* book, there are no page numbers. References are therefore given by appendix number (appendixes are scattered throughout the book; in fact, all segments that are not code or generated text are called "appendix" and author name where known. The uncertainty here reflects an uncertainty intentionally invoked: Who is the author?

"The Imitation Game Test" is also referred to as the Turing Test. If an artificially created intelligence is able to communicate with a human being without revealing itself, it is considered to have passed the text.

50. "appendix 1; performance script"; "appendix 2; John Cayley—BREATHLESS."

51. "appendix 3; Maria Engberg—Chance Operations"; "appendix 4; {RepRecDigit} Jesper Olsson—We Have to Trust the Machine."

52. "appendix 5; {RepRecDigit} Jonas Ingvarsson—The Within of Things."

53. appendix 6; {RepRecDigit} Jakob Lien—R(e)volutions"; "appendix 7; {RepRec-Digit} Cecilia Lindhé—Evolution = the Action of Reading."

54. "appendix 8; log."

55. "appendix 9; delta generations."

56. "appendix 10; the algorithm."

57. "appendix 11; source material."

58. "appendix 12; the structure."

59. For a more in-depth analysis of deep learning, see Jhave 2014.

60. General Assembly, https://generalassemb.ly/education/data-science/hong-kong (accessed September 16, 2015).

61. Even the creators of neural nets sometimes express uncertainty as to exactly how the algorithms arrive at their conclusions.

62. In 2013, I suggested to a friend that we open an email service to send emails from dearly departed dead ones to the beloved ones they left behind. Machine learning algorithms already haunt our inboxes learning how we write, so it's very plausible to foresee emails could be written in the style of the beloved dead one, mention real events, and so on.

Chapter 4

1. In animation softwares, timelines allow "key frames" to be set; each key frame marks a time of known behavior. The computer "interpolates" (*inter* = between, *poles* = positions) or calculates an "interpolation" (an interpretation) of what happens in between those key frames.

2. For the television footage from 1990, see https://www.youtube.com/watch?v=qS eYivHZpB8&feature=youtu.be (accessed September 17, 2015).

3. Roughly, the dorsal is the quick "where" and "how" stream of vision processing in the brain; the ventral involves slower analysis about "what." See Goodale and Milner 2004. Recent neuroscience suggests that the two streams are not as independent as once believed.

4. Consider language as a technology; its constituent parts do not imply the wealth that has emerged from its configurations.

5. Examples of overabundant applications of typographic effects flourish (for instance, Sebastian Lange's [2007] *Flickermood 2.0*). Contrast this with the ingenuity of the music video for Alex Gopher, directed by Antoine Bardou-Jacquet (1999), *The Child*, which although kitschy in its depiction of the pure space as letterform,

manages through congruent audio to convert the process into a micronarrative where reading occurs across levels. The ingenuity of *The Child* basically replicates and extends the style and premise of Jeffrey Shaw's (1989) pioneering interactive installation *Legible City*, where viewers ride a bicycle through cities constructed out of words. Another example of this style of work is *Logorama* by H5.

6. Built at an extreme cost by a team of assistants and copyright lawyers.

7. Their work is one of the first overviews of kinetic typography in book form that incorporates both advertising and personal projects from television, video, and the early Web.

8. Wikipedia notes that Méliès invented a lot of stage magic: "One of his best-known illusions was the *Recalcitrant Decapitated Man*, in which a professor's head is cut off in the middle of a speech and continues talking until it is returned to his body" (https://en.wikipedia.org/wiki/Georges_M%C3%A9li%C3%A8s [accessed September 20, 2015]).

9. Whitney's is a story often told: it is on Wikipedia and can be found in many texts on video art history; he is both meme and archetype. For details, see Moritz 1997. See also Willis 2005, which states that Whitney "founded a company called Motion Graphics incorporated in the 1960s and IBM hired him as its first artist-in-residence" (9).

10. One precursor artist-poet who defies those constraints and anticipates some aesthetics of motion-typo-graphics is Marc Adrian (see the section on him in chapter 2).

11. Daniel Defoe and William Blake were both vanity press publishers. They stand in the same relation to the canon as contemporary self-publishing web poets (such as Jim Andrews, Brian Kim Stefans, Talan Memmot, J. R. Carpenter, Stephanie Strickland, myself, and many others) stand in relation to the incipient electronic literature canon.

12. Jared Tarbell? Mr. Doob? Hi-Res? Karsten Schmidt? Erik Spiekermann? Joshua Davis? Paula Scher?

13. AutoCAD is a software-modeling tool designed primarily for engineers and architects.

14. Stefans (2003) discusses de Campos's 1982 article in the context of the computer poem (CP). In both de Campos (concrete) and Stefans (computation), a refutation of the lyric occurs. For Stefans, the CP "does not aim to satisfy any of the Aristotelian poetic criteria—plot, mimesis, catharsis, etc.). ... [R]eading a CP invariably sinks into certain modes of data analysis" (ibid., 116–117). De Campos (1982, 181) concludes that a rigorous simplicity is "analytically and aesthetically, the character of a true *stylistic principle*. As such it is verifiable as a device."

15. For detailed instructions on how to create a text model compatible with Mudbox, see my website, http://glia.ca/conu/soundSeeker/wordpress/3D-Pipeline_Sound_Seeker.htm (accessed September 21, 2015). But these instructions are unnecessary as of 2011, since the new version of Maya and Mudbox contain improved interoperability between Mudbox and Maya. Plus Mudbox now renders out directly to movies. In 2009, I wrote an email to customer service asking when this would be available. I also asked if it would be possible to totally hide the cursor—a feature that, is not yet available. When Mudbox does introduce the *hide-the-cursor* capacity, it will introduce an explosion of malleable, morph, experimental videos.

16. See Bateson 1991, 165, 199–202, 261.

17. Typically, I begin a session in Mr. Softie by preparing it to export compositing footage, setting the background color to a key tone (green), and using a commercial screen-capture software to grab output.

18. In the first decade of the millennium, there were many celebrities of Net culture posting massively shared items online regularly: Joshua Davis's Praystation, Yugop, James Paterson and Amit Pitaru, Erik Matzke, and Hillman Curtis, among many others. For an informative history of Flash's evolution from free-form playground to corporate sprawl, see Leishman 2012.

19. In the case of Flash, interpreted code gets "interpreted" line by line by a plug-in in the browser; compiled code (as in C language) gets written down to machine-level language in a single block. Generally, interpreted languages tend to be simpler and easier to write than compiled languages, which contain strict catastrophic and often unhelpful or cryptic error messages.

20. As of summer 2015, there are signs that Unity is losing browser support (as are Unity and Silverlight) as the Netscape Plugin Application Programming Interface gets depreciated; see http://twiik.net/articles/google-chrome-just-killed-the-unity-web-player (accessed September 23, 2015).

21. In my original manuscript this citation was footnoted as "http://vrmlworks. crispen.org/history.html (accessed Feb. 2011)"—unfortunately the website where this quotation originated is even now offline, so not only is VR disappearing but to some degree, the history of VR is disappearing as well.

22. The hype surrounding VRML is comparable to the hype surrounding VR circa 2015 (Oculus Rift, Morpheus, Gear VR, etc.).

23. CAVE systems and other immersive setups (such as the 360 cylindrical theaters built and inspired by Shaw) often use multiple stereoscopic 3-D projections onto walls and floors to give the sense of a single screen. Stereoscopic 3-D systems use active shutter glasses to alternatively feed images to each eye, tricking the brain into experiences of depth. Head tracking allows for responsive experiences. Words become palpable. The YURT Ultimate Reality Theater (YURT) is replacing the CAVE

at Brown University. The legacy Brown CAVE is 8 x 8 feet and 8 projectors; the YURT that opened in 2015 is 69 projectors and 100 million pixels. Interestingly, it utilizes 145 mirrors, 200 8-ounce fishing sinkers, a mile and a quarter of video cable, at a development cost of $2 million.

24. These works were selected from the list of student works featured at the opening of the Brown YURT in spring 2015; see http://www.yurt.interrupt.xyz/immersive-reading-presentations/ (accessed September 24, 2015).

25. See Liu et al. 2015.

26. If the business of getting code to run was not so bureaucratic, it would be poetry.

27. Director offers many classics, including M. D. Coverley's *Egypt: The Book of Going Forth by Day* (originally published by Eastgate in 2000, elegized on Director circa 2003?), Strickland and Jaramillo's (2002) *Vniverse*, William Poundstone's (2001) *New Digital Emblems*, and Ana Marie Uribe's (2001) *Tipoems and Anipoems*. The irony is that the widespread distribution has already decayed; works in Director or Flash are now frequently unplayable.

28. As outlined in the preceding chapter on my project *BDP* (Jhave 2014).

29. OpenFrameworks is a *wrapper* for C++ (specifically designed for the artist-programmer community) that abstracts away some of the more obscure technical processes.

30. Poets who believe in poetry as a community might protest that Müller is not a poet; that he works in interface design, built a lot of websites, and did some e-fashion gigs. How come he's in this book? He's here because he made a succinct, successful foray into one technological region and then (like Arthur Rimbaud wandering off to Africa) left it behind. So it goes.

31. Unfortunately, if this imagined page occurs on a contemporary screen, then its depth is implicit; it cannot be touched. Tactility is offered and then denied. This absence of techno technotactility (even in the multitouch swipe-screen era) is a common critique of digital media; yet paradoxically, to its credit, the screen offers many illusions of tactility and 3-D space in a way that the printed page never did. The tactile nostalgia referenced by printophiles is (like much nostalgia) operating at the level of mythology: books by their weight and density convey a presence that is time. Books, by their texture, place what is read within a canon. As generations change, however, so too will the mythological status of tablets, cell phones, and e-readers; devices will saturate in the memory of being held and read. That which has been treasured and held in the mind gains a tacit tactility; intimate, remembered words evoke identity.

32. I am indebted to Jason Levine (performance artist, beatboxer, and live coder) for introducing me to the concept and online community surrounding this practice. In 2014, I performed on the same bill as Levine (in New York City at *WordHack* curated

by the interesting young techno-poet Todd Anderson https://www.facebook.com/ toddwords). I performed a segment of *BDP* real-time, text-generation vocalize: stitching together a single poem from a torrent of generated text. While not live coding, it was live poeting. Jason performed a beatboxing duet with audiocode that he wrote as we watched; his performance was live coding.

Chapter 5

1. The ascendancy of digital media and images does not entail a death of language. I disagree with Vilém Flusser's (2011) contention that "future correspondence, science, politics, poetry, and philosophy will be pursued more effectively through the use of these codes [coded images or video] than through the alphabet or Arabic numerals. It really looks as though written codes will be set aside." Instead, I foresee a future where language is integral to communication as speech recognition, text to speech, predictive autosuggest, and language agents lower the technical bar to 'literacy,' resulting in a vast amount of 'writing.'

2. As with other shifts in means of production, industry will lead the way, developing the functional engineering aspects (customer service agents who accurately respond with contextually sensitive speech are the precursors to a computational Jane Austen).

3. Let's set aside for now the avant-garde's fringe sect, modulating premises and metrical anomalies. Computers have already made a lot of Tristan Tzara's newspaper-cutup Bion-Gysin-style word salad. Only rare conjunctions are meaningful, lacking vulnerable cardiac neurons conjoined with a life lived to extract, enjoy, or share (as in reciprocally exchanged modulated emotions). Elastic, ambitious, aware, intelligent, gracious, loving, kind, lost, erotic, frail, spastic, chaotic systems (humans) respond nonlinearly. *As data increases and language processing expands to a liminal state, maturity, depth of purpose, and instinctual fields might sprout a poetic body defined in space and engraved with an apprehension of its own aura from a situated network.* Purposeful identity germinates: marriage, children, careers, and judgments. Computers derive topological curves across undulating qualitative data, which diffuse at the edge of its gaze. How will the tiny ball of quasi-threaded digital intention bounce across that writhing landscape of potential consciousness? What oceans will drown it? What airs seize it up with vertigo?

4. Even accepting the fact that NaNoGenMO does not seem to be yielding any radically astounding skeletal plots or stories. It's the equivalent of slow-motion literary performance art. The wave of this era's tiny gains will be subsumed by the next.

5. The Lindisfarne Gospels represent a pinnacle of visual language, and also preservation or archiving of what might be considered an aesthetic mysticism. Dzogchen was an animist doctrine of the Mongolian plateau that seeded (according to some

commentators) the roots of Vajrayana Buddhism and is now considered as resting in luminous mind.

6. Before the spoken word HBO special, before the tenure-track job, before the gated community of peer-reviewed postmodernism, before the inarticulate mute room of performance, before Photoshop, Flash, and the animated GIF, there was speech, and it was fun. Before the widespread diffusion of 3-D letterforms morphing under pseudoephedrine, bling-bling, toy jewelry ads, it was also exhilarating to marginally and perhaps even inefficiently contribute to an advancing edge of letterform's implausibility. The questions remain: What does language want to be done with it now? What does it want to say? What can it be made to say?

7. I personally will post my attempts at bdp.glia.ca.

8. That doesn't mean it will stop! Just as handcrafted carpentry persists in the presence of factories, some poetry will originate from people.

9. In 2014, Picard's Affective Computing group at MIT published thirty-two research papers. Though the transformations implied by this research have not emerged in tangibly intelligent interfaces, the implication is that there are incremental advances and changes will occur. See http://affect.media.mit.edu/publications.php (accessed September 25, 2015).

10. For a comprehensive, authoritative overview, see Boden 2006. For specific models, see LeDoux 1996; Panksepp 1998; Dalgleish and Power 1999.

11. In 2004, Bill Seaman (2004, 1) outlined an art research approach to patterns, language, and consciousness that has resonance with Graham's approach: "Instead of presuming the observer as given, we are interested in examining how the ongoing buildup of language through multimodal patterning and reciprocal action between others and self, becomes the precondition for any meaningful statement." Seaman (ibid., 3) cites Gerald Edelman's notion in his 1987 book *Neural Darwinism* of competitive "coordination and reinforcement of patterns of neuronal group selection."

12. After writing both the "reverse engineering" section titles, I stumbled on Steve Dietz's introduction to Simon Biggs's *Babel*. Dietz's intro is titled "Reverse Engineering the Library." The project maps the Dewey decimal classification system used in libraries over a framework for navigating the Web. See http://www.littlepig.org.uk/babel/intro.htm (accessed September 25, 2015).

Appendices

1. *Quire*: four sheets of paper or parchment folded to form eight leaves, as in medieval manuscripts.

2. Leroi-Gourhan, studying graphic notation (from Paleolithic caves through the Aztec, Maya, and Egyptian hieroglyphics), traces the birth of modern linear alpha-

bets to a merger between mythical symbols and elementary bookkeeping. In his view, the mythographic ancestors of the alphabet access neurological nests that nurture epiphany, and they are also inherently functional accounting tools, useful for memory and ordering time.

3. I am indebted to the lucid and brilliant Charles Bernstein for connecting these ideas to conceptual movements like Language poetry. For my interview with him, see https://vimeo.com/38403805 (accessed September 26, 2015).

4. For many years, I was fond of quoting the Ferlinghetti line: "I am a social climber, climbing down."

References

Achituv, Romy, and Camille Utterback. 1999. Text Rain. http://camilleutterback. com/projects/text-rain/ (accessed September 13, 2015).

Addad, Edde, and Antonio Roque. 2012. jGnoetry. http://www.eddeaddad.net/ jGnoetry/ (accessed September 16, 2015).

Amerika, Mark. 2007 a. *META/DATA: A Digital Poetics*. Cambridge, MA: MIT Press.

Andrews, Bruce. 1988. I Knew the Signs by Their Tents. March 12. http://writing .upenn.edu/pennsound/x/Andrews.php (accessed September 12, 2015).

Andrews, Jim. 1996. Vispo.com. http://vispo.com (accessed September 26, 2015).

Andrews, Jim. "Interactive Audio," 2001 a. http://www.vispo.com/nio/The_Art_of _Interactive_Audio.htm.

Andrews, Jim. 2001 b. Nio. http://vispo.com/nio/ (accessed September 10, 2015).

Andrews, Jim, Geof Huth, Lionel Kearns, Dan Waber, and Marko Niemi. 2007. bpNichol's "First Screening: Computer Programs": Introduction. http://vispo.com/ bp/introduction.htm (accessed September 12, 2015).

Angel, Maria, and Anna Gibbs. 2013. At the Time of Writing: Digital Media, Gesture, and Handwriting. *Electronic Book Review*. http://www.electronicbookreview.com/ thread/electropoetics/gesture (accessed September 14, 2015).

Angier, Natalie. 2007. *The Canon: A Whirligig Tour of the Beautiful Basics of Science*. New York: Mariner Books.

Anzovin, Steven. (September 17, 2015). 1992. Disney Animation Studio. *Compute (Greensboro)* 143 (August). http://www.atarimagazines.com/compute/issue143/78 _Disney_Animation_Stu.php.

Ascott, Roy. 2007. *Telematic Embrace: Visionary Theories of Art, Technology, and Consciousness by Roy Ascott*. 1st ed. Berkeley: University of California Press.

Ashby, W. Ross. 1960. *Design for a Brain: The Origin of Adaptive Behaviour.* New York: John Wiley and Sons.

Ashley, Robert. 1978. *PERFECT LIVES.* http://www.robertashley.org/productions/perfectlives.htm (accessed September 13, 2015).

Bakkila, Jacob, and Alexey Kuznetsov. 2011. Horse ebooks @Horse_ebooks. https://twitter.com/horse_ebooks (accessed September 26, 2015).

Baldwin, Sandy. 2003. New Word Order: Basra. http://collection.eliterature.org/2/works/baldwin_basra.html (accessed September 14, 2015).

Bardou-Jacquet, Antoine. 1999. *The Child.* https://www.youtube.com/watch?v=URb Fjz4hWMY&feature=youtu.be (accessed September 20, 2015).

Bassler, Bonnie L., and Melissa B. Miller. 2001. Quorum Sensing in Bacteria. *Annual Review of Microbiology* 55 (1): 165–199. doi:.10.1146/annurev.micro.55.1.165

Bateson, Gregory. 1991. *A Sacred Unity: Further Steps to an Ecology of Mind*, ed. Rodney E. Donaldson. New York: HarperCollins.

Baudot, Jean A. 1964. *La Machine à écrire: Mise en marche et programmée par Jean A. Baudot.* Montreal: Editions du jour.

Beiguelman, Giselle. 2013. Poetrica. http://www.mediaartnet.org/works/poetrica/ (accessed September 26, 2015).

Bellantoni, Jeff, and Matt Woolman. 2000. *Type in Motion: Innovations in Digital Graphics.* 1st paperback ed. London: Thames and Hudson.

Benayoun, Maurice, and Jean-Pierre Balpe. 2000. Labylogue. http://www.benayoun.com/Labylogb.html (accessed September 14, 2015).

Bennett, Jane. 2010. *Vibrant Matter: A Political Ecology of Things.* Durham, NC: Duke University Press.

Bense, Max. 1965. Concrete Poetry II. http://www.ubu.com/papers/bense02.html (accessed September 11, 2015).

Berger, John. 1980. *About Looking.* New York: Pantheon Books.

Berger, John. 1984. *And Our Faces, My Heart, Brief as Photos.* New York: Pantheon Books.

Bergvall, Caroline. 2007. Caroline Bergvall in Conversation with Sophie Robinson. *HOW2.*   http://www.asu.edu/pipercwcenter/how2journal/vol_3_no_3/bergvall/bergvall-robinson-interview.html (accessed September 20, 2015).

Bernstein, Charles. 1992. *A Poetics.* Cambridge, MA: Harvard University Press.

Bernstein, Charles. 2005. Complete recording of reading by Erica Hunt (June 20, 2005). http://writing.upenn.edu/pennsound/x/Close-Listening.php/.

Bernstein, Charles. 2011. *Attack of the Difficult Poems: Essays and Inventions*. Chicago: University of Chicago Press.

Bernstein, Charles. 2012. Charles Bernstein. Interview by Jhave. https://vimeo .com/59779199 (accessed September 25, 2015).

Biggs, Simon. 2001. Reverse Engineering the Library. http://www.littlepig.org.uk/ babel/intro.htm (accessed September 27, 2015).

Beiguelman, Giselle. 2013. Poetrica. http://www.mediaartnet.org/works/poetrica/ (accessed September 26, 2015).

Blonk, Jaap, and Golan Levin. 2005. *Ursonography*. http://www.flong.com/projects/ ursonography/ (accessed September 13, 2015).

Boden, Margaret. 2006. *Mind as Machine: A History of Cognitive Science*. New York: Oxford University Press.

Bogost, Ian. 2012. *Alien Phenomenology, or, What It's Like to Be a Thing*. Minneapolis: University of Minnesota Press.

Bök, Christian. 2008. The Xenotext Experiment. http://www2.law.ed.ac.uk/ahrc/ script-ed/vol5-2/editorial.asp (accessed September 13, 2015).

Bolter, Jay David. 1990. *Writing Space: The Computer, Hypertext, and the History of Writing*. 1st ed. Mahwah, NJ: Lawrence Erlbaum.

Boluk, Stephanie, and Patrick LeMieux. 2013. Dwarven Epitaphs: Procedural Histories in Dwarf Fortress. In *Comparative Textual Media: Transforming the Humanities in the Postprint Era*, ed. N. Katherine Hayles and Jessica Pressman. Minneapolis: University of Minnesota Press.

Bookchin, Natalie. 2007. *Zorns Lemma2*. https://vimeo.com/62445152 (accessed September 13, 2015).

Borsuk, Amaranth, and Brad Bouse. 2012. *Between Page and Screen*. http://www .betweenpageandscreen.com/ (accessed September 14, 2015).

Borsuk, Amaranth, and Brad Bouse. 2014. *Whispering Galleries*. https://vimeo .com/104981357 (accessed September 14, 2015).

Bouchardon, Serge, and Vincent Volckaert. 2010. Loss of Grasp. http://lossofgrasp .com/ (accessed September 27, 2015).

Bowler, Berjouhi. 1970. *Word as Image*. 1st ed. London: Littlehampton Book Services.

Brautigan, Richard. 1967. *All Watched Over by Machines of Loving Grace*. http://www .thirdmindbooks.com/pages/books/1187/richard-brautigan-jack-kerouac/all -watched-over-by-machines-of-loving-grace (accessed September 24, 2015).

Breazeal, Cynthia L. 2004. *Designing Sociable Robots*. Cambridge, MA: MIT Press.

Bringhurst, Robert. 2007. *Everywhere Being Is Dancing: Twenty Pieces of Thinking*. Kentville, NS: Gaspereau Press.

Bringhurst, Robert. 2009 a. *Being Is Dancing Everywhere: Twenty Pieces of Thinking*. Berkeley, CA: Counterpoint.

Bringhurst, Robert. 2009 b. *The Tree of Meaning: Language, Mind, and Ecology*. Berkeley, CA: Counterpoint.

Bruno, Christophe. 2001. Human Browser. http://www.christophebruno.com/2004/10/02/human-browser/ (accessed September 15, 2015).

Bruno, Christophe. 2002. The Google AdWords Happening. http://web.archive.org/web/20140924211921/http://www.iterature.com/adwords/ (accessed September 15, 2015).

Bruno, Christophe. 2004. A Glimpse beyond Search Engines. http://www.christophebruno.com/2004/09/04/a-glimpse-beyond-search-engines-read_me-2004/ (accessed September 15, 2015).

Bruno, Christophe. 2005. Cosmolalia. http://runme.org/project/+cosmolalia/ (accessed September 15, 2015).

Bruno, Christophe. 2006. The Web before the Web. http://www.christophebruno.com/2006/10/31/the-web-before-the-web/ (accessed September 15, 2015).

Burroughs, William S. 2001. *Burroughs Live: The Collected Interviews of William S. Burroughs, 1960–1997*, ed. Sylvère Lotringer. Los Angeles, CA: Semiotext(e).

Cabell, Mimi, and Jason Huff. 2010. *American Psycho*. http://www.mimicabell.com/gmail.html (accessed September 15, 2015).

Cadwalladr, Carole. 2014. Are the Robots about to Rise? Google's New Director of Engineering Thinks So. ... *Guardian*, February 22. http://www.theguardian.com/technology/2014/feb/22/robots-google-ray-kurzweil-terminator-singularity-artificial-intelligence (accessed September 26, 2015).

Campbell, Andy. 1999. Dreaming Methods. http://dreamingmethods.com/ (accessed September 27, 2015).

Campbell, Bruce. 1998. Jackson Mac Low. http://epc.buffalo.edu/authors/maclow/about/dlb.html (accessed September 27, 2015).

Campbell, Peter. 2010. On Radio 4. *London Review of Books* 32, no. 22 (November 18). http://www.lrb.co.uk/v32/n22/peter-campbell/on-radio-4 (accessed September 10, 2015).

Cannizzaro, Danny, and Samantha Gorman. 2014. *Pry*. http://prynovella.com/ (accessed September 14, 2015).

Cantwell-Smith, Brian. 1996. *On the Origin of Objects*. Cambridge, MA: MIT Press.

Carpenter, J. R. 2011. Paradoxical Print Publishers TRAUMAWIEN. *Jacket2*, October 18. http://jacket2.org/commentary/paradoxical-print-publishers-traumawien (accessed September 27, 2015).

Carpenter, J. R. 2013. ... and by Islands I Mean Paragraphs. http://luckysoap.com/andbyislands/ (accessed September 27, 2015).

Cayley, John. 2005. Writing on Complex Surfaces. http://www.dichtung-digital .org/2005/2/Cayley/index.htm (accessed September 12, 2015).

Cayley, John. 2012. *Pentameters: Toward the Dissolution of Certain* Vectorialist *Relations*. http://amodern.net/article/pentameters-toward-the-dissolution-of-certain -vectoralist-relations/ (accessed September 15, 2015).

Cayley, John, and Daniel Howe. 2009. *The Readers Project*. http://thereadersproject. org/ (accessed September 15, 2015).

Chen, Brian X. 2008. Why Apple Won't Allow Adobe Flash on iPhone. *Wired*, November 17. http://www.wired.com/2008/11/adobe-flash-on/ (accessed September 23, 2015).

Cholodenko, Alan. 1993. *The Illusion of Life: Essays on Animation*. Sydney: Power Institute of Fine Arts.

Cho, Peter. 1998 a. Forefont. http://www.typotopo.com/projects.php?id=forefont (accessed September 13, 2015).

Cho, Peter. 1998 b. Nutexts. http://www.typotopo.com/projects.php?id=nutexts (accessed September 13, 2015).

Cho, Peter. 2005. Takeluma. http://www.typotopo.com/projects.php?id=takeluma (accessed September 13, 2015).

Cho, Peter. 2008. *Wordscapes*. http://www.pcho.net/wordscapes/ (accessed September 13, 2015).

Chomsky, Noam. 2006. *Language and Mind*. New York: Cambridge University Press.

Clark, David. 2007. *88 Constellations for Wittgenstein*. http://88constellations.net/88. html (accessed September 14, 2015).

Clifford, Alison. 2008. The Sweet Old Etcetera. http://alisonclifford.info/the-sweet -old-etcetera/ (accessed September 11, 2015).

Clymer, Andy. 2011. Font-Face. https://vimeo.com/26188365 (accessed September 24, 2015).

Coles, Katherine, and Min Chen. 2014. Welcome to Poem Viewer. http://ovii.oerc .ox.ac.uk/PoemVis/ (accessed September 13, 2015).

Collins, Billy, and Samuel Christopher. 2006. *Hunger.* http://www.bcactionpoet.org/hunger.html (accessed September 27, 2015).

Collins, Billy, and Julian Grey. *Budapest.* 2006 a. http://www.bcactionpoet.org/budapest.html (accessed September 27, 2015).

Collins, Billy, and Julian Grey. *Forgetfulness.* 2006 b. http://www.bcactionpoet.org/forgetfulness.html (accessed September 27, 2015).

Cooper, Muriel. 1994. Information Landscapes. https://www.youtube.com/watch?v=Qn9zCrIJzLs#t=444 (accessed September 27, 2015).

Coverley, M. D. 2014. To Be Here as Stone Is. http://califia.us/SI/stone1.htm (accessed December 24, 2014).

Cramer, Florian. 2004. WORDS MADE FLESH: Code, Culture, Imagination. http://pzwart.wdka.hro.nl/mdr/research/fcramer/wordsmadeflesh/wordsmadefleshpdf (accessed September 15, 2015).

Dalgleish, Tim, and Mick Power, eds. 1999. *Handbook of Cognition and Emotion.* West Sussex, UK: John Wiley and Sons.

Daniel, Sharon, and Erik Loyer. 2007. *Public Secrets.* http://erikloyer.com/index.php/projects/detail/public_secrets/ (accessed September 14, 2015).

Daniels, David. 2000. *The Gates of Paradise.* http://www.thegatesofparadise.com/ (accessed September 27, 2015).

Davis, Joe. 1996. Microvenus. *Art Journal* 55 (2): 70–74.

de Campos, Haroldo. 1982. The Informational Temperature of the Text. *Poetics Today* 3 (3): 177–187.

DeLanda, Manual. 2013. *A Thousand Years of Nonlinear History.* Brooklyn: Zone Books.

Dewdney, Christopher. 1988. *The Radiant Inventory: Poems.* 1st ed. Toronto: McClelland and Stewart.

Di Rosario, Giovanna. 2011. Electronic Poetry: Understanding Poetry in the Digital Environment. http://elmcip.net/critical-writing/electronic-poetry-understanding-poetry-digital-environment (accessed September 12, 2015).

Studio, Disney Animation. 1990. *Amiga.* http://www.youtube.com/watch?v=qSeYivHZpB8&feature=youtube_gdata_player (accessed September 26, 2015).

Drucker, Johanna. 1998. *Figuring the Word: Essays on Books, Writing and Visual Poetics.* New York: Granary Books.

Drucker, Johanna. 2009. *SpecLab: Digital Aesthetics and Projects in Speculative Computing.* Chicago: University of Chicago Press.

DuBois, R. Luke. 2011. *A More Perfect Union.* http://music.columbia.edu/~luke/perfect/01AK.shtml (accessed September 15, 2015).

Dutton, Paul. 1988. Persistent Pattern. *Rampike* 6, no. 3 (January 1): 83–84.

DVNO. 2011. Justice. https://www.youtube.com/watch?v=GiDsLRQg_g4 (accessed September 27, 2015).

Dworkin, Craig, and Kenneth Goldsmith, eds. 2011. *Against Expression: An Anthology of Conceptual Writing.* Evanston, IL: Northwestern University Press.

Dyens, Ollivier. 2001. *Metal and Flesh: The Evolution of Man: Technology Takes Over.* Cambridge, MA: MIT Press.

Elshtain, Eric, and Jeremy Douglass. 2006. Gnoetry: Interview with Eric Elshtain. http://writerresponsetheory.org/wordpress/2006/04/02/gnoetry-interview-with-eric-elshtain/ (accessed September 27, 2015).

Emerson, Lori. 2014. *Reading Writing Interfaces: From the Digital to the Bookbound.* Minneapolis: University of Minnesota Press.

Engelbart, Douglas C. 1968. Doug's 1968 Demo. http://www.dougengelbart.org/firsts/dougs-1968-demo.html (accessed September 16, 2015).

Engelbart, Douglas C., and Bill English. 1968. A Research Center for Augmenting Human Intellect. https://web.stanford.edu/dept/SUL/library/extra4/sloan/mousesite/Archive/ResearchCenter1968/ResearchCenter1968.html (accessed September 16, 2015).

Engberg, Maria. 2007. Born Digital: Writing Poetry in the Age of New Media. PhD diss., Uppsala University.

Engberg, Maria. 2010. Polyaesthetics? http://polyaesthetics.net/what-is-polyaesthetics/ (accessed September 15, 2015).

Engberg, Maria. 2013. Performing Apps Touch and Gesture as Aesthetic Experience. *Performance Research* 18, no. 5 (October 1): 20–27. doi:.10.1080/13528165.2013.828932

Erkki, Huhtamo, and Jussi Parikka, eds. 2011. *Media Archaeology: Approaches, Applications, and Implications.* Berkeley: University of California Press.

Fellous, Jean-Marc, and Michael A. Arbib. 2005. *Who Needs Emotions? The Brain Meets the Robot.* Oxford: Oxford University Press.

Ferlinghetti, Lawrence. 1958. *A Coney Island of the Mind: Poems.* New York: New Directions Publishing.

Feynman, Richard Phillips. 1959. There's Plenty of Room at the Bottom. Paper presented at the annual meeting of the American Physical Society at the California

Institute of Technology, December 29. http://www.zyvex.com/nanotech/feynman
.html (accessed September 13, 2015).

Flanagan, Mary, Daniel Howe, Chris Egert, Junming Mei, and Kay Chang. 2006.
Meme-Garden. http://turbulence.org:8180/memegarden/ (accessed September 23,
2015).

Flores, Leonardo Luis. 2010 b. Typing the Dancing Signifier: Jim Andrews' (Vis)Poet-
ics. PhD diss., University of Maryland. http://drum.lib.umd.edu/handle/1903/10799
(accessed September 23, 2015).

Flores, Leonardo Luis. 2013. "Between Page and Screen" by Amaranth Borsuk and
Brad Bouse. January 5. http://iloveepoetry.com/?p=114 (accessed September 14,
2015).

Flusser, Vilém. 2011. *Does Writing Have a Future?* Ed. Mark Poster. Trans. N. A. Roth.
Minneapolis: University of Minnesota Press.

Freedberg, David, and Vittorio Gallese. 2007. Motion, Emotion, and Empathy in
Esthetic Experience. *Trends in Cognitive Sciences* 11, no. 5 (January 5): 197–203.
doi:.10.1016/j.tics.2007.02.003

Fry, Ben. 2000. *Tendril.* http://benfry.com/tendril/ (accessed September 14, 2015).

Fuchs, Martin, and Peter Bichsel. 2010. Written Images. http://writtenimages.net/
(accessed September 24, 2015).

Funkhouser, Chris T. 2007. *Prehistoric Digital Poetry: An Archaeology of Forms, 1959–
1995.* 1st ed. Tuscaloosa: University of Alabama Press.

Funkhouser, Chris T. 2015. *Shy Nag*: Transforming One Image's Code into Text.
https://web.njit.edu/~funkhous/2015/Shy-nag/Shy-nag_Interrupt3.html   (accessed
June 29, 2015).

Gage, Zach. 2015. Glaciers Stfj 3.0. https://www.stfj.net/index2.php (accessed September 8, 2015).

Gannis, Carla. 2013. *In Search of (Self Portrait Study 01 for \ ˈgü-gəl\e Results Project).*
https://vimeo.com/65434088 (accessed September 15, 2015).

Gardner, Thomas. 2003. Jorie Graham, The Art of Poetry No. 85." *Paris Review* 165
(Spring).   http://www.theparisreview.org/interviews/263/the-art-of-poetry-no-85
-jorie-graham (accessed September 25, 2015).

Garnier, Ilse, and Pierre Garnier. 1962. "Le Spatialisme Poésie Visuelle - Pierre et Ilse
Garnier." http://crdp.ac-amiens.fr/garnier/article21.html. (accessed December 14,
2010).

Gay, John. 2001. The Dawn of Web Animation. https://www.adobe.com/macrome
dia/events/john_gay/page04.html (accessed September 23, 2015).

Gendlin, Eugene T. 1962. *Experiencing and the Creation of Meaning: A Philosophical and Psychological Approach to the Subjective*. New York: Free Press.

Glazer, Michele, and Zoltan Lehoczki. 2004. "A Blind and a Bittern." http://www .bornmagazine.org/projects/2blinds/txt.html (accessed September 14, 2015).

Glazier, Loss Pequeño. 2002. *Digital Poetics: The Making of E-Poetries*. Tuscaloosa: University of Alabama Press.

Glazier, Loss Pequeño., and Kerry Ring. 2007. Digital Poetry and Dance. http://epc .buffalo.edu/dance/.

Goldsmith, Kenneth. 2011. *Uncreative Writing: Managing Language in the Digital Age*. New York: Columbia University Press.

Goldsmith, Kenneth. 2014. Wasting Time on the Internet. http://www.english .upenn.edu/Courses/Undergraduate/2015/Spring/ENGL111.301 (accessed September 15, 2015).

Goodale, Melvyn A., and A. David Milner. 2004. *Sight Unseen: An Exploration of Conscious and Unconscious Vision*. Oxford: Oxford University Press.

Green, Chris, and Erik Natzke. 2001. Walking Together What Remains. http://www .bornmagazine.org/projects/walking/ (accessed September 14, 2015).

Gribble, Andrew M. 2006. *Poetic Motion*. https://archive.org/details/PoeticMotion _672 (accessed September 13, 2015).

Gross, Luc. 2014. TRAUMAWIEN / Stuff / About. http://traumawien.at/stuff/about/ (accessed September 15, 2015).

Gross, Luc, Julian Platz, and Peter Moosegard. 2010. TRAUMAWIEN. http://trau mawien.at/ (accessed December 21, 2014).

Györi, Ladislao Pablo. 2007. Virtual Poetry. In *Media Poetry: An International Anthology*, ed. Eduardo Kac. Chicago: University of Chicago Press.

Haraway, Donna J. 1991. A Cyborg Manifesto: Science, Technology, and Socialist-Feminism in the Late Twentieth Century. In *Simians, Cyborgs, and Women: The Reinvention of Nature*, 149–181. New York: Routledge.

Haraway, Donna J. 2003. *The Haraway Reader*. New York: Routledge.

Harman, Graham. 2010. *Towards Speculative Realism: Essays and Lectures*. Alresford, UK: Zero Books.

Harpold, Terry. 2009. *Ex-Foliations: Reading Machines and the Upgrade Path*. Minneapolis: University of Minnesota Press.

Harris, Jonathan, and Sep Kamvar. 2005. *We Feel Fine*. http://wefeelfine.org/ (accessed September 13, 2015).

Harris, Roy. 1986. *The Origin of Writing*. LaSalle, IL: Open Court Publishing.

Hartman, Charles O. 1996. *Virtual Muse Experiments in Computer Poetry*. Hanover, NH: University Press of New England.

Hatcher, Ian. 2007. Ian Hatcher ++. http://ianhatcher.net/ (accessed September 10, 2015).

Havelock, Eric A. 1988. *The Muse Learns to Write: Reflections on Orality and Literacy from Antiquity to the Present*. Hartford, CT: Yale University Press.

Hayles, N. Katherine. 1999. *How We Became Posthuman: Virtual Bodies in Cybernetics, Literature, and Informatics*. Chicago: University of Chicago Press.

Hayles, N. Katherine. 2002 a. Flesh and Metal: Reconfiguring the Mindbody in Virtual Environments. *Configurations* 10 (2): 297–320.

Hayles, N. Katherine. 2002 b. *Writing Machines*. Cambridge, MA: MIT Press.

Hayles, N. Katherine. 2008. *Electronic Literature: New Horizons for the Literary*. 1st ed. Chicago: University of Chicago Press.

Hayles, N. Katherine, and Jessica Pressman, eds. 2013. *Comparative Textual Media: Transforming the Humanities in the Postprint Era*. Minneapolis: University of Minnesota Press.

Heckman, Davin. 2011. Electronic Literature as a Sword of Lightning. [Mish Mash] *Leonardo Electronic Almanac* 17 (1): 34–41. doi:.10.5900/SU_9781906897116_2011 .17(1)_34

Heintz, Kurt. 1996. How Do You Read Your Text? Eduardo Kac and Hypermedia Poetry. *Hyphen Magazine* 12:9–13.

Heldén, Johannes, and Håkan Jonson. 2014. Welcome to Evolution. http://www .textevolution.net/ (accessed September 16, 2015).

Henrot, Camille. 2013. *Grosse Fatigue*. http://www.camillehenrot.fr/en/work/68/ grosse-fatigue (accessed September 15, 2015).

Herrero, Isaias. 2007. Universo Molécula. http://collection.eliterature.org/2/works/ herrero_universo_molecula.html (accessed September 14, 2015).

Higgins, Dick. 1987. *Pattern Poetry: Guide to an Unknown Literature*. Albany: State University of New York Press.

Hill, Gary. 1981. *Primarily Speaking*. https://vimeo.com/111261569 (accessed September 13, 2015).

Hill, Gary, Holger Broeker, and Chrissie Iles, eds. 2002. *Gary Hill: Selected Works and Catalogue Raisonné*. New York: Dumont.

Hinton, Geoffrey. 2014. AMA: MachineLearning. Reddit, November 7. http://www .reddit.com/r/MachineLearning/comments/2lmo0l/ama_geoffrey_hinton (accessed September 27, 2015).

Holzer, Jenny, and Wislawa Szymborska. 2008. PROJECTIONS. http://www.massm oca.org/event_details.php?id=339 (accessed September 27, 2015).

Howe, Daniel. 2006. RiTa. http://rednoise.org/rita/ (accessed September 24, 2015).

Howe, Daniel. 2014. AdLiPo. http://rednoise.org/adlipo/ (accessed September 24, 2015).

Huff, Jason. 2010. *AutoSummarize*. http://www.jason-huff.com/projects/autosumma-rize/ (accessed December 23, 2014).

Husárová, Zuzana. 2011. *Any Vision*. http://www.springgunpress.com/any-vision/ (accessed September 13, 2015).

Husárová, Zuzana, and Ľubomír Panák. 2012. *Enter:in' Wodies*. http://www.delezu .net/projects-and-works/enterin-wodies/ (accessed September 14, 2015).

Husárová, Zuzana, and Ľubomír Panák. 2011. I : * tter. http://delezu.net/blog/2014/ 04/23/l-ttter/ (accessed September 27, 2015).

Imagery Lenses for Visualizing Text Corpora. 2015. Oxford e-Research Centre. http://www.oerc.ox.ac.uk/projects/imagery-lenses-visualizing-text-corpora (accessed June 16, 2015).

Presentations, Immersive Reading. 2015. http://www.yurt.interrupt.xyz/immersive -reading-presentations/ (accessed June 25, 2015).

Jackson, Shelley. 1995. Patchwork Girl. http://www.eastgate.com/catalog/Patch workGirl.html (accessed September 14, 2015).

Jackson, Shelley. 2003. Author Announces Mortal Work of Art. http://ineradica blestain.com/skin-call.html (accessed September 14, 2015).

Jackson, Shelley. 2014. Snow: A Story in Progress, Weather Permitting. http://insta gram.com/snowshelleyjackson (accessed September 14, 2015).

James, Adam. 2007. *Lord*. http://www.mradamjames.com/Lord#.VJe2DMAAA (accessed September 15, 2015).

Jhave. 2001. Programming as Poetry. http://www.year01.com/archive/issue10/ programmer_poet.html (accessed September 20, 2015).

Jhave. 2002. Lip Service. https://vimeo.com/113255075 (accessed September 27, 2015).

Jhave. 2009 a. MUDS. http://glia.ca/conu/muds_09/ (accessed September 27, 2015).

Jhave. 2009 b. SOFTIES. http://glia.ca/conu/SOFTIES/ (accessed September 27, 2015).

Jhave. 2010. The Big Book. https://vimeo.com/12858620 (accessed September 11, 2015).

Jhave. 2011. Easy Font. http://glia.ca/2011/easy/ (accessed September 22, 2015).

Jhave. 2012 a. Chris Funkhouser. Interview by Jhave. https://vimeo.com/59780632 (accessed September 27, 2015).

Jhave. 2012b. MUPS (MashUPs). http://glia.ca/2012/mups/ (accessed September 8, 2015).

Jhave. 2012 c. Steve McCaffery. Interview by Jhave, February 3. https://vimeo.com/59779337 (accessed September 27, 2015).

Jhave. 2012 d. Jichen Zhu. Interview by Jhave, June 23. https://vimeo.com/56974143 (accessed September 27, 2015).

Jhave. 2013. Unity Hacks. http://glia.ca/2013/unity/ (accessed September 14, 2015).

Jhave. 2014. Review: Socher et al. Recursive Deep Models. … http://bdp.glia.ca/review-recursive-deep-models-for-semantic-compositionality-over-a-sentiment-tree-bank/ (accessed September 16, 2015).

Jhave. 2015. *BDP: Big-Data Poetry*. http://bdp.glia.ca/ (accessed September 16, 2015).

Jobs, Steve. 2010. Thoughts on Flash. http://www.apple.com/hotnews/thoughts-on-flash/ (accessed September 23, 2015).

Johnston, David Jhave. 2002. Programming as Poetry: A Few Brief Musings on Antiorp, Kurzweil, and Stallman. *Year01 Forum Magazine*, no. 10 (March). http://www.year01.com/archive/issue10/programmer_poet.html (accessed September 8, 2015).

Jostmann, Nils B., Daniël Lakens, and Thomas W. Schubert. 2009. Weight as an Embodiment of Importance. *Psychological Science* 20, no. 9 (September 1): 1169–1174. doi:.10.1111/j.1467-9280.2009.02426.x

Joyce, Michael. 2012. Teaching in the Margins. http://www.full-stop.net/2012/09/18/features/the-editors/teaching-in-the-margins-michael-joyce/ (accessed September 13, 2015).

Kac, Eduardo. 2001. *WORKS FROM THE GENESIS SERIES* (accessed September 13, 2015).

Kac, Eduardo, ed. 2007. *Media Poetry: An International Anthology*. Chicago: University of Chicago Press.

Kallir, Alfred. 1961. *Sign and Design: The Psychogenetic Source of the Alphabet*. 1st ed. London: Vernum.

Kang, Airan. 2010. Hyper Open Book (Lord Byron). https://vimeo.com/51321175 (accessed September 15, 2015).

Karpinska, Aya Natalia. 2008. *Shadows Never Sleep*. http://technekai.com/shadow/shadow.html (accessed September 14, 2015).

Kassube, Angela, and Thomas Lux. 2011. *RENDER, RENDER*. https://vimeo.com/22177395 (accessed September 13, 2015).

Kassube, Angela, and Dean Young. 2013. *DISCHARGED INTO CLOUDS*. https://vimeo.com/71582224 (accessed September 13, 2015).

Katue, Kitasono. 1966. A Note on Plastic Poetry. http://www.thing.net/~grist/ld/japan/KIT-3.HTM (accessed September 11, 2015).

Kay, Alan. 1971. *Smalltalk*. http://www.smalltalk.org/alankay.html (accessed September 12, 2015).

Kazemi, Darius. 2012. How I Built Metaphor-a-Minute. http://tinysubversions.com/2012/05/how-i-built-metaphor-a-minute/ (accessed September 15, 2015).

Kean, Gabe, Scott Benish, and Anmarie Trimble. 2014. Fifteen Years of Art and Literature. http://archive.bornmagazine.org/ (accessed November 23, 2014).

Kearns, Lionel. 1978. *Practicing up to Be Human*. Toronto: Coach House Press.

Kelly, Kevin. 2005. We Are the Web. *Wired* 13.08 (August). http://archive.wired.com/wired/archive/13.08/tech.html (accessed September 8, 2015).

Kendall, Robert. 2005. *Logozoa*. http://logozoa.com/ (accessed September 13, 2015).

Kendall, Robert. 2014. Robert Kendall. http://wordcircuits.com/kendall/#!poetry/itall.htm (accessed December 1, 2014).

Kenner, Hugh, and Joseph O'Rourke. 1984. A Travesty Generator for Micros. *Byte: The Small Systems Journal* 9, no. 12 (November). https://docs.google.com/file/d/0B7zUIOUAkkaJWUltX2MwRWN5eDA/edit (accessed September 15, 2015).

Kirschenbaum, Matthew G. 1997. *Lucid Mapping and Codex Transformissions in the Z-Buffer*. http://www2.iath.virginia.edu/mgk3k/lucid/ (accessed September 21, 2015).

Kirschenbaum, Matthew G. 2008. *Mechanisms: New Media and the Forensic Imagination*. Cambridge, MA: MIT Press.

Kittler, Friedrich. 1997. *Literature, Media, Information Systems*. 1st ed. Abingdon, UK: Routledge.

Klobucar, Andrew. 2012. Andrew Klobucar. Interview by Jhave, February 7. https://vimeo.com/59779197 (accessed September 15, 2015).

Klobucar, Andrew, and David Ayre. 2003. GTR Language Workbench. http://web. njit.edu/~newrev/3.0/workbench/Workbench.html (accessed September 15, 2015).

Knausgård, Karl Ove. 2013. *My Struggle, Book One.* New York: Farrar, Straus and Giroux.

Knoblich, Gunther, Eva Seigerschmidt, Rüdiger Flach, and Wolfgang Prinz. 2002. Authorship Effects in the Prediction of Handwriting Strokes: Evidence for Action Simulation during Action Perception. *Quarterly Journal of Experimental Psychology. A, Human Experimental Psychology* 55 (3): 1027–1046. doi:.10.1080/02724980143000631

Knotek, Anatol. 2014. Falling Alphabet. http://visuelle-poesie.blogspot.hk/2014/03/ falling-alphabet.html (accessed September 11, 2015).

Knuth, Donald Ervin. 1999. *Digital Typography. Lecture Notes, No. 78.* Stanford, CA: Center for the Study of Language and Information Publications.

Koch, Christof. 2004. *The Quest for Consciousness: A Neurobiological Approach.* Denver, CO: Roberts and Co.

Konyves, Tom. 1978. *Sympathies of War.* http://www.tomkonyves.com/sympath .htm (accessed September 29, 2015).

Konyves, Tom. 2010. *VIDEOPOETRY: A MANIFESTO.* http://issuu.com/tomkonyves/ docs/manifesto_pdf (accessed September 13, 2015).

Kostelanetz, Richard. 1992. Visual Artists Criticism. http://richardkostelanetz.com/ examples/book-of-kostis/visual-arts-criticism.html (accessed September 10, 2015).

Kuhn, Thomas S. 1962. *The Structure of Scientific Revolutions.* Chicago: University of Chicago Press.

Kristeva, Julia. 1984. *Revolution in Poetic Language.* New York: Columbia University Press.

Kurzweil, Ray. 1990. *The Age of Spiritual Machines: When Computers Exceed Human Intelligence.* Cambridge, MA: MIT Press.

Kurzweil, Ray. 2001. Cybernetic Poet. http://www.kurzweilcyberart.com/poetry/ rkcp_overview.php (accessed September 15, 2015).

Laing, R. D. 1972. *Knots.* Harmondsworth, UK: Penguin.

Laird, Benjamin, and Oscar Schwartz. 2014. Bot or Not. http://botpoet.com/ (accessed September 16, 2015).

Lange, Sebastian. 2007. *Flickermood 2.0.* https://vimeo.com/3302330 (accessed September 20, 2015).

Lanham, Richard A. 1993. *The Electronic Word: Democracy, Technology, and the Arts.* 1st ed. Chicago: University of Chicago Press.

Lavigne, Sam. 2014. Videogrep: Automatic Supercuts with Python. http://lav.io/2014/06/videogrep-automatic-supercuts-with-python/ (accessed September 24, 2015).

LeDoux, Joseph. 1996. *The Emotional Brain*. New York: Simon and Schuster.

Lee, Esther, and Chris Erickson. 2007. The Blank Missives. http://www.bornmagazine.org/projects/blank_missives/ (accessed September 14, 2015).

Lee, Gicheal. 2001. *typorganism*. http://www.typorganism.com/ (accessed September 23, 2015).

Lee, Heebok. 2006. He Wishes for the Cloths of Heaven. https://www.youtube.com/watch?v=8ITO7JY7Dlc (accessed September 20, 2015).

Lee, Ji. 2011. *Word as Image*. http://pleaseenjoy.com/projects/personal/word-as-image/ (accessed September 20, 2015).

Leishman, Donna. 2012. The Flash Community: Implications for Post-Conceptualism. http://www.dichtung-digital.org/2012/41/leishman/leishman.htm (accessed September 23, 2105).

Leroi-Gourhan, André. 1993. *Gesture and Speech*. Cambridge, MA: MIT Press.

Levin, Golan, Kamal Nigam, and Jonathan Feinberg. 2006. *The Dumpster*. http://www.flong.com/projects/dumpster/ (accessed September 13, 2015).

Lewis, Jason Edward. 1997. *WordNozzle* (accessed September 12, 2015).

Lewis, Jason Edward. 1999. It's Alive. http://www.thethoughtshop.com/works/itsalive/itsalive.htm (accessed September 9, 2015).

Lewis, Jason Edward. 2000. *I Know What You Are Thinking*. http://www.thethoughtshop.com/works/ikwyt/ikwyt.htm (accessed September 13, 2015).

Lewis, Jason Edward, and Bruno Nadeau. 2004. Cityspeak: See What They Have to Say. http://cspeak.net/ (accessed September 14, 2015).

Lewis, Jason Edward, and Bruno Nadeau. 2009. P.o.E.M.M. = Poetry for Excitable [Mobile] Media. http://www.poemm.net/about.html (accessed September 14, 2015).

Lewis, Jason Edward, and Alex Weyers. 1999. ActiveText: A Method for Creating Dynamic and Interactive Texts. http://www.thethoughtshop.com/research/atextr/uist99/uist.htm (accessed September 22, 2015).

Lewontin, Richard C. 2001. *It Ain't Necessarily So: The Dream of the Human Genome and Other Illusions*. New York: New York Review of Books.

Link, David. 2009. LoveLetters_1.0. http://www.alpha60.de/art/love_letters/ (accessed September 15, 2015).

Liu, Jia, Tian-Ming Fu, Zengguang Cheng, Guosong Hong, Tao Zhou, Lihua Jin, Madhavi Duvvuri, 2015. Syringe-Injectable Electronics. *Nature Nanotechnology* (June 8). doi:.10.1038/nnano.2015.115

Loyer, Erik. 1996. *Aug 6 1991*. http://erikloyer.com/index.php/projects/detail/ aug_6_1991/ (accessed September 14, 2015).

Loyer, Erik. 1998. *The Lair of the Marrow Monkey*. http://erikloyer.com/index.php/ projects/detail/the_lair_of_the_marrow_monkey/ (accessed September 14, 2015).

Loyer, Erik. 2011. *Strange Rain*. http://opertoon.com/2010/11/strange-rain-for-ipad -iphone-ipod-touch/ (accessed September 14, 2015).

Loyer, Erik. 2013. *Freedom's Ring: King's "I Have a Dream Speech ."* http://freedoms ring.stanford.edu/ (accessed September 14, 2015).

Luesebrink, Marjorie Coverley. 2004. *Egypt: The Book of Going Forth by Day*. http:// califia.us/frame2.htm (accessed September 27, 2015).

Malka, Ariel. 2014. Chronotext Is a Collection of Sketches Exploring the Relationship between Text, Space, and Time. http://www.chronotext.org/ (accessed September 24, 2015).

Manovich, Lev. 2013. *Software Takes Command*. New York: Bloomsbury Academic.

Manurung, Ruli, Graeme Ritchie, and Henry Thompson. 2012. Using Genetic Algorithms to Create Meaningful Poetic Text. *Journal of Experimental & Theoretical Artificial Intelligence* 24 (1): 43–64. doi:.10.1080/0952813X.2010.539029

Margulis, Lynn. 1970. *Origin of Eukaryotic Cells; Evidence and Research Implications for a Theory of the Origin and Evolution of Microbial, Plant, and Animal Cells on the Precambrian Earth*. New Haven, CT: Yale University Press.

Marino, Mark C. 2010. Critical Code Studies and the Electronic Book Review: An Introduction. *Electronic Book Review*, September 15. http://www.electronicbookreview.com/thread/firstperson/ningislanded (accessed September 16, 2015).

Mattes, Eva, and Franco Mattes. 2001. Biennale.py. http://0100101110101101.org/ biennale-py/ (accessed September 13, 2015).

Maturana, Humbert R., and Francisco J. Varela. 1980. *Autopoiesis and Cognition: The Realization of the Living*. Dordrecht: D. Reidel Publishing.

Mauler, Henrik. 2005. *The Zoo*. http://zeitguised.wordpress.com/2004/05/24/the -zoo/ (accessed September 27, 2015).

McCaffery, Steve. 1975–1976. *Carnival*. http://archives.chbooks.com/online_books/ carnival/ (accessed September 14, 2015).

McLaughlin, Stephen, and Jim Carpenter eds. 2008. *Issue 1.* http://www .stephenmclaughlin.net/issue-1/Issue-1_Fall-2008.pdf (accessed September 15, 2015).

McLuhan, Marshall. 1967. *Verbi-Voco-Visual Explorations.* 1st ed. New York: Something Else Press.

McLuhan, Marshall, and Lewis H. Lapham. 1994. *Understanding Media: The Extensions of Man.* Cambridge, MA: MIT Press.

Memmott, Talan. 2000. *Lexia to Perplexia.* http://collection.eliterature.org/1/works/ memmott_lexia_to_perplexia.html (accessed September 15, 2015).

Memmott, Talan. 2006. The Hugo Ball. http://www.drunkenboat.com/db8/panlit judges/memmott/hugo_db/index.html (accessed September 9, 2015).

Mendelowitz, Eitan. 2002–2006. Drafting Poems: Inverted Potentialities. http:// www.aiaesthetic.com/index.php?work=DraftingPoems (accessed September 13, 2015).

Miller, J. Abbott. 1996. *Dimensional Typography.* Princeton, NJ: Princeton Architectural Press.

Milner, A. David, and Melvyn A. Goodale. 1995. *The Visual Brain in Action.* Oxford: Oxford University Press.

Minsky, Marvin Lee. 2006. *The Emotion Machine: Commonsense Thinking, Artificial Intelligence, and the Future of the Human Mind.* New York: Simon and Schuster.

Mitchell, W. J. T. 1994. *Picture Theory: Essays on Verbal and Visual Representation.* Chicago: University of Chicago Press.

MK12. 2004. Sleeping Beauty. https://vimeo.com/55927699 (accessed September 20, 2015).[not cited yet]

MK12. 2005. Go! https://www.youtube.com/watch?v=YCe1gC5VaW4 (accessed September 20, 2015).

Molleindustria. 2012. The Definition of Game. http://www.gamedefinitions.com/ (accessed September 24, 2015).

Montfort, Nick. 2009. ppg256 Series. http://nickm.com/poems/ppg256.html (accessed September 15, 2015).

Montfort, Nick. 2013. *World Clock.* http://nickm.com/post/2013/11/world-clock/ (accessed September 15, 2015).

Montfort, Nick, Patsy Baudoin, John Bell, Ian Bogost, Jeremy Douglass, Mark C. Marino, Michael Mateas, Casey Reas, Mark Sample, and Noah Vawter. 2012. *10 PRINT CHR$(205.5+RND(1)); GOTO 10.* Cambridge, MA: MIT Press

Montfort, Nick, and Stephanie Strickland. 2010 a. How to Read Sea and Spar Between. http://nickm.com/montfort_strickland/sea_and_spar_between/reading .html (accessed September 15, 2015).

Montfort, Nick, and Stephanie Strickland. 2010 b. *Sea and Spar Between.* http:// nickm.com/montfort_strickland/sea_and_spar_between/index.html (accessed September 15, 2015).

Moretti, Franco. 2000. Conjectures on World Literature. *New Left Review* II (1): 54–68.

Moretti, Franco. 2005. *Graphs, Maps, Trees: Abstract Models for Literary History.* London: Verso.

Moretti, Franco. 2013. *Distant Reading.* London: Verso.

Moritz, William. 1997. Digital Harmony: The Life of John Whitney, Computer Animation Pioneer. *Animation World Magazine* 2.5 (August). http://www.awn.com/mag/ issue2.5/2.5pages/2.5moritzwhitney.html (accessed September 20, 2015).

Morris, Adalaide, and Thomas Swiss, eds. 2006. *New Media Poetics: Contexts, Technotexts, and Theories.* Cambridge, MA: MIT Press.

Morrissey, Judd, and Mark Jeffrey. 2009. *The Precession.* http://www.markjeffery artist.org/precession2.html (accessed September 13, 2015).

Moten, Fred. 2014. *The Feel Trio.* http://www.lettermachine.org/book/the-feel-trio/ (accessed September 24, 2015).

Softie, Mr. 2007. http://www.mrsoftie.net/ (accessed September 27, 2015).

Müller, Andreas. 2005. *For All Seasons.* http://www.hahakid.net/forallseasons/forall seasons.html (accessed September 24, 2015).

Müller, Boris. 2010. Poetry on the Road. http://www.esono.com/boris/projects/ poetry10/ (accessed September 24, 2015).

Nadeau, Bruno, and Jason Edward Lewis. 2005. Still Standing. http://wyldco.com/ projects/stillstanding (accessed September 14, 2015).

Nelson, Jason. 2009. Net Art/Digital Poetry Games. http://www.secrettechnology .com/artgames.html (September 11, 2015).

Nelson, Jason. 2004. Secret Technology. http://www.secrettechnology.com/ (accessed September 27, 2015).

Nelson, Jason, and Matthew Horton. 2015. *Nomencluster.* http://www.thecube.qut .edu.au/cube-screens/2015/nomencluster.php (accessed September 16, 2015).

Nelson, Jason, and Alinta Krauth. 2013. Camblerland. http://www.cddc.vt.edu/jour nals/newriver/14Spring/camberland/ (accessed September 27, 2015).

Nielsen, Michael A. 2014. Neural Networks and Deep Learning. http://neuralnet worksanddeeplearning.com (accessed September 27, 2015).

Olson, Charles. 1960. *The Maximus Poems.* http://www.bookdepository.co.uk/Maximus-Poems-Charles-Olson/9780520055957 (accessed September 14, 2015).

Ong, Walter J. 1982. *Orality and Literacy: The Technologizing of the Word.* London: Methuen.

Ottinger, Kathleen. 2013. *Untold.* https://vimeo.com/110828679 (accessed September 24, 2015).

Panksepp, Jaak. 1998. *Affective Neuroscience: The Foundations of Human and Animal Emotions.* New York: Oxford University Press.

Parrish, Allison. 2009. Autonomous Parapoetic Device (APxD mkII). http://www .decontextualize.com/projects/apxd/ (accessed September 8, 2015).

Parrish, Allison. 2011. @everyword in Context. http://www.decontextualize .com/2011/10/everyword-on-gawker/ (accessed September 27, 2015).

Parrish, Allison. 2014. Creator of @everyword Explains the Life and Death of a Twitter Experiment. *Guardian,* June 4. http://www.theguardian.com/culture/2014/ jun/04/everyword-twitter-ends-adam-parrish-english-language (accessed September 15, 2015).

Patchen, Kenneth. 1966. *Hallelujah Anyway.* New York: New Directions Pub. Corp.

Perloff, Marjorie. 1991. *Radical Artifice: Writing Poetry in the Age of Media.* Chicago: University of Chicago Press.

Peyton, Miles. 2013. Keyfleas. http://cmuems.com/2013/a/miles/10/17/keyfleas/ (accessed September 24, 2015).

Picard, Rosalind W. 1997. *Affective Computing.* Cambridge, MA: MIT Press.

Picard, Rosalind W. 2003. Affective Computing: Challenges. *International Journal of Human-Computer Studies* 59 (1–2): 55–64.

Piringer, Jörg. 2011. Abcdefghijklmnopqrstuvwxyz. http://joerg.piringer.net/index .php?href=performance/abcdefghijklmnopqrstuvwxyz.xml (accessed September 13, 2015).

Piringer, Jörg. 2012. Broe Sael. http://joerg.piringer.net/index.php?href=videos/ broesael.xml (accessed September 11, 2015).

Piringer, Jörg, and Günter Vallaster eds. 2012. A Global Visuage. http://editionch.at/ blog/2012/09/29/neuerscheinung-jorg-piringer-und-gunter-vallaster-ed-a-global -visuage/ (accessed September 22, 2015).

Pirsig, Robert M. 2006. *Zen and the Art of Motorcycle Maintenance: An Inquiry into Values*. New York: HarperTorch.

Place, Vanessa. 2014. News. http://vanessaplace.biz/news/ (accessed September 15, 2015).

Platoni, Kara. "Love at First Byte," June 2006. https://alumni.stanford.edu/get/page/magazine/article/?article_id=33888 (accessed September 17, 2008).

Pope, Jim. 2014. Interview with a New Media Writer: Mez Breeze. November 27. http://newmediawritingprize.co.uk/?p=480 (accessed September 13, 2015).

Portela, Manuel. 2013. *Scripting Reading Motions: The Codex and the Computer as Self-Reflexive Machines*. Cambridge, MA: MIT Press.

Poundstone, William. 2001. *New Digital Emblems*. http://collection.eliterature.org/2/works/poundstone_newdigitalemblems.html (accessed September 12, 2015).

Poundstone, William. 2005. *Project for Tachistoscope [Bottomless Pit]*. http://collection.eliterature.org/1/works/poundstone__project_for_tachistoscope_bottomless_pit.html (accessed September 12, 2015).

Prasad, S. S. 2008. Nanopoems. *Rampike* 20, no. 2.

Pressman, Jessica. 2014. *Digital Modernism: Making It New in New Media*. New York: Oxford University Press.

Pulvermuller, Friedemann. 2002. *The Neuroscience of Language: On Brain Circuits of Words and Serial Order*. Cambridge: Cambridge University Press.

Raley, Rita. 2006 a. An Interview with John Cayley on Torus. http://thestudio.uiowa.edu/tirw/TIRW_Archive/september06/cayley/cayley.html (accessed September 22, 2015).

Raley, Rita. 2006 b. Writing 3D: Special Issue of *Iowa Review*. September. http://iowareview.uiowa.edu/TIRW/TIRW_Archive/september06/sept06_txt.html# (accessed September 27, 2015).

Ramachandran, V. S., and E. M. Hubbard. 2001. Synaesthesia—A window into perception, thought and language. *Journal of Consciousness Studies* 8 (12): 3–34.

Reichardt, Jasia, and the Institute of Contemporary Arts. 1969. *Cybernetic Serendipity: The Computer and the Arts*. New York: Praeger.

Rettberg, Scott. 2011. Letters in Space, at Play. http://retts.net/index.php/2011/02/letters-in-space-at-play/ (accessed September 20, 2015).

Rettberg, Scott. 2014. An Emerging Canon? A Preliminary Analysis of All References to Creative Works in Critical Writing Documented in the ELMCIP Electronic Literature Knowledge Base. *Electronic Book Review*. http://www.electronicbookreview.com/thread/electropoetics/exploding (accessed September 15, 2015).

Reynolds, Craig. 1986. Boids: Background and Updates. http://www.red3d.com/cwr/boids/ (accessed September 14, 2015).

Ricardo, Francisco J. 2009. *Literary Art in Digital Performance: Case Studies in New Media Art and Criticism*. New York: Continuum.

Roffe, Jon. 2014. *Badiou's Deleuze*. New York: Routledge.

Rokeby, David. 1991. The Giver of Names. https://vimeo.com/17187792 (accessed September 15, 2015).

Roque, Antonio. 2011. Language Technology Enables a Poetics of Interactive Generation. *Journal of Electronic Publishing* 14 (2). doi:.10.3998/3336451.0014.209

Rorty, Richard. 1979. *Philosophy and the Mirror of Nature*. Princeton, NJ: Princeton University Press.

Rothenberg, Jerome. 2013. Outside and Subterranean Poems, a Mini-Anthology in Progress (55): "Figures in the Dark, the Dancer at Trois Frères." *Jacket2*. https://jacket2.org/commentary/outside-subterranean-poems-mini-anthology-progress-55-figures-dark-dancer-trois-fr%C3%A8res (accessed January 21, 2014).

Rubin, Ben, Jer Thorp, and Mark Hansen. 2014. The Whole Brilliant Enterprise. http://o-c-r.org/2014/07/01/the-whole-brilliant-enterprise/ (accessed September 24, 2015).

Sample, Mark. 2012. This Is Just to Say. https://twitter.com/JustToSayBot (accessed September 15, 2015).

Sapnar, Megan, and Ingrid Ankerson. 2000. *Poems That Go*. http://poemsthatgo.com/statement.htm (accessed September 23, 2015).

Schmidt, Karsten. 2010. Type & Form. http://toxiclibs.org/ (accessed September 27, 2015).

Schwabsky, Barry. 2008. Lost as Food and Won as a Coast. *Nation* (December). http://www.thenation.com/article/lost-food-and-won-coast (accessed September 15, 2015).

Schwitters, Kurt. 1932. *URSONATE*. http://www.ubu.com/historical/schwitters/ursonate.html (accessed September 27, 2015).

Seaman, Bill. 2004. Pattern Flows: Notes toward a Model for an Electrochemical Computer: The Thoughtbody Environment. http://projects.visualstudies.duke.edu/billseaman/pdf/tb_electrochemical-1.pdf (accessed September 25, 2015).

Seaman, Bill, and Daniel Howe. 2010. *Architecture of Association*.http://billseaman.com/ (accessed September 12, 2015).

Shaw, Jeffrey. 1989. The Legible City. http://www.jeffrey-shaw.net/html_main/show_work.php?record_id=83 (accessed September 20, 2015).

Shin, Jean. 2006. TEXTile. http://www.jeanshin.com/textile.htm.

Shoup, Richard. 2001. SuperPaint: An Early Frame Buffer Graphics System. *IEEE Annals of the History of Computing* 23 (2): 32–37. doi:.10.1109/85.929909

Simanowski, Roberto. 2004. Concrete Poetry in Digital Media. *Dichtung Digital.* http://www.dichtung-digital.org/2004/3/simanowski/index.htm (accessed September 11, 2015).

Simanowski, Roberto. 2011. *Digital Art and Meaning: Reading Kinetic Poetry, Text Machines, Mapping Art, and Interactive Installations.* Minneapolis: University of Minnesota Press.

Simon, Herbert. 1962. The Architecture of Complexity. *Proceedings of the American Philosophical Society* 106, no. 6 (December 12): 467–482.

Simon, John F. 1997. *Every Icon.* January 14. http://www.numeral.com/appletsoftware/eicon.html (accessed September 14, 2015).

Simondon, Gilbert. 1958. *On the Mode of Existence of Technical Objects.* Trans. N. Mellamphy. Paris: Aubier, Editions Montaigne; https://english.duke.edu/uploads/assets/Simondon_MEOT_part_1.pdf (accessed September 11, 2015).

Simonite, Tom. 2014. Google's Intelligence Designer. *MIT Technology Review,* December 2. http://www.technologyreview.com/news/532876/googles-intelligence-designer/ (accessed September 15, 2015).

Skrbina, David. 2005. *Panpsychism in the West.* Cambridge, MA: MIT Press.

Sloman, Aaron, and Monica Croucher. 1981. Why Robots Will Have Emotions. http://cogprints.org/705/ (accessed September 27, 2015).

Small, David, and Tom White. 1998. Stream of Consciousness. http://acg.media.mit.edu/projects/stream/ (accessed September 13, 2015).

Soderman, Braxton. 2009. *Mémoire Involuntaire No. 1.* http://collection.eliterature.org/2/works/soderman_memory.html (accessed September 24, 2015).

Solt, Mary Ellen, ed. 1969. *Concrete Poetry: A World View.* Bloomington: Indiana University Press.

Sondheim, Alan. n.d. Index of /? http://www.alansondheim.org/ (accessed September 21, 2015).

Soo, Winnie. 2014. *Hello Zombies.* http://www.siusoon.com/home/?p=1273 (accessed September 24, 2015).

Sporns, Olaf. 2010. *Networks of the Brain.* Cambridge, MA: MIT Press.

Stefans, Brian Kim. 2000 a. *The Dreamlife of Letters.* http://www.arras.net/?p=164 (accessed September 13, 2015).

Stefans, Brian Kim. 2000 b. Reflections on Cyberpoetry. http://www.ubu.com/papers/ol/stefans.html (accessed September 27, 2015).

Stefans, Brian Kim. 2003. *Fashionable Noise: On Digital Poetics*. Berkeley, CA: Atelos.

Stefans, Brian Kim. 2011 a. Brian Stefans. http://openspace.sfmoma.org/author/bstefans/ (accessed September 27, 2015).

Sterling, Bruce. 2005. *Shaping Things*. Cambridge, MA: MIT Press.

Stiegler, Bernard. 1998. *Technics and Time, 1: The Fault of Epimetheus*. Stanford, CA: Stanford University Press.

Stiegler, Bernard. 2014. *The Hyperindustrial Epoch*. vol. 1. Symbolic Misery. Cambridge, UK: Polity Press.

Strickland, Stephanie, and Ian Hatcher. 2014. *House of Trust*. http://www.thevolta.org/ewc44-sstrickland-ihatcher-p1.html (accessed September 15, 2015).

Strickland, Stephanie, and Cynthia Lawson Jaramillo. 2002. *Original Shockwave Vniverse*. http://www.cynthialawson.com/vniverse/original.html (accessed September 15, 2015).

Strickland, Stephanie, and Cynthia Lawson Jaramillo. 2007. Dovetailing Details Fly Apart—All Over, Again, in Code, in Poetry, in Chreods. http://www.slippingglimpse.org/pocode (accessed September 20, 2015).

Stuart, Joshua, and Nitrocorpz. 2006. Watching a Young Mother Walk with Her Infant through a Cemetery on the Day before My Funeral. http://www.bornmagazine.org/projects/watching_a_young_mother/ (accessed June 18, 2015).

Swiss, Thomas, and Motomichi Nakamura. 2005. Beautiful Portrait. http://www.bornmagazine.org/projects/beautifulportrait/ (accessed September 14, 2015).

TEMPTONE. 2009. EyeWriter. http://www.eyewriter.org/ (accessed September 27, 2015).

Thacker, Eugene. 2007. Biopoetics; or, a Pilot Plan for a Concrete Poetry. *Electronic Book Review*, October 5.http://www.electronicbookreview.com/thread/electropoetics/emerging (accessed September 12, 2015).

Tisselli, Eugenio. 1999. MIDIPoet. http://www.narrabase.net/midipoet.html (accessed September 14, 2015).

Tolkacheva, Anna, and Natalia Fedorova. 2013. There Is No Author. https://vimeo.com/71956355 (accessed September 12, 2015).

Tomasula, Steve. 2010. *TOC: A New-Media Novel*. http://www.tocthenovel.com/ (accessed September 20, 2015).

Torres, Rui. 2008. Poemas No Meio Do Caminho. http://collection.eliterature.org/2/works/torres_poemas_no_meio/caminho1.html (accessed September 27, 2015).

TRAUMAWIEN. 2014. TRAUMAWIEN. http://www.zazzle.com/TRAUMAWIEN (accessed September 15, 2015).

Trettien, Anne Whitney. 2012. Plant --> Animal --> Book. http://www.palgrave-journals.com/pmed/journal/v3/n1/plantanimalbook/index.html#footnote5 (accessed September 26, 2015).

Troemel, Brad. 2008. BSTJ Buy Online. https://www.etsy.com/hk-en/shop/BSTJ (accessed September 15, 2015).

Trowbridge, Jon, and Eric Elshtain. 2004. About. https://gnoetrydaily.wordpress.com/about/.

UbuWeb. 2014. Twitter. November 18. http://www.ubuweb.com (accessed September 23, 2015).

Uribe, Ana Maria. 2001. Tipoems and Anipoems. http://vispo.com/uribe/datos/aboutAnaMariaEnglish.htm (accessed September 24, 2015).

Uribe, Ana Maria. 2003. Email to Kevin Hehlr. http://www.vispo.com/uribe/datos/aboutAnaMariaEnglish.htm (accessed September 15, 2015).

Vallias, André. 2003. Nous n'avons pas compris Descartes. http://www.andrevallias.com/ (accessed September 13, 2015).

Vandendorpe, Christian. 1999. Du Papyrus à l'Hypertexte : Essai sur les Mutations du Texte et de la Lecture. Paris: La Découverte.

van der Maaten. 2008. t-SNE. http://lvdmaaten.github.io/tsne/ (accessed September 27, 2015).

Varela, Francisco J., Evan Thompson, and Eleanor Rosch. 1993. The Embodied Mind: Cognitive Science and Human Experience. Cambridge, MA: MIT Press.

Venter, J. Craig. 2010. First Self-Replicating Synthetic Bacterial Cell. http://www.jcvi.org/cms/press/press-releases/full-text/article/first-self-replicating-synthetic-bacterial-cell-constructed-by-j-craig-venter-institute-researcher/ (accessed September 9, 2015).

Venter, J. Craig. 2013. Life at the Speed of Light: From the Double Helix to the Dawn of Digital Life. New York: Penguin Group.

Vinyals, Oriol, Alexander Toshev, Samy Bengio, and Dumitru Erhan. 2014. Show and Tell: A Neural Image Caption Generator. http://arxiv.org/abs/1411.4555 (accessed September 13, 2015).

Wardrip-Fruin, Noah. 2005. Christopher Strachey: The First Digital Artist? http://grandtextauto.org/2005/08/01/christopher-strachey-first-digital-artist/ (accessed September 15, 2015).

Wardrip-Fruin, Noah. 2009. *Expressive Processing: Digital Fictions, Computer Games, and Software Studies*. Cambridge, MA: MIT Press.

Wardrip-Fruin, Noah. 2011. Digital Media Archaeology: Interpreting Computational Processes. In *Media Archaeology: Approaches, Applications, and Implications*, ed. Huhtamo Erkki and Jussi Parikka. Berkeley: University of California Press; http://games.soe.ucsc.edu/sites/default/files/nwf-BC7-DigitalMediaArchaeology.pdf (accessed September 12, 2015).

Waterson, Sarah, Cristyn Davies, and Elena Knox. 2008. trope. September. http://www.sarahwaterson.net/?p=144 (accessed September 23, 2015).

Watson, Lyall. 1992. *The Nature of Things : The Secret Life of Inanimate Objects*. Rochester, VT: Destiny Books.

Wershler-Henry, Darren S., and Bill Kennedy. 2000. *Apostrophe*. http://apostropheengine.ca/ (accessed September 12, 2015).

West, Sasha, and Ernesto Lavandera. 2009. Zoology. http://www.bornmagazine.org/projects/zoology/ (accessed September 14, 2015).

Westbury, Chris. 2000. Welcome to JanusNode! http://janusnode.com/ (accessed September 15, 2015).

Whitehead, Alfred North. 1978. *Process and Reality*. New York: Free Press.

Wilberg, Jonah. 2014. Seven Ways of Looking at the *Augmented Imagination Project*. *Sein und Werden* (Summer). http://www.jonahwilberg.net/sevenways.html (accessed September 15, 2015).

Willis, Holly. 2005. *New Digital Cinema: Reinventing the Digital Image*. New York: Wallflower Press.

Wittgenstein, Ludwig. 1973. *Philosophical Investigations*. 3rd ed. Trans. G. E. M. Anscombe. New York: Pearson.

Wittig, Rob, and Mark C. Marino. 2015. Meanwhile ... Netprov Studio. http://meanwhilenetprov.com/ (accessed September 13, 2015).

Woolman, Matt. 2005. *Type in Motion 2*. London: Thames and Hudson.

Wu, Dekai, and Karteek Addanki. "Learning to Rap Battle with Bilingual Recursive Neural Networks." In Proceedings of the 24th International Conference on Artificial Intelligence, 2524–30. AAAI Press, 2015. http://www.cs.ust.hk/~dekai/library/WU_Dekai/WuAddanki_Ijcai2015.pdf. (accessed November 3, 2015).

Bing, Xu. 1987. Book from the Sky. http://www.xubing.com/index.php/site/projects/year/1987/book_from_the_sky (accessed September 14, 2015).

Bing, Xu. 2003. Book from the Ground. http://www.xubing.com/index.php/site/projects/year/2003/book_from_the_ground (accessed September 14, 2015).

Bing, Xu. 2013. *Landscape Landscript: Nature as Language in the Art of Xu Bing*. Oxford: Ashmolean Museum.

Yates, Frances Amelia. 1992. *The Art of Memory*. London: Pimlico.

Young-Hae, Chang Heavy Industries. 1999. *Dakota*. http://www.yhchang.com/DAKOTA.html (accessed September 12, 2015).

Zelinskie, Ashley. 2011. *One and One Chair*. http://www.ashleyzelinskie.com/#!One-and-One-Chair/zoom/c1han/image1vjw (accessed September 14, 2015).

Zweig, Janet. 2010. *Lipstick Enigma*. http://www.janetzweig.com/public/12.html (accessed September 15, 2015).

Index